Free Video  **Free Video**

Essential Test Tips Video from Trivium Test Prep

Dear Customer,

Thank you for purchasing from Trivium Test Prep! We're honored to help you prepare for your exam.

To show our appreciation, we're offering a **FREE** *HESI Essential Test Tips* **Video by Trivium Test Prep.*** Our video includes 35 test preparation strategies that will make you successful on the HESI exam. All we ask is that you email us your feedback and describe your experience with our product. Amazing, awful, or just so-so: we want to hear what you have to say!

To receive your **FREE** *HESI Essential Test Tips* **Video**, please email us at 5star@triviumtestprep.com. Include "Free 5 Star" in the subject line and the following information in your email:

1. The title of the product you purchased.
2. Your rating from 1 – 5 (with 5 being the best).
3. Your feedback about the product, including how our materials helped you meet your goals and ways in which we can improve our products.
4. Your full name and shipping address so we can send your **FREE** *HESI Essential Test Tips* **Video**.

If you have any questions or concerns please feel free to contact us directly at 5star@triviumtestprep.com.

Thank you!

– Trivium Test Prep Team

*To get access to the free video please email us at 5star@triviumtestprep.com, and please follow the instructions above.

HESI A^2 PRACTICE TEST QUESTIONS 2021–2022

4 Full-Length Practice Tests for the HESI Admission Assessment Exam

E.M. Falgout

TABLE OF CONTENTS

Want More?

INTRODUCTION

The HESI Admission Assessment (HESI A^2) exam is a part of the admissions process for nursing and allied health programs around the country. Schools use the test to assess applicants' capabilities in high-school level reading, writing, math, and science. This guide will allow you to review your knowledge in these subject areas, apply your knowledge, and answer test questions.

What's on the HESI A^2?

The HESI A^2 is a computer-based exam with eight sections. Different schools require different sections as part of their applications. Check with the institution or program you are interested in to find out what sections you need to take on test day.

You can work through the sections on the HESI A^2 in any order.

Most candidates take about four hours to complete the HESI A^2. Some programs allow candidates more time, depending on the required tests, or do not impose a time limit at all. The time limits listed below are suggested by the administrators of the HESI A^2 exam.

HESI A^2 Content

Subject	Topics	Number of Questions	Suggested Time Limit
Mathematics	arithmetic, fractions and decimals, proportions, units and measurements, calculating dosages	55	50 minutes
Reading	main idea, supporting idea, inferences, details, interpreting information	55	60 minutes
Vocabulary	knowledge of English vocabulary, particularly related to health and medicine	55	50 minutes
Biology	biological molecules, cells, cellular respiration, genetics, photosynthesis	30	25 minutes
Chemistry	atomic structure, chemical bonding, chemical equations, chemical reactions, nuclear chemistry, the periodic table	30	35 minutes

Subject	Topics	Number of Questions	Suggested Time Limit
Anatomy and Physiology	body systems (muscular, skeletal, nervous, renal/urinary, reproductive, endocrine, circulatory, and respiratory)	30	25 minutes
Physics	mechanics, energy, forces, waves, and light (This section is typically excluded by many programs; the mathematics and other sciences are more important.)	30	25 minutes

OTHER UNSCORED SECTIONS

Learner profile exams are **UNSCORED** tests to help students better understand their strengths and weaknesses, learning styles and habits, and other personality traits. Some schools may require them.

All sections on the HESI A² will include some pilot, unscored questions. The test writers use these questions to test new material. These questions do not count toward your final score. However, these questions are not indicated on the exam, so you must answer every question.

How is the HESI A² Scored?

There is no way to pass or fail the HESI A². A candidate's score simply shows their level of comprehension and skill. Schools and programs have their own entrance requirements, so candidates must check with the institutions that they want to attend for details on required scores.

Ascencia Test Prep

With health care fields such as nursing, pharmacy, emergency care, and physical therapy becoming the fastest-growing industries in the United States, individuals looking to enter the health care industry or rise in their field need high-quality, reliable resources. Ascencia Test Prep's study guides and test preparation materials are developed by credentialed industry professionals with years of experience in their respective fields. Ascencia recognizes that health care professionals nurture bodies and spirits, and save lives. Ascencia Test Prep's mission is to help health care workers grow.

ONE: PRACTICE TEST ONE

Mathematics

Directions: Work the problem carefully, and choose the best answer.

1. Solve: $8x + 2 = 3x + 17$
    A) −3
    B) 3
    C) 5
    D) −6

2. A pharmacy technician fills 13 prescriptions in 30 minutes. At that rate, how many prescriptions can he fill in a 7-hour shift?
    A) 91
    B) 45
    C) 182
    D) 208

3. The diameter of a round table is 60 inches. What is the diameter of the table in meters?
    A) 1.667 m
    B) 2.5 m
    C) 1.524 m
    D) 0.75 m

4. Alice ran $3\frac{1}{2}$ miles on Monday, and she increased her distance by $\frac{1}{4}$ mile each day. What was her total distance from Monday to Friday?
    A) $17\frac{1}{2}$ mi
    B) 20 mi
    C) $18\frac{1}{2}$ mi
    D) 19 mi

5. $\$75.00 − \$39.73 =$
    A) $36.73
    B) $46.27
    C) $44.73
    D) $35.27

6. Simplify the following expression:
    $5 − 7(3^2 − 4)$
    A) −5
    B) 1
    C) −9
    D) −30

7. Fried's rule for computing an infant's dose of medication is:

$$\frac{\text{child's age in months} \times \text{adult dosage}}{150}$$

If the adult dose is 25 milligrams, how much should be given to a one-and-a-half-year-old child?

A) 3 mg

B) 6 mg

C) 4 mg

D) 5 mg

8. Cotton swabs can be ordered in boxes of 125. If the doctor's office needs to order 4,250 cotton swabs, how many boxes should be ordered?

A) 34 boxes

B) 17 boxes

C) 42 boxes

D) 40 boxes

9. Simplify the following expression:

$16 + 10 \div 2$

A) 13

B) 21

C) 19

D) 11

10. Find the total weight of three cartons weighing 6.5 kilograms, 3.59 kilograms, and 2 kilograms.

A) 4.26 kg

B) 0.91 kg

C) 10.11 kg

D) 12.09 kg

11. Solve: $-9b - 4 = 2b + 7$

A) 11

B) 3

C) -1

D) 1

12. Evaluate the following expression for $a = -10$: $\frac{a^2}{4 - 3a + 4}$

A) 54

B) 9

C) -1

D) 59

13. A carpenter is planning to add wood trim along three sides of a doorway. The sides of the doorway measure $7\frac{1}{2}$ feet, $2\frac{5}{8}$ feet, and $7\frac{1}{2}$ feet. How much wood trim is needed?

A) $16\frac{5}{8}$ ft

B) $17\frac{5}{8}$ ft

C) $16\frac{1}{2}$ ft

D) $17\frac{1}{2}$ ft

14. Which of the following rational numbers is the least?

A) $-3\frac{1}{3}$

B) 2.73

C) 0

D) $-\frac{24}{5}$

15. What fraction is equivalent to 0.7?

A) $\frac{7}{5}$

B. $\frac{3}{10}$

C) $\frac{7}{10}$

D) $\frac{7}{100}$

16. The average high temperature in Paris, France, in July is 25°C. Convert the temperature to Fahrenheit.

A) 13°F

B) 43°F

C) 77°F

D) 57°F

17. Evaluate the following expression for $x = -7$, $y = -9$, and $z = -4$: $x + y - z$

    A) –2

    B) 6

    C) –12

    D) 8

18. In a class of 25 students, four students were absent. What percent of the students were absent?

    A) 4%

    B) 16%

    C) 21%

    D) 84%

19. A patient's chart indicates that she was administered pain medication at 1400 hours. The patient can have another dose in 4 hours. At what time can the patient have another dose?

    A) 8:00 p.m.

    B) 12:00 a.m.

    C) 6:00 p.m.

    D) 2:00 p.m.

20. The ratio of fiction to nonfiction books in a small public library is 2 to 5. If there are 735 total books in the library, how many are fiction?

    A) 294 books

    B) 210 books

    C) 184 books

    D) 257 books

21. A food label says that the box holds 2.5 servings. How many boxes would be needed to provide 10 servings?

    A) 4 boxes

    B) 25 boxes

    C) 10 boxes

    D) 6 boxes

22. In 2016, LeBron James averaged 26.4 points per game over 74 games. How many points did James score that year? (Round to the nearest whole number.)

    A) 1954 points

    B) 2803 points

    C) 100 points

    D) 2640 points

23. A patient weighs 110 pounds. What is her weight in kilograms?

    A) 55 kg

    B) 50 kg

    C) 11 kg

    D) 20 kg

24. If $285.48 will be shared equally by six people, how much will each person receive?

    A) $1712.88

    B) $47.58

    C) $885.46

    D) $225.48

25. A hardcover best-selling book is on sale for $18. If the book is discounted 25%, what was its original price?

    A) $20.50

    B) $24.00

    C) $4.50

    D) $30.00

26. One day during flu season, 23% of a company's staff was absent. If the company employs 127 people, how many staff members were present on that day? (Round your answer to the nearest whole number.)

    A) 98 people

    B) 29 people

    C) 104 people

    D) 46 people

27. What is $\frac{2}{3}$ of $\frac{3}{10}$?

A) $\frac{9}{20}$

B) $\frac{5}{13}$

C) $\frac{2}{5}$

D) $\frac{1}{5}$

28. A nurse records a patient's vital signs during a 3:00 p.m. to 11:00 p.m. shift. The clock in the patient's room reads 6:45. What time should be written in the patient's chart?

A) 0645

B) 1845

C) 1645

D) 1045

29. $\frac{1}{2} \div \frac{2}{3} =$

A) $\frac{1}{3}$

B) $\frac{3}{4}$

C) $\frac{3}{5}$

D) $\frac{5}{6}$

30. On a history test, Robert answered fifteen questions correctly. If he answered approximately 94% of the questions correctly, how many questions were on the test?

A) 20 questions

B) 25 questions

C) 16 questions

D) 32 questions

31. Solve: $12x + 5 = 77$

A) -6

B) 6

C) 10

D) 8

32. Simplify the following expression:
$\frac{4x^2}{2x} + 7x$

A) $11x^2$

B) $2x^3 + 7$

C) $2x + 7$

D) $9x$

33. Convert 0.64 to a fraction in lowest terms.

A) $\frac{8}{125}$

B) $\frac{16}{25}$

C) $\frac{2}{3}$

D) $\frac{4}{5}$

34. Solve: $5(x + 3) - 12 = 43$

A) 8

B) 12

C) 9

D) 10

35. $7\frac{1}{3} \div \frac{4}{5} =$

A) $9\frac{1}{6}$

B) $5\frac{13}{15}$

C) $\frac{6}{55}$

D) $\frac{15}{88}$

36. Marcus works maintenance for a large apartment complex. He averages $\frac{2}{3}$ hour per maintenance call. How many calls can he take in an 8-hour work day?

A) 6 calls

B) 12 calls

C) 24 calls

D) 36 calls

37. How many fluid ounces are in a 300-milliliter bottle of shampoo?

A) 10.15 fl oz

B) 101.5 fl oz

C) 8.87 fl oz

D) 20.7 fl oz

38. Solve: $\frac{x}{4} + \frac{2}{3} = \frac{29}{12}$

A) 5

B) 12

C) 7

D) 10

39. Carlos spent $1.68 on bananas. If bananas cost 48 cents per pound, how many pounds of bananas did he buy?

A) 2.06 lb

B) 1.2 lb

C) 8.1 lb

D) 3.5 lb

40. Angelica bought a roast weighing 3.2 pounds. If the roast cost $25.44, how much did it cost per pound?

A) $5.95

B) $7.95

C) $7.44

D) $8.14

41. The instructions for an over-the-counter liquid medication say to take 15 milliliters every four hours. If Janice has only standard measuring spoons, how many teaspoons of the medication should she take? (Note: 1 m = 0.2 tsp)

A) 7.5 tsp

B) 2 tsp

C) 3 tsp

D) 1.5 tsp

42. Simplify the following expression: $3xy(x^2 - 11xy + 10y^2)$

A) $3x^4y^4$

B) $3x^3y - 33x^2y^2 + 30xy^3$

C) $3x^3y - 11xy + 10y^2$

D) $3x^3y + 33x^2y^2 - 30xy^3$

43. Simplify the following expression: $\frac{10x^9y^6}{5x^3y^2}$

A) $2x^6y^4$

B) $2x^3y^3$

C) $5x^3y^3$

D) $5xy$

44. Find 9% of 81.

A) 9

B) 7.29

C) 90

D) 72

45. An old TV ad states, "Four out of five dentists surveyed recommend sugarless gum for their patients who chew gum." If 450 dentists were surveyed, how many recommended sugarless gum?

A) 360 dentists

B) 400 dentists

C) 50 dentists

D) 90 dentists

46. $17 - 4\frac{3}{5} =$

A) $6\frac{1}{5}$

B) $13\frac{2}{5}$

C) $12\frac{2}{5}$

D) $13\frac{3}{5}$

47. Terrence has 63 hours of sick leave. If he donates 15.75 hours to a coworker with a long-term illness, how much sick leave does he have left?

A) 78.75 hr

B) 48.75 hr

C) 15.12 hr

D) 47.25 hr

48. $(-9)(-4) =$

A) -13

B) 13

C) -36

D) 36

49. $-2(11) =$

A) 22

B) -22

C) 18

D) -18

50. $8.653 + 2 + 1.06 =$

A) 8.761

B) 11.713

C) 9.715

D) 9.913

51. $\frac{1}{2} + \frac{5}{6} - \frac{3}{4} =$

A) $\frac{7}{12}$

B) $\frac{3}{4}$

C) $\frac{7}{36}$

D) $\frac{25}{36}$

52. The electric company uses the formula $C = 0.057k + 23.50$, where k represents the number of kilowatt-hours used by the customer, to determine the amount of a customer's bill. Find the bill amount for a customer who uses 1210 kilowatt-hours.

A) $68.97

B) $713.20

C) $30.40

D) $92.47

53. Jim is taking care of 8 patients during his shift. So far it has taken him 25 minutes to see two patients. At this rate, how long will it take Jim to check in on all 8 patients?

A) 2 hr

B) 50 min

C) 100 min

D) 1 hr

54. Jack missed 5% of 260 work days last year, some for illness and some for vacation. How many days did Jack work?

A) 13 days

B) 208 days

C) 247 days

D) 255 days

55. A patient enters the emergency room at 11:15 a.m. The patient is discharged 4 hours later. Express the time the patient left the ER in military time.

A) 1515

B) 0315

C) 0515

D) 0715

Reading

Directions: Read the passage carefully, and then read the questions that follow and choose the most correct answer.

The endocrine system is made up of glands—such as the parathyroid, thyroid, pituitary, and adrenals—that produce hormones. Men and women have different reproductive glands: men have testes and women have ovaries. The pituitary gland serves as the "master gland" of the endocrine system.

The endocrine system's function is to produce and distribute hormones. Endocrine glands release hormones into the bloodstream, where they are carried to other tissues or organs. When the hormones reach other tissues, they catalyze certain chemical reactions, stimulating various processes or activities. For instance, hormones are responsible for important bodily processes such as puberty and menstruation. Hormones are also released in humans in moments of fear or anxiety and can trigger the fight-or-flight response. The endocrine system is the primary source of a wide range of physiological activities and is sometimes referred to as the "hardworking chemical control center" of the human body.

1. What is the best summary of the passage?

A) The endocrine system controls hormones that stimulate processes in the body.

B) Endocrine glands differ in men and women.

C) The pituitary gland is the "master gland" of the endocrine system.

D) Hormones are responsible for puberty and menstruation.

2. What is the author's primary purpose in writing this essay?

A) to warn people about the dangers of hormonal imbalance

B) to persuade people to take care of their endocrine glands

C) to advise people about different hormones and what they do

D) to inform people about the endocrine system's parts and functions

3. What is the meaning of the word *stimulating* in the second paragraph?

A) to make something happen

B) to reproduce something

C) to create fear or anxiety

D) to destroy or diminish a tissue

4. Which of the following statements can be considered a statement of FACT according to the content offered in the paragraphs above?

A) The endocrine system is the most important system in the human body.

B) The endocrine system is the only "chemical control center in the body."

C) The endocrine system only has one organ: the pancreas.

D) The endocrine system stimulates reactions in the body by releasing hormones.

5. According to the passage, what is true about hormones?

A) They are only secreted by the pancreas.

B) They can help trigger fight-or-flight responses.

C) They almost always cause negative reactions.

D) Their sole purpose is to stimulate reproductive activities.

6. According to the passage, what serves as the major organ associated with the endocrine system?

A) the pituitary gland

B) the testicles

C) the ovaries

D) the spinal cord

Every medical professional should understand the root causes and potential effects of hypoglycemia because it can actually be a matter of life or death for a patient with diabetes. Hypoglycemia—which literally means low (*hypo*) blood sugar (*glycemia*)—is one of the most common medical emergencies for patients who have diabetes. Hypoglycemia can occur when a patient either takes too much insulin or has not consumed enough sugar. At other times, hypoglycemia stems from overexertion. A person can even become hypoglycemic if they vomit an important meal, depriving the body of the sugar and nutrients it needs to stay balanced.

Any medical professional interacting with diabetic patients should know the telltale signs of hypoglycemia. When a diabetic patient's blood sugar plummets, their mental state becomes altered. This can lead to unconsciousness or, in more severe cases, a diabetic coma and/or brain damage. If you notice the rapid onset of nervousness or anxiety, shakiness, and/or profuse sweating in someone with diabetes, you will likely need to help administer glucose to them as soon as possible (as long as they are conscious enough to swallow). Most diabetic patients manage their condition by using glucometers.

Glucometers measure the level of glucose in the bloodstream. During a potential hypoglycemic episode, if at all possible, ask the person if they have used their glucometer lately or encourage them to use it immediately. If the person is still cognizant but looks "out of it," you may have to assist in the process. A blood glucose value of less than 80 milligrams per deciliter can be considered a hypoglycemic episode. This kind of reading would prompt a swift glucose administration and, in worst-case scenarios, a trip to the emergency room.

7. What is the main idea of the passage?

A) Medical professionals should know what causes hypoglycemia and how to manage it.

B) Glucometers help patients with diabetes monitor their glucose levels.

C) Patients with diabetes can slip into a diabetic coma if they do not monitor their glucose levels.

D) Profuse sweating is one of the most telltale signs of a hypoglycemic episode.

8. Which of the following is NOT listed as a detail in the passage?

A) Glucometers help patients and medical professionals measure the level of glucose in the bloodstream.

B) Any blood glucose value that reads less than 80 milligrams per deciliter can be considered a hypoglycemic episode.

C) Only people with diabetes can become hypoglycemic.

D) Hypoglycemia literally means low (*hypo*) blood sugar (*glycemia*).

9. What is the author's primary purpose in writing this essay?

A) to inform health care workers and the public about the symptoms of hypoglycemia and how to respond to it

B) to persuade people to purchase more glucometers so that they can properly handle all hypoglycemic episodes

C) to dramatize a hypoglycemic episode so readers will know what to expect if they encounter a patient with diabetes who is undergoing one

D) to recount a time when a medical professional failed to properly respond to a hypoglycemic episode

10. What is the meaning of the word *administer* in the second paragraph?

A) adorn

B) give

C) revive

D) withdraw

11. Which of the following statements can the reader infer from the passage?

   A) Diabetic comas, which can be triggered by untreated episodes of hypoglycemia, can cause permanent brain damage.

   B) Glucometers are too expensive for most diabetic patients to purchase, making cases of hypoglycemia frequent.

   C) Medical professionals should ignore the personal perspectives of people experiencing hypoglycemic episodes.

   D) Diabetes is a dangerous disease that cannot be managed properly.

12. Which of the following statements is a fact stated in the passage?

   A) Profuse sweating is the number one sign that tells a medical professional a hypoglycemic episode has concluded.

   B) Any blood glucose value that reads less than 80 milligrams per deciliter can be considered a hypoglycemic episode.

   C) Most diabetic patients do not know how to monitor their own condition, so health care workers must help them.

   D) Most personal glucometers are outdated, and medical professionals should purchase their own.

Communicating with any human being in crisis—whether that crisis is physical or emotional—is going to be more difficult than normal, everyday communication. Thus, emergency responders and medical practitioners, like many other social service providers, need to learn how to be sensitive in interpersonal communication. Here are some tips about how to hone your craft as a communicator while working with people in crisis. These tips can also be used for everyday communication.

First, it is essential that you are aware of cultural differences. In some cultures, direct eye contact can be unsettling or disrespectful. People from different cultures may have different comfort levels with personal space: some might find physical closeness comforting; others might find it threatening. Your body language speaks volumes. Be sure you are aware of the symbolic nature of your posture, hand motions, and gestures.

It is also important to enunciate your verbal statements and directions in a clear, relevant way. Use terminology and directions that a patient will understand, and avoid lofty medical jargon. Believe it or not, you also want to be honest with the person in crisis, even if the conditions are dire. Also explain, if possible, what you might do to help alleviate even the most drastic conditions so that the person feels supported. Lastly, and most importantly, be prepared to listen. Even if there is a language barrier, condition, or disability limiting your communication with the person in crisis, try to position yourself as an active listener. These tips will help you support people who need clarity and sensitivity.

13. What is the meaning of the phrase *speaks volumes* in the second paragraph?

   A) talks too much

   B) reads instructions

   C) communicates many things

   D) reads novels in several volumes

14. According to the passage, what do most people in crisis need?

   A) medical care

   B) psychological counseling

   C) cultural understanding

   D) sensitivity and clarity

15. Which of the following statements can be considered a statement of FACT according to the content offered in the paragraphs above?

    A) Most people cannot handle it if you look them in the eye and tell "dire" truths.

    B) Communicating with someone in crisis is more difficult than normal communication.

    C) The most important part of sensitive communication is establishing physical contact.

    D) Communicating with patients is not as important as dealing quickly with their injuries.

16. According to the passage, what is true about cultural differences?

    A) People from most cultures can recognize a thumbs-up gesture.

    B) In some cultures, people are uncomfortable with direct eye contact.

    C) When a crisis occurs, cultural differences usually disappear.

    D) No matter what someone's culture is, everyone needs a hug in a crisis.

17. What is the best summary of the passage?

    A) In some cultures, direct eye contact can be unsettling or disrespectful.

    B) Posture, hand motions, and gestures can symbolize respect or disrespect.

    C) Medical practitioners must learn to be sensitive with people who are in crisis.

    D) Medical practitioners should give clear directions and avoid using lofty medical jargon.

18. What is the author's primary purpose in writing this essay?

    A) to warn people about the dangers of disrespectful communication

    B) to persuade medical personnel to speak only when it is necessary

    C) to tell an interesting story about a paramedic who offended a patient

    D) to advise medical practitioners about communicating with patients in crisis

A variety of environmental factors can inhibit the body's ability to naturally keep itself cool. Humid conditions, for instance, mean that sweat evaporates slowly, reducing the body's ability to radiate heat. On the other hand, extremely dry heat may encourage people to push beyond their normal boundaries of exertion because they do not "feel" the heat as much as in humid environments. Overexertion in either moist or dry heat forces the body to alter its heat-coping mechanisms, placing people at risk of experiencing heat cramps, heat exhaustion, or heat stroke. These physiological responses to heat exposure can impair important bodily functions and can even result in death.

Heat cramps occur when an excessive amount of water and salts are released from the body—in the form of sweat—in hot conditions. Prolonged loss of water and salts will lead to muscle cramps, usually in the legs or abdomen. Excessive loss of fluids and salts can also lead to heat exhaustion, a state in which a person experiences shallow breathing, an altered mental state, unresponsiveness, dizziness or faintness, and/or moist and cool skin. These symptoms occur as a result of circulatory dysfunction; the overexposure to heat combined with the loss of fluids disrupts normal blood flow.

If not addressed promptly, heat exhaustion can lead to heatstroke, which is a life-threatening heat-exposure emergency. Heatstroke occurs when the body gets so overheated that it becomes hyperthermic; the patient stops sweating and the skin becomes hot and can appear flushed. Heatstroke can lead to loss of consciousness, muscle twitching, seizures, or even cardiac arrest. For these reasons, it is essential to immediately remove a person experiencing heat exposure from the hot environment so they can cool off and replenish fluids. The best prevention for heat-exposure illnesses is to limit time spent in the heat (for example, by taking frequent breaks), limit exertion, and hydrate regularly.

19. What is the main idea of the passage?

A) Heat exhaustion can lead to heatstroke, a life-threatening emergency.

B) A range of environmental conditions can prevent the body from cooling itself.

C) The best prevention for heat exposure is to limit time spent in the heat.

D) Overexposure to heat can lead to circulatory dysfunction.

20. Which of the following is NOT listed as a detail in the passage?

A) Humidity can cause sweat to evaporate too slowly, and this can impede natural cooling.

B) Dry heat may allow people to overexert themselves because they do not "feel" the heat.

C) Heat cramps occur when people drink too much water before exercising.

D) A hyperthermic patient stops sweating and has hot skin that looks flushed.

21. What is the author's primary purpose in writing this essay?

A) to inform readers about symptoms of heat exposure and how to respond to it

B) to persuade older readers to move to regions with cooler climates

C) to dramatize a hyperthermic episode so readers will know what to expect if they treat a patient who is undergoing one

D) to recount a time when a medical professional failed to properly respond to a hyperthermic episode

22. What is the meaning of the word *inhibit* in the first sentence?

A) embarrass

B) cause

C) enhance

D) hinder

23. Which of the following statements is a FACT stated in the passage?

A) While heat exposure can impair important bodily functions, it rarely results in death.

B) A patient who is experiencing heat exposure should not be moved; instead, the hot environment should be cooled immediately.

C) The best treatment for heat-exposure illnesses is to acclimate to high temperatures.

D) A patient who has heat exhaustion may have shallow breathing, an altered mental state, and dizziness.

24. Which of the following statements can the reader infer from the passage?

A) Some people die because they do not know how dangerous overexposure to heat can be.

B) Most of the patients who die as a result of overexposure to heat are over sixty years old.

C) Athletes who train in hot climates can tolerate heat better than those who train in cooler places.

D) Excessive sweating is a sign that a patient is hyperthermic and needs immediate treatment.

Medical professionals not only have to handle physical medical emergencies; they also have to be prepared to manage behavioral emergencies. Behavioral emergencies occur when a person's behavior—an observable response to the environment—is unreasonable to the point that it disrupts normal, everyday activities. Extreme cases of a behavioral emergency may result when someone's behavior is creating a danger to themselves or others. Chronic cases of extreme behavioral emergencies may eventually be classified as a mental disorder. Psychological and behavioral effects can result from any number of illnesses; they can also be the result of a chemical imbalance, genetic disorder, or psychological disturbance. People suffering from mental disorders are at risk for increased incidents of behavioral emergencies because their behavioral patterns are typically impaired or disrupted. Consequently, medical professionals must be trained in crisis management to deal with behavioral emergencies that may increase the possibility of self-harm or interpersonal conflict. While medical practitioners must be trained for emergency situations that demand physical restraint, extreme cases of behavioral emergency may be directed to police for appropriate support.

25. What is the author's primary purpose in writing this paragraph?

   A) to warn readers about dangerous behavioral emergencies

   B) to persuade family members to call 911 to prevent suicides

   C) to advise readers about ways to treat someone who is mentally ill

   D) to inform readers about managing patients in behavioral emergencies

26. Which of the following statements can be considered a statement of FACT according to the content offered in the paragraph above?

   A) It is unlawful for a medical professional to attempt to treat a violent, mentally ill patient without calling for police assistance.

   B) When a person's actions pose a threat to him- or herself—or to others— professionals consider this an extreme form of behavioral emergency.

   C) People suffering from mental illness almost always cause behavioral emergencies because they cannot stop themselves from picking fights with others.

   D) Medical professionals with crisis-management training are better equipped to deal with behavioral emergencies than police officers are.

27. According to the passage, what is true of genetic disorders?

   A) They are one cause of mental illness.

   B) They do not cause mental illness.

   C) They almost always cause mental illness.

   D) They are the main cause of mental illness.

28. Which of the following statements can the reader infer from the passage?

   A) People who are mentally ill are harder to deal with than physically ill patients.

   B) Most people who are psychologically disturbed try to harm themselves or others.

   C) In a behavioral emergency, police officers may have to put handcuffs on a mentally ill person.

   D) Most medical professionals are unwilling or unable to cope with violent or suicidal patients.

29. According to the passage, when should a medical professional call for police support in dealing with a behavioral emergency?

   A) in every case

   B) very rarely

   C) when the medical professional needs help with physically restraining someone

   D) when the patient is irrational to the extent that it interferes with everyday activities

1) The thyroid is an important endocrine gland located in the neck. 2) Normally, when thyroid hormones drop below a certain level, the pituitary gland releases thyroid-stimulating hormone. 3) Once stimulated, the thyroid gland floods the body with another hormone, thyroxine. 4) Thyroxine is one of the drivers of weight loss and weight gain; it affects the increase or decrease of the metabolic rate in the body tissues. 5) However, when something goes wrong, the thyroid can either produce too much thyroxine or not enough. 6) An excess of thyroxine in the circulatory system

may result in a condition known as hyperthyroidism, which produces a rapid metabolic rate. 7) Hyperthyroidism may result in extended periods of irritability and anxiety. 8) A deficit of thyroxine in the circulatory system may result in a condition known as hypothyroidism. 9) People with hypothyroidism typically suffer from obesity and fatigue. 10) Fortunately, medications are available to help patients regulate their thyroid function when they have been diagnosed with hyperthyroidism or hypothyroidism.

30. Which sentence best summarizes the paragraph's main idea?

A) Sentence 1: "The thyroid is an important endocrine gland located in the neck."

B) Sentence 2: "Normally, when thyroid hormones drop below a certain level, the pituitary gland releases thyroid-stimulating hormone."

C) Sentence 4: "Thyroxine is one of the drivers of weight loss and weight gain; it affects the increase or decrease of the metabolic rate in the body tissues."

D) Sentence 10: "Fortunately, medications are available to help patients regulate their thyroid function when they have been diagnosed with hyperthyroidism or hypothyroidism."

31. Which of the following is NOT listed as a detail in the passage?

A) When thyroid hormones drop below normal, the pituitary gland releases a hormone that stimulates the thyroid to produce more thyroxine.

B) Too much thyroxine in the circulatory system is a condition called hyperthyroidism.

C) Too little thyroxine in the circulatory system is a condition called hypothyroidism.

D) Patients with hyperthyroidism are usually very overweight and easily tired.

32. What is the meaning of the word *deficit* in sentence 8?

A) surplus

B) trade

C) insufficiency

D) budget

33. What is the author's primary purpose in writing this paragraph?

A) to inform readers about the thyroid's normal function and disorders of the gland

B) to persuade readers with hypothyroidism to take medication and lose weight

C) to encourage readers with thyroid disorders by telling them that medication is available

D) to recount a time when a patient was successfully treated for a serious thyroid disorder

34. Which of the following statements is a FACT stated in the passage?

A) Most older patients have either hyperthyroidism or hypothyroidism.

B) Hypothyroidism is common among children who do not get enough exercise.

C) Hyperthyroidism is common among young parents with busy, stressful lives.

D) Medications are available to help patients regulate their thyroid function.

35. Which of the following statements can the reader infer from the passage?

A) The pituitary gland's main function is regulating the thyroid gland.

B) Thyroxine is one of the medications patients can take to regulate thyroid function.

C) The prefix *hyper* means "too much" and the prefix *hypo* means "not enough."

D) Hyperthyroidism is one cause of eating disorders such as anorexia and bulimia.

The spinal cord is the central messaging stem of the nervous system. Almost all sensory information the human body experiences must pass through the spinal cord in order to reach the brain. The spinal cord also coordinates reflexes, or motor responses.

When the spinal cord is cross-sectioned, it becomes apparent that it possesses an outer layer of myelinated motor and sensory axons (also referred to as white matter) and an inner layer of nerve cell bodies (gray matter). Sensory information the body takes in enters the spinal cord through neurons located on its dorsal plane (the back side). The cell bodies of these dorsally located neurons form a cluster called a dorsal root ganglion. Motor information, on the other hand, exits the spinal cord ventrally, meaning from the front side. Every nerve branch that enters and exits the spinal cord is called a nerve root.

The entire spinal cord has five regions. From top to bottom, these regions are cervical, thoracic, lumbar, sacral, and coccygeal. Each region innervates a corresponding area of the body. Spinal nerves "direct" the incoming and outgoing messages of the central nervous system, making the spinal cord the main neurological conduit of the human body.

36. Which of the following statements can the reader infer from the passage?

   A) When the human body is in pain, the spinal cord conveys that information to the brain.

   B) Orthopedic surgeons cross-section patients' spinal cords to treat spinal injuries.

   C) The coccygeal region is located near the top of the spinal cord, below the cervical region.

   D) Dorsally located neurons can be found on the front side of the spinal cord, near the top.

37. According to the passage, what is true of the spinal cord's cervical region?

   A) It is in the middle of the spinal cord.

   B) It is the lowest region of the spinal cord.

   C) It is at the top of the spinal cord.

   D) It is on the back side of the spinal cord.

38. What is the meaning of the word *conduit* in the last sentence?

   A) current

   B) channel

   C) artery

   D) area

39. Which sentence best summarizes the passage's main idea?

   A) "The spinal cord also coordinates reflexes, or motor responses."

   B) "The spinal cord is the central messaging stem of the nervous system."

   C) "Sensory information the body takes in enters the spinal cord through neurons located on its dorsal plane (the back side)."

   D) "The cell bodies of these dorsally located neurons form a cluster called a dorsal root ganglion."

40. What is the author's primary purpose in writing this essay?

   A) to show that the spinal cord is more important than other body parts

   B) to persuade readers to take better care of their spines and spinal cords

   C) to advise readers about ways to treat spinal cord disorders

   D) to inform readers about the spinal cord's functions and parts

41. According to the passage, which part of the spinal cord coordinates reflexes, or motor responses?

   A) the cervical region

   B) the lumbar region

   C) the back side

   D) the front side

Scientists only partially understand carcinogenesis—the process by which normal cells become cancer cells. Yet most scientists agree that this malignant transformation results from damaged genetic material within a cell. In a normal cell, DNA helps control processes such as mitosis, or cell division, and protein synthesis. DNA provides the "master codes" for these two biological processes.

However, cells that are becoming cancerous demonstrate disturbances in these processes. The damage to the genetic material can cause unchecked growth and reproduction, continuing to pass the abnormalities on to further generations of cells. Altered cellular programs and altered DNA can lead cancerous cells to proliferate, invade, move, or spread. Anaplasia, a process by which cells become undifferentiated, is characteristic of some cancerous tumors. Some cells even mutate in a way in which they lose elements of programmed cell death, or apoptosis. In fact, apoptosis is what causes cancer to grow at such high rates and, in some extreme cases, live indefinitely.

42. According to the passage, what is something scientists do NOT know?

   A) what happens to cells during carcinogenesis

   B) all aspects of the process of carcinogenesis

   C) the fact that damaged DNA helps to cause carcinogenesis

   D) the fact that normal DNA helps to control mitosis and protein synthesis

43. What is the meaning of the word *malignant* in the first paragraph?

   A) damaged

   B) undifferentiated

   C) cancerous

   D) fast-growing

44. Which sentence best summarizes the passage's main idea?

   A) "Scientists only partially understand carcinogenesis—the process by which normal cells become cancer cells."

   B) "Yet most scientists agree that this malignant transformation results from damaged genetic material within a cell."

   C) "In a normal cell, DNA helps control processes such as mitosis, or cell division, and protein synthesis."

   D) "In fact, apoptosis is what causes cancer to grow at such high rates and, in some extreme cases, live indefinitely."

45. Which of the following is NOT listed as a detail in the passage?

   A) DNA helps control mitosis, or cell division, and protein synthesis.

   B) Cells going through carcinogenesis show disturbances in mitosis and protein synthesis.

   C) Normal DNA, too, can cause abnormal unchecked growth and reproduction of cells.

   D) Apoptosis (losing aspects of programmed cell death) causes cancer to grow at high rates.

46. What is the author's primary purpose in writing this essay?

   A) to speculate on environmental—rather than genetic—causes for cancer

   B) to recount times when genetic testing saved the lives of cancer patients

   C) to inform readers about cause-effect relationships between genetic material and cancer

   D) to persuade readers to undergo genetic testing to predict whether they will develop cancer

47. Which of the following statements can the reader infer from the passage?

    A) Scientists disagree about the cause-effect relationship between damaged genetic material and carcinogenesis.

    B) All human diseases and disorders can be traced back to damaged DNA.

    C) Scientists do not yet know exactly how genetic material becomes damaged.

    D) Most cancerous tumors are the result of anaplasia, a process by which cells become undifferentiated.

Most people think of respiration as the mechanical exchange of air between human lungs and the environment. They think about oxygen filling up the tiny air sacs in the lungs. They think about how this process feeds the capillaries surrounding the air sacs, which then infuse the bloodstream with the oxygen it needs. They may even think about how carbon dioxide is exhaled from the lungs back into the environment. But this process—known as external respiration—is just one form of respiration that occurs in the human body. Did you know there are actually two types of respiration in humans? The second form of respiration is equally important; it is known as internal, or cellular, respiration.

Whereas external respiration centers on an exchange between the lungs and the environment, internal respiration centers on a molecular exchange between cells and capillaries. All organs inside the human body rely on cellular respiration to function properly. Cells within the organs are surrounded by thousands of tiny capillaries that act as channels for the exchange of gases. Oxygen is carried through these microscopic blood vessels, moving from red blood cells to the surrounding tissue. Additionally, built-up carbon dioxide in the tissues flows through the capillaries back to the lungs. This second form of respiration may be invisible to the human eye, but it is crucial for the maintenance of human life.

48. Which of the following statements can the reader infer from the passage?

    A) The author believes that most people know what capillaries are.

    B) The idea that the human lungs contain tiny air sacs is a myth.

    C) The term "external respiration" does not accurately describe breathing.

    D) The author believes that most people have never heard of internal respiration.

49. What is the author's primary purpose in writing this essay?

    A) to inform readers about external and internal respiration

    B) to advise readers about ways to treat patients with lung disease

    C) to prove that most people are ignorant about internal respiration

    D) to persuade readers to take better care of their lungs and other organs

50. How does the author define the word *capillaries* in the passage?

    A) "tiny air sacs" (paragraph 1)

    B) "two types of respiration" (paragraph 1)

    C) "[a]ll organs inside the human body" (paragraph 2)

    D) "these microscopic blood vessels" (paragraph 2)

51. According to the passage, external respiration is an exchange between what and what?

    A) the lungs and the environment

    B) oxygen and carbon dioxide

    C) capillaries and cells

    D) blood vessels and blood cells

52. Which sentence best summarizes the passage's main idea?

A) "Most people think of respiration as the mechanical exchange of air between human lungs and the environment."

B) "They may even think about how carbon dioxide is exhaled from the lungs back into the environment."

C) "The second form of respiration is equally important; it is known as internal, or cellular, respiration."

D) "Cells within the organs are surrounded by thousands of tiny capillaries that act as channels for the exchange of gases."

53. According to the passage, how does carbon dioxide escape during internal respiration?

A) The lungs draw it into tiny air sacs.

B) The lungs release it into the bloodstream.

C) It travels from the tissues through the capillaries back to the lungs.

D) It travels from the capillaries into the red blood cells to the tissues.

Scientists separate hormones into two major categories: peptide hormones and steroid hormones. Peptide hormones are made of amino acids, while steroid hormones are made of cholesterol. Two examples of peptide hormones are insulin and glucagon. Insulin decreases glucose levels in the blood, while glucagon increases glucose levels. They work together as part of a feedback system to regulate blood sugar. An increase in insulin may cause a decrease in glucagon and vice versa.

Hormone feedback systems can also involve steroid hormones. For example, testosterone is a steroid hormone that influences male secondary sexual characteristics that develop during puberty. Its level is influenced by the production of follicle-stimulating hormone (FSH) and luteinizing hormone (LH) in a negative feedback loop. The release of FSH and LH stimulates the production of testosterone. When testosterone reaches a certain level, it inhibits the production of FSH and LH. As testosterone levels fall, FSH and LH begin to be released again, starting the cycle over. A similar but more complex feedback loop occurs in women with FSH and LH stimulating the production of estrogen, resulting in the cycle of ovulation and menstruation.

54. According to the second paragraph, what happens immediately after "testosterone reaches a certain level [by rising]"?

A) "[T]estosterone levels fall."

B) "FSH and LH begin to be released again."

C) "[I]t inhibits the production of FSH and LH."

D) "[It stimulates] the production of estrogen."

55. What does the word *feedback* mean in the passage?

A) criticism

B) reaction

C) advice

D) opinion

Vocabulary

Directions: Read the question and then choose the most correct answer.

1. Which word is not spelled correctly in the context of this sentence?

   The six-toed Hemingway cats are an exseption among domestic cat species, which usually have five toes.

   A) exseption
   B) domestic
   C) species
   D) usually

2. Select the meaning of the underlined word in the sentence.

   The administration of the HPV vaccination before the onset of adolescence is recommended as a <u>precaution</u> against the sexually transmitted human papillomavirus.

   A) warning
   B) detriment
   C) prevention
   D) diagnosis

3. Select the meaning of the underlined word in the sentence.

   The triage system gives <u>priority</u> to patients based on the severity of their condition.

   A) medical care
   B) transportation
   C) precedence
   D) insurance

4. A patient with co-morbidities

   A) has chronic pain.
   B) is near death.
   C) presents with two disorders.
   D) has no symptoms of a disorder.

5. Select the word that means "dependent on something else."

   The contract specified that the nurse's hiring was conditional on her passing a drug test.

   A) contract
   B) specified
   C) conditional
   D) passing

6. Select the word that best completes the sentence.

   The scaly rash on the child's forearm was a _____ of eczema.

   A) laceration
   B) manifestation
   C) treatment
   D) transmission

7. Which word means "reduce in strength"?

   A) restore
   B) dilute
   C) combine
   D) suppress

8. Select the meaning of the underlined word in the sentence.

   A constant <u>prone</u> state, coupled with respiratory co-morbidities, may lead to pneumonia.

   A) excited
   B) flat
   C) unconscious
   D) uncomfortable

9. Select the meaning of the underlined word in the sentence.

Excess consumption of salt can cause patients to <u>retain</u> water.

A) excrete

B) shed

C) filter

D) hold

10. Select the meaning of the underlined word in the sentence.

<u>Excessive</u> supplements can be harmful and may interfere with the effectiveness of medications.

A) too many

B) a variety of

C) prescribed by a doctor

D) taken orally

11. Select the word that best completes the sentence.

She was told that the procedure would be endoscopic and therefore minimally _____ .

A) effective

B) invasive

C) inflamed

D) expensive

12. Which word is not spelled correctly in the context of this sentence?

Tests of mental ability in the elderly often include recalling the placment of objects.

A) ability

B) recalling

C) placment

D) objects

13. What best describes the term *predispose*?

A) to get rid of

B) to wash thoroughly

C) to make susceptible

D) to have a poor attitude

14. Select the meaning of the underlined word in the sentence.

<u>Asymmetric</u> moles are often indications of an underlying pathology.

A) patterned

B) unbalanced

C) circular

D) aligned

15. Select the meaning of the underlined word in the sentence.

The patient asked the nightshift nurse for a <u>soporific</u>.

A) stimulant

B) muscle relaxer

C) sleeping pill

D) anti-diarrheal

16. A collateral blood vessel is a vessel that

A) carries blood from the limbs to the heart.

B) moves blood around vessels that are impaired.

C) is easily obstructed by blood clots.

D) has been damaged by trauma.

17. What best describes the term *syndrome*?

A) a disease that is getting worse

B) a set of symptoms characteristic of a disease

C) a series of tests used to diagnose an illness

D) a condition inherited from a parent

18. Select the meaning of the underlined word in the sentence.

Many pharmacists recommend taking vitamin B-12 <u>sublingually</u> to promote absorption.

A) by mouth

B) with meals

C) under the tongue

D) after eating

19. Select the word that best completes the sentence.

The Ebola virus is a(n) _____ disease requiring strict protocols to prevent its spread.

A) asymptomatic

B) neurologic

C) innocuous

D) pathogenic

20. When a physician orders a hematologic study on a patient,

A) a study will be conducted on the patient's neurovascular system.

B) the nurse will take the patient's blood pressure.

C) the lab will do a blood workup on the patient.

D) the lab will examine the patient's urine for blood.

21. Select the meaning of the underlined word in the sentence.

Health care workers must remain poised, professional, and <u>pragmatic</u> under pressure.

A) practical

B) logical

C) emotional

D) aloof

22. Select the meaning of the underlined word in the sentence.

After extensive physical therapy, the patient was once again <u>ambulatory</u>.

A) healthy

B) recovered

C) symptomatic

D) walking

23. A room equipped with special acoustic equipment may be used for

A) cardiovascular procedures.

B) procedures related to sound or hearing.

C) oral surgery.

D) ocular surgery.

24. Select the meaning of the underlined word in the sentence.

<u>Progress</u> is being made in developing effective treatments for triple-negative breast cancer.

A) an agreement

B) an improvement

C) a decision

D) a description

25. Select the word that means "severe and destructive."

The virulent infection worsened rapidly, and the patient was admitted to the Intensive Care Unit.

A) virulent

B) worsened

C) admitted

D) Intensive

26. Which word means "the tearing of soft body tissue resulting in a wound"?

A) paroxysmal

B) precipitous

C) laceration

D) surgical

27. Select the meaning of the underlined word in the sentence.

Some medicines are best administered via a transdermal patch.

A) in the muscle

B) under the tongue

C) through the skin

D) in the mouth

28. Select the meaning of the underlined word in the sentence.

Dysfunctional bureaucracies in a hospital can endanger patients.

A) vast

B) expensive

C) intricate

D) flawed

29. What is the best description of the term external?

A) totally open

B) hidden action

C) occurring once

D) located outside

30. Select the meaning of the underlined word in the sentence.

Following strokes that cause vascular damage, patients can suffer shock or heart failure.

A) circulatory

B) digestive

C) respiratory

D) endocrine

31. Select the meaning of the underlined word in the sentence.

The interview process was an amalgam of performance tasks, psychological tests, and one-to-one meetings.

A) blend

B) process

C) schedule

D) conference

32. Select the word that means "to widen."

Vasodilators are drugs that dilate blood vessels, increasing blood flow and lowering blood pressure.

A) vasodilators

B) dilate

C) increasing

D) pressure

33. Select the meaning of the underlined word in the sentence.

Studies show that the normal respiration rate in relaxed adults varies with cardiovascular health.

A) breathing

B) sleeping

C) digestion

D) heart beat

34. Select the word that means "unobstructed."

In an emergency, maintaining a patent airway is often the priority nursing intervention.

A) emergency

B) patent

C) priority

D) intervention

35. What best describes the term *paroxysmal*?
    A) occurring on the left side
    B) experiencing a seizure
    C) undergoing a procedure
    D) experiencing confusion

36. Select the meaning of the underlined word in the sentence.
    Rather than showing improvement, the patient's ability to walk <u>regressed</u> after his knee replacement.
    A) got better
    B) strengthened
    C) worsened
    D) failed

37. When using a cannula, a nurse would be
    A) measuring the patient's blood pressure.
    B) applying compression where necessary.
    C) cleaning a wound of debris and dead tissue.
    D) inserting a thin tube into the body to drain fluid.

38. Which word means "unstable"?
    A) obverse
    B) enteral
    C) labile
    D) occult

39. Which word means "the opposite"?
    A) primary
    B) obverse
    C) intact
    D) distended

40. Select the word that best completes the sentence.
    The patient requested a _____ drug in the hopes of getting some sleep.
    A) soporific
    B) localized
    C) systemic
    D) stimulating

41. Select the meaning of the underlined word in the sentence.
    Many high school teachers who want to show a movie must <u>justify</u> their decision and receive approval.
    A) understand
    B) explain
    C) organize
    D) introduce

42. Select the meaning of the underlined word in the sentence.
    Daily exercise is <u>sensible</u> for those striving for health and well-being.
    A) confusing
    B) prohibited
    C) necessary
    D) wise

43. A manipulation of a patient with abduction requires
    A) the movement of a limb away from the body's midline.
    B) assisting the patient with ambulation.
    C) palpation of the patient's peripheral arteries.
    D) attenuation of the heart muscle.

44. Select the meaning of the underlined word in the sentence.

The wound proved to be <u>superficial</u> and did not require sutures.

A) shallow

B) impressive

C) gruesome

D) jagged

45. Select the meaning of the underlined word in the sentence.

The boss <u>succumbed</u> to pressure from his employees and let them leave early for the holiday.

A) ignored

B) fought

C) surrendered

D) enjoyed

46. Select the meaning of the underlined word in the sentence.

The surgeon had to <u>resect</u> a portion of the intestine due to a diagnosis of volvulus.

A) remove

B) repair

C) replace

D) relocate

47. Select the meaning of the underlined word in the sentence.

A nutritional <u>deficiency</u> will slow down the bone healing process in adults and children.

A) foundation

B) solution

C) injury

D) shortage

48. Which word means "affecting only the surface"?

A) superficial

B) persistent

C) transdermal

D) occult

49. What is the best description of the term *ossify*?

A) loss of bone density

B) a bone fracture

C) to remedy

D) to harden

50. Select the meaning of the underlined word in the sentence.

Long-distance swimming requires attention to <u>hydration</u>, as excessive sweating can go unnoticed.

A) measuring temperature

B) maintaining cleanliness

C) consuming fluids

D) taking vitamins

51. Select the meaning of the underlined word in the sentence.

The medicine affected the patient <u>adversely</u>, exacerbating the pain rather than relieving it.

A) consequently

B) harmfully

C) helpfully

D) expectedly

52. What best describes the term *superficial*?

A) concerning the face

B) serious in demeanor

C) thorough and complete

D) on the surface

53. Select the meaning of the underlined word in the sentence.

Delayed recognition of <u>subtle</u> changes in a patient's appetite can lead to patient deterioration.

A) obvious

B) rapid

C) slight

D) large

54. Select the meaning of the underlined word in the sentence.

Many <u>cardiac</u> conditions are emergent and require immediate medical care.

A) pertaining to the lungs

B) pertaining to the heart

C) pertaining to respiration

D) pertaining to the chest

55. Select the word that best completes the sentence.

The patient's _____ was affected by his stroke, and he could not recall simple facts.

A) hydration

B) acuity

C) balance

D) temperament

Grammar

Directions: Read the question and then choose the most correct answer.

1. Which of the following sentences is grammatically correct?

   A) Kiana went to class; but Lara stayed home.

   B) Kiana went to class, but Lara stayed home.

   C) Kiana went to class, Lara stayed home though.

   D) Kiana went to class but Lara stayed home.

2. Which word from the following sentence is an adverb?

   Our boss has recently hired two new employees.

   A) Our

   B) boss

   C) has

   D) recently

3. Which two words are used incorrectly in the following sentence?

   After the bus driver spoke to the passenger, she realized that she might have acted rudely.

   A) After/realized

   B) spoke/acted

   C) she/she

   D) realized/rudely

4. Which is a list of <u>only</u> homophones?

   A) accept, except, expect

   B) aloud, allowed, louder

   C) they're, there, their

   D) where, wear, weary

5. Which of the following sentences is grammatically correct?

   A) I'm sorry, but I can't drive any further today.

   B) I'm sorry, but I can't drive any father today.

   C) I'm sorry, but I can't drive any fatter today.

   D) I'm sorry, but I can't drive any farther today.

6. Select the best punctuation marks for the blanks in the following sentence.

   "Jean ____" I asked, "Can you come over for dinner ____"

   A) a colon and an exclamation point

   B) a comma and a question mark

   C) a semicolon and a period

   D) a period and a question mark

7. Which word is used incorrectly in the following sentence?

   Liz's love about praise was reflected in how happy she seemed during the birthday toasts in her honor.

   A) love

   B) about

   C) reflected

   D) toasts

8. Which of the following is a dependent clause?

   A) I want to get something hot to eat.

   B) Sometimes we hike in the mountains.

   C) She drives straight home every day.

   D) If you are ready to leave the party.

9. Select the best words for the blanks in the following sentence.

   Mateo was _____ busy studying for an exam _____ attend the party with his roommate.

   A) too, too

   B) two, too

   C) to, two

   D) too, to

10. Select the best words for the blanks in the following sentence.

    It is not a good idea to throw a _____ indoors; when Sam did it, he knocked over a _____ full of cereal and milk.

    A) bull, bawl

    B) bowl, ball

    C) ball, bowl

    D) bawl, bull

11. Which word from the following sentence is an adverb?

    Don't wolf down your food so hastily—you will get a stomachache.

    A) wolf

    B) food

    C) hastily

    D) stomachache

12. Select the best words for the blanks in the following sentence.

    _____ I love tomato sauces, I dislike the texture of raw tomatoes, _____ I avoid salads that contain them.

    A) Because, yet

    B) Although, so

    C) If, but

    D) So, nor

13. Which word is used incorrectly in the following sentence?

    I wish I could except your invitation, but I am going out of town that weekend.

    A) wish

    B) could

    C) except

    D) town

14. Which punctuation mark is used incorrectly in the following sentence?

    I continued, "Lets' wait until 8:00 p.m. to eat dinner."

    A) , (comma)

    B) " (opening quotation mark)

    C) ' (apostrophe)

    D) " (closing quotation mark)

15. Which of the following sentences is grammatically correct?

    A) The cat eat their food while the dog sleep in their bed.

    B) The cats eats its food while the dog sleep in their bed.

    C) The cat eat their food while the dogs sleep in their bed.

    D) The cat eats its food while the dogs sleep in their beds.

16. Select the best words for the blanks in the following sentence.

    _____ is nobody over _____. Did you think you saw someone?

    A) They're, their

    B) Their, they're

    C) They're, there

    D) There, there

17. Which word from the following sentence is a preposition?

Whenever they get scared, our cats hide under the bed.

A) whenever

B) our

C) hide

D) under

18. Which is the best way to rewrite the following incorrectly written sentence?

Walking to school, Javi's basketball was stolen by a gang of mean older boys.

A) As Javi was walking to school, a gang of mean older boys stole his basketball.

B) Walking to school, a gang of mean older boys stole Javi's basketball.

C) When Javi and a gang of mean older boys were walking to school, the gang of mean older boys noticed Javi's basketball, so they stole it.

D) Javi took his basketball to school one day, and it got stolen.

19. Select the best words for the blanks in the following sentence.

Finding a _____ in your sock is not enough to ruin your _____ day, I hope!

A) whole, hole

B) hole, whole

C) howl, whale

D) whale, howl

20. Select the best words for the blanks in the following sentence.

The _____ teammates were practicing _____ the big game on the following Friday.

A) fore, four

B) four, for

C) fewer, for

D) four, fore

21. Which of the following sentences is grammatically correct?

A) My teacher and the school principal has worked together for many years.

B) My teacher and the school principal have worked together for many years.

C) My teacher and the school principal have been worked together for many years.

D) My teacher and the school principal had working together for many years.

22. Which of the following sentences uses capitalization correctly?

A) We're going to Austin, Texas, next weekend so that we can attend my brother's graduation.

B) We're going to Austin, Texas, next Weekend so that we can attend my brother's Graduation.

C) We're going to austin, Texas, next weekend so that we can attend my Brother's graduation.

D) We're going to Austin, texas, next Weekend so that we can attend my brother's graduation.

23. Which word is used incorrectly in the following sentence?

How are you feeling on this sunny Saturday mourning?

A) How

B) feeling

C) Saturday

D) mourning

24. Which of the following sentences is grammatically correct?

A) Is that purple jacket Shelby's or yours?

B) Is that purple jacket Shelbys or yours?

C) Is that purple jacket Shelby's or your?

D) Is that purple jacket Shelby's or you?

25. Select the best words for the blanks in the following sentence.

My mechanic says that if a driver _____ incorrectly, he or she might eventually _____ the car's brakes by wearing them out.

A) brains, bray

B) brays, brain

C) breaks, brake

D) brakes, break

26. Which word is used incorrectly in the following sentence?

There was a heat wave in October, even though Summer was long over.

A) wave

B) October

C) Summer

D) long

27. Which word from the following sentence is a subordinating conjunction?

Because we love animals, our family has adopted a rescue dog and four rescue cats.

A) Because

B) love

C) family

D) and

28. Which of the following is a compound sentence?

A) The ferryboat ride from Oakland to San Francisco does not take long at all.

B) Last weekend we took the ferry to San Francisco, and we stayed in the city for two nights.

C) Although the BART train is convenient, too, the ferryboat ride is more enjoyable.

D) If you decide to drive over the Bay Bridge, it will probably take you far longer, and you will not enjoy being stuck in traffic.

29. Which word is used incorrectly in the following sentence?

You're rite: the best time to write a thank-you note is right after you receive a gift or a big favor.

A) You're

B) rite

C) write

D) right

30. Which of the following choices uses punctuation correctly?

A) My cat Katrina isn't the only female in our home, there's Hollie the dog, and I am female, too.

B) My cat Katrina isnt the only female in our home: theres Hollie the dog, and I am female, too.

C) My cat Katrina isn't the only female in our home: there's Hollie the dog, and I am female, too.

D) My cat Katrina isnt' the only female in our home? There's Hollie the dog, and I am female, too.

31. Which two words from the following sentence are homophones?

It rained hard during the afternoon, so I reined in my horse, turned her toward home, and we galloped for shelter.

A) rained, reined

B) It, I

C) turned, toward

D) horse, home

32. Which of the following sentences is grammatically correct?

A) It is so hot today that I can scarcely bare it.

B) It is so hot today that I can scarcely bore it.

C) It is so hot today that I can scarcely bear it.

D) It is so hot today that I can scarcely burn it.

33. Which of the following sentences is grammatically correct?

   A) One of my teammates hope to be the star player tonight.

   B) Two of my teammates hopes to be star players tonight.

   C) All my teammates hopes to play their best tonight.

   D) Of course, no one on our team wants to play poorly.

34. Which of the following sentences contains a possessive pronoun?

   A) I love thin-crust pizza topped with roasted red peppers and caramelized onions.

   B) Ana's favorite pizza is the deep-dish kind they sell at the Chicago airport.

   C) Mom makes pizza dough from scratch; it contains flour, yeast, and other ingredients.

   D) Go ahead and take the last slice—it's yours!

35. Select the best words for the blanks in the following sentence.

   One medication _____ me poorly, but the other medication had no _____ at all.

   A) effected; affect

   B) affected; effect

   C) effected; effect

   D) affected; affect

36. Which of the following sentences is grammatically correct?

   A) I have about six sweaters, and the most soft one is cashmere.

   B) My softest sweater is made of cashmere.

   C) I have about six sweaters, and the softer one is cashmere.

   D) My most softest sweater is made of cashmere.

37. Which word is incorrectly capitalized or lowercased in the following sentence?

   The Summer season is made up of June, July, and August.

   A) Summer

   B) season

   C) June

   D) August

38. Which word or phrase is used incorrectly in the following sentence?

   We could have went out last night, but it was raining.

   A) could have

   B) went

   C) but

   D) was raining

39. Select the best words for the blanks in the following sentence.

   After the king received a ____ wound in battle and died, his whole country was in ____ for a year.

   A) mortal, mourning

   B) mourning, mortal

   C) morning, mooring

   D) mooring, mourning

40. Which word is used incorrectly in the following sentence?

   There are two bedrooms, a bathroom, and a sitting room in our hotel sweet.

   A) There

   B) bathroom

   C) hotel

   D) sweet

41. Which words from the following sentence are pronouns?

I offered to help her study for the test, but she was too busy.

A) I, her, she

B) offered, help, study

C) to, for, but, was

D) test, too, busy

42. Select the best word or phrase for the blank in the following sentence.

By the time Emma arrived at my house, we _____ already late for the party, so I was irritated with her.

A) were

B) was

C) had been

D) were being

43. Which word is used incorrectly in the following sentence?

Please bring that unsafe toy away from your little brother.

A) Please

B) bring

C) unsafe

D) brother

44. Which of the following sentences is grammatically correct?

A) I don't think the outcome will effect me much, so I won't worry about it.

B) I don't think the outcome will infect me much, so I won't worry about it.

C) I don't think the outcome will inspect me much, so I won't worry about it.

D) I don't think the outcome will affect me much, so I won't worry about it.

45. Which of the choices is a homophone for a word in the sentence below?

The new member of the royal family has a sweet smile and a poised manner.

A) knew

B) rayon

C) sweat

D) manure

46. Select the best words for the blanks in the following sentence.

I _____ busy studying for my exam, and my brothers _____ busy studying for theirs.

A) are, are

B) are, am

C) am, am

D) am, are

47. Which word is used incorrectly in the following sentence?

My elementary school principle's name was Mrs. Woodnancy.

A) elementary

B) school

C) principle's

D) Mrs.

48. Which word from the following sentence is an interjection?

I was considering majoring in English, but then I thought, hey, why not major in biology?

A) considering

B) English

C) hey

D) biology

49. Which of the following sentences is grammatically correct?

A) DeQuan loves eating pizza, but meat toppings make him feel queasy.

B) Though he avoids meat toppings, pizza is one of DeQuan's favorite foods.

C) Meat toppings on pizza makes DeQuan feel queasy.

D) Pizza is one of DeQuan's favorite foods but he can't put meat on it.

50. Select the best words for the blanks in the following sentence.

Our _____ says she lives by this _____: "Honesty is the best policy."

A) principle, principal

B) prince, principle

C) principal, invincible

D) principal, principle

51. Which of the following sentences is correctly punctuated?

A) "Im so relieved that the storm is over!" Robyn exclaimed.

B) "I'm so relieved that the storm is over! Robyn exclaimed.

C) "I'm so relieved that the storm is over?" Robyn exclaimed.

D) "I'm so relieved that the storm is over!" Robyn exclaimed.

52. Which word is used incorrectly in the following sentence?

Hundreds of years ago (in days of yore), if you were female, you're destiny was not yours to decide: your father, brother, or husband made all your decisions for you.

A) Hundreds

B) yore

C) you're

D) yours

53. Which of the following sentences is grammatically correct?

A) I used flour to bake a cake, and I decorated it with flowers.

B) I used flower to bake a cake, and I decorated it with flour.

C) I used fleer to bake a cake, and I decorated it with flowing.

D) I used flair to bake a cake, and I decorated it with flours.

54. Select the best word for the blank in the following sentence.

Gold is a valuable precious _____ used in jewelry, medicine, and technology.

A) meddle

B) medal

C) mettle

D) metal

55. Which of the following is a compound-complex sentence?

A) This mug, the large, pale-blue ceramic one, is my favorite cup from which to drink coffee.

B) First I pour in about two inches of coffee, and then I fill the rest of the cup with hot milk.

C) Although it is not a good idea to consume sweets in the morning, I always add two teaspoons of raw sugar.

D) Because caffeine keeps me awake, I can't have it in the evening, but I need one cup of coffee in the morning.

Biology

Directions: Read the question carefully, and then choose the most correct answer.

1. Water molecules are considered polar because they:

   A) form hydrogen bonds.

   B) are held together by a covalent bond.

   C) have a high specific heat.

   D) have partial positive and negative charges.

2. Why do the tails of phospholipids not interact with water?

   A) The phospholipids' tails are too large to interact with water.

   B) Nonpolar molecules do not interact with water.

   C) Inorganic molecules interact with each other.

   D) Water molecules have a high specific heat.

3. Which of the following is found in plant cells but not in animal cells?

   A) cell wall

   B) Golgi apparatus

   C) plasma membrane

   D) proteins

4. Tay-Sachs disease is caused by a four-codon insertion that causes errors in the production of the enzyme beta-hexosaminidase. What kind of mutation causes Tay-Sachs disease?

   A) point mutation

   B) base substitution

   C) frameshift mutation

   D) deletion

5. The purpose of oxygen in the electron transport chain is to:

   A) form water.

   B) drive the proton gradient.

   C) act as the final electron acceptor.

   D) carry protons.

6. To form nucleosomes, DNA is wrapped around:

   A) histones.

   B) chromatin.

   C) centromeres.

   D) ATP.

7. In which phase of the cell cycle do chromosomes become visible?

   A) S

   B) G2

   C) interphase

   D) prophase

8. Which of the following is produced during transcription?

   A) DNA

   B) mRNA

   C) lipids

   D) proteins

9. If an egg cell has 14 chromosomes, how many chromosomes would a skin cell from the same organism contain?

   A) 7

   B) 14

   C) 28

   D) 56

10. Which type of bond holds the oxygen and hydrogen atoms in water molecules together?

    A) ionic bond

    B) covalent bond

    C) hydrogen bond

    D) metallic bond

11. Red-green color blindness is an X-linked recessive trait. If the mother is a carrier and the father is color blind, what is the percent chance that they will have a child who has red-green color blindness?

    A) 0 percent

    B) 25 percent

    C) 50 percent

    D) 75 percent

12. Organic molecules must contain which element?

    A) carbon

    B) phosphorous

    C) nitrogen

    D) oxygen

13. Where do the light reactions of photosynthesis occur in plants?

    A) mitochondria

    B) chloroplast

    C) cytoplasm

    D) vacuole

14. Which molecule is produced during the Calvin cycle?

    A) carbon dioxide

    B) glucose

    C) water

    D) ATP

15. Why is one strand of DNA synthesized in Okazaki fragments?

    A) DNA is synthesized in the 5' to 3' direction.

    B) Replication of DNA occurs one strand at a time.

    C) Synthesis of one of the strands is incomplete.

    D) Large strands of DNA cannot be ligated.

16. The primary purpose of meiosis is to:

    A) replicate DNA.

    B) grow specialized tissues.

    C) prevent mutations in DNA.

    D) produce gametes.

17. During protein synthesis, the purpose of tRNA is to:

    A) carry the mRNA to the ribosome.

    B) align the next amino acid with the growing protein.

    C) detach the finished protein from the ribosome.

    D) package the protein for transport out of the cell.

18. Cystic fibrosis is a recessive trait. If the mother does not carry the recessive gene, but the father carries a single copy, what are the chances that their child will have cystic fibrosis?

    A) 0 percent

    B) 25 percent

    C) 50 percent

    D) 75 percent

19. Which of the following is a carbohydrate?

    A) DNA polymerase

    B) vegetable oil

    C) fructose

    D) mRNA

20. Which organelle produces energy in the form of ATP?

A) mitochondria

B) nucleus

C) vacuole

D) Golgi apparatus

21. Which of the following is removed from ATP to release energy?

A) adenosine

B) a phosphate group

C) oxygen

D) an electron

22. Which of the following is found at the end of a chromosome?

A) telomere

B) centromere

C) centrosome

D) promoter

23. During meiosis, the number of chromosomes is reduced from 2n to 1n during:

A) metaphase I.

B) anaphase II.

C) prophase II.

D) telophase I.

24. Protein synthesis takes place at which organelle?

A) nucleus

B) vacuole

C) ribosome

D) chloroplast

25. How many nucleotides are in a codon?

A) 3

B) 4

C) 5

D) 6

26. During cellular respiration, electrons are carried by:

A) NADH.

B) ADP.

C) cyclic AMP.

D) glucose.

27. The codon for the amino acid methionine is AUG. Which anticodon would be found on the tRNA that carries methionine?

A) AUG

B) TAC

C) UAC

D) TUG

28. An organism has 8 pairs of chromosomes. How many chromosomes does each egg or sperm cell contain?

A) 4

B) 8

C) 16

D) 32

29. In which phase of the cell cycle is DNA replicated?

A) G1

B) S

C) G2

D) mitosis

30. When a scientist crosses a red flower with a white flower, the F1 generation has pink flowers. In this flower, the allele for red is:

A) dominant over white.

B) codominant with white.

C) incompletely dominant over white.

D) recessive to white.

Chemistry

Directions: Read the question carefully, and then choose the most correct answer.

1. Which element has the greatest number of protons? Refer to the periodic table.

   A) Mg^{2+}

   B) Br^-

   C) Na^+

   D) N^{3-}

2. Which of the following elements will form an ion with a charge of −2? Refer to the periodic table.

   A) F and Be

   B) Cl and Br

   C) Se and Br

   D) Se and O

3. What type of bond is formed between one positively charged atom and one negatively charged atom?

   A) ionic bond

   B) hydrogen bond

   C) covalent bond

   D) metallic bond

4. A solution that contains less than the maximum amount of solute that can be dissolved in it is:

   A) heterogeneous.

   B) homogeneous.

   C) unsaturated.

   D) saturated.

5. Which of the following elements is the most electronegative?

   A) radon (Rn)

   B) tin (Sn)

   C) sulfur (S)

   D) fluorine (F)

6. Which of the following is a chemical property?

   A) viscosity

   B) density

   C) toxicity

   D) color

7. What are the coefficients needed to balance the equation below?

   $\_Pb(NO_3)_2 + \_K_2CrO_4 \rightarrow \_PbCrO_4 + \_KNO_3$

   A) 1, 1, 1, 2

   B) 2, 2, 2, 3

   C) 1, 1, 1, 1

   D) 3, 3, 3, 1

8. Which of the following is a base?

   A) $Ba(OH)_2$

   B) HCl

   C) $HClO_4$

   D) HI

9. If 10 moles of $Pb(NO_3)_2$ react completely with K_2CrO_4, how many moles of KNO_3 are produced?

   $Pb(NO_3)_2 + K_2CrO_4 \rightarrow PbCrO_4 + 2KNO_3$

   A) 2 moles of KNO_3

   B) 5 moles of KNO_3

   C) 10 moles of KNO_3

   D) 20 moles of KNO_3

10. A particular substance has a half-life of twenty days. If the initial sample was 100 g, how many grams will remain after forty days?

    A) 75 g

    B) 50 g

    C) 33 g

    D) 25 g

11. The half-life of an unknown radioactive element X is four days. How much of a 100 g sample of element X will remain after four days?

A) 25 g

B) 50 g

C) 75 g

D) 100 g

12. The identity of an element is determined by its number of:

A) neutrons.

B) nuclei.

C) protons.

D) electrons.

13. Which of the following elements will form an ion with a charge of +2? Refer to the periodic table.

A) Ca and Mn

B) Li and Be

C) Na and Mg

D) Mg and Ca

14. Which type of bond occurs when electrons are shared between two atoms?

A) hydrogen bond

B) covalent bond

C) metallic bond

D) ionic bond

15. The number of neutrons in an atom is equal to:

A) the atomic mass minus the number of electrons.

B) the number of protons plus the number of electrons.

C) the number of protons minus the number of electrons.

D) the atomic mass minus the atomic number.

16. What state of matter has a definite shape and definite volume?

A) solid

B) liquid

C) gas

D) plasma

17. Solutions that have a sour taste and react strongly with metals are:

A) acidic.

B) basic.

C) neutral.

D) salts.

18. What type of reaction is shown below?

$2Li + Cl_2 \rightarrow 2LiCl$

A) synthesis reaction

B) decomposition reaction

C) single displacement reaction

D) double displacement reaction

19. Which of the following is a negatively charged subatomic particle?

A) neutron

B) proton

C) cation

D) electron

20. How many electrons are needed to complete the valence shell of the halogens?

A) 1

B) 2

C) 6

D) 7

21. The weak attraction between temporary dipoles creates:

   A) the London dispersion force.

   B) a hydrogen bond.

   C) dipole-dipole interactions.

   D) a covalent bond.

22. How many moles of O_2 are needed to produce 20 moles of $KClO_3$?

   $2KCl + 3O_2 \rightarrow 2KClO_3$

   A) 1.5 moles of O_2

   B) 15 moles of O_2

   C) 20 moles of O_2

   D) 30 moles of O_2

23. Which process occurs when a substance goes from gas to liquid, such as when dew forms on grass in the morning?

   A) condensation

   B) sublimation

   C) evaporation

   D) deposition

24. Which of the following is a heterogeneous mixture?

   A) sugar water

   B) air

   C) vegetable oil

   D) cereal in milk

25. What type of reaction is shown below?

   $2H_2O_2 \rightarrow 2H_2O + O_2$

   A) synthesis reaction

   B) decomposition reaction

   C) single displacement reaction

   D) double displacement reaction

26. Which elements have the same number of electrons in their valence shell? Refer to the periodic table.

   A) Na, K, Ca

   B) Mg, Be, Cr

   C) F, Cl, Br

   D) P, N, C

27. What type of reaction is shown below?

   $2K(s) + Cl_2(g) \rightarrow 2KCl(s)$

   A) decomposition

   B) synthesis

   C) single displacement

   D) double displacement

28. How many electrons are needed to complete the valence shell of the noble gases?

   A) 0

   B) 1

   C) 2

   D) 3

29. Which process occurs when water vapor becomes a solid?

   A) condensation

   B) sublimation

   C) evaporation

   D) deposition

30. What type of reaction is shown below?

   $Zn + CuCl_2 \rightarrow ZnCl_2 + Cu$

   A) synthesis reaction

   B) decomposition reaction

   C) single displacement reaction

   D) double displacement reaction

Anatomy and Physiology

Directions: Read the question carefully, and then choose the most correct answer.

1. Which of the following heart valves prevents blood from going back into the right ventricle?

A) aortic

B) mitral

C) pulmonary

D) tricuspid

2. Which of the following is the layer of bone that houses blood vessels and nerve endings?

A) periosteum

B) compact bone

C) spongy bone

D) trabecula

3. Which part of the digestive system is the appendix attached to?

A) stomach

B) cecum

C) jejunum

D) ileum

4. Which of the following statements is anatomically correct?

A) The knees are superior to the shoulder.

B) The stomach is lateral to the kidneys.

C) The fingers are proximal to the shoulders.

D) The urethral meatus is anterior to the anus.

5. Which artery branches off directly from the aortic arch?

A) right common carotid

B) right subclavian

C) pulmonary

D) left subclavian

6. Which type of nerve allows a person to determine the temperature of an object?

A) interneurons

B) cranial nerves

C) spinal nerves

D) afferent neurons

7. Which of the following is a response by the innate immune system when tissue is damaged?

A) The skin dries out.

B) The temperature increases.

C) The blood flow to the area decreases.

D) The heart rate slows.

8. Which layer of the skin contains large numbers of blood vessels?

A) epidermis

B) dermis

C) hypodermis

D) subcutaneous

9. Which of the following is released when bone is broken down?

A) phosphorous

B) iron

C) calcium

D) zinc

10. Which part of a nerve cell holds the cellular organelles?

A) soma

B) dendrite

C) axon

D) synapse

11. Which hormone produced by the pineal gland causes drowsiness?

A) oxytocin

B) dopamine

C) thyroxine

D) melatonin

12. Where are apocrine glands of the integumentary system located?

A) armpit

B) hands

C) feet

D) abdomen

13. Which zone of the sarcomere has myosin filaments that are thick and do not shorten during muscle contraction?

A) Z-line

B) A-band

C) I-band

D) H-zone

14. Which of the following secretes progesterone and estradiol after the egg is fertilized?

A) oocyte

B) corpus luteum

C) fallopian tube

D) fimbriae

15. Which of the following describes a function of the large intestine?

A) It absorbs approximately 25 percent of the available nutrients from food.

B) It secretes enzymes that break down nucleic acids.

C) It produces enzymes that regulate blood sugar level.

D) It absorbs water and electrolytes before waste is expelled.

16. Which of the following is the largest and outermost part of the brain?

A) pons

B) cerebellum

C) cerebrum

D) thalamus

17. Which of the following connects the ribs to the sternum?

A) costal cartilage

B) synovial joint

C) cardiac muscle

D) collagen fiber

18. Which of the following is true about air in the lungs?

A) During expiration, air completely leaves the lungs.

B) There is always about a liter of air in the lungs.

C) Shallow breathing does not circulate any air through the lungs.

D) Deep breathing moves a maximum of two liters of air through the lungs.

19. Which of the following bones are directly connected to the ulna and radius?

A) carpal

B) metacarpal

C) tarsal

D) metatarsal

20. Which of the following stores oxygen to help muscles perform work under stress?

A) myofibril

B) transverse tube

C) myoglobin

D) filament

21. Which of the following provides the energy muscles need to contract?

   A) sarcolemma

   B) mitochondria

   C) myofibril

   D) sarcomere

22. Which of the following joins the left and right hemispheres of the cerebrum?

   A) corpus callosum

   B) corpus luteum

   C) corpus sulci

   D) corpus gyri

23. A patient has recently been diagnosed with a bone marrow disorder that leads to slow blood clotting. The patient is likely low in which of the following?

   A) red blood cells

   B) plasma

   C) platelets

   D) hemoglobin

24. A patient came to the emergency department complaining of severe lower back pain after a fall. Which vertebrae has the patient most likely injured?

   A) cervical

   B) thoracic

   C) cranial

   D) lumbar

25. Which of the following describes the triceps when the elbow is extended?

   A) agonist

   B) antagonist

   C) fixator

   D) synergist

26. Which of the following is the outer and most durable layer of the meninges?

   A) pia mater

   B) dura mater

   C) arachnoid mater

   D) subarachnoid space

27. What type of muscle is found in the external sphincter of the bladder?

   A) involuntary

   B) voluntary

   C) undifferentiated

   D) multinucleated

28. What is the role of the liver in digestion?

   A) It produces the bile needed to digest fats.

   B) It stores bile produced by the gallbladder.

   C) It regulates feelings of hunger.

   D) It collects the waste that is the end product of digestion.

29. Which granular leukocyte digests bacteria?

   A) neutrophil

   B) eosinophil

   C) basophil

   D) lymphocyte

30. What is the role of the thyroid gland?

   A) It controls the release of hormones from the pituitary gland.

   B) It regulates the sleep cycle.

   C) It controls the body's metabolic rate.

   D) It regulates blood sugar level.

Physics

Directions: Read the question carefully, and then choose the most correct answer.

1. A race car accelerates from 0 miles per hour to 60 miles per hour in 4 seconds. What is the race car's acceleration?

   A) 6.7 m/s²
   B) 15.0 m/s²
   C) 15.7 m/s²
   D) 240.0 m/s²

2. A mover exerts a constant 400 newton force to push a sofa up a 10 meter-long truck ramp. How much work does the mover do?

   A) 40 J
   B) 400 J
   C) 4000 J
   D) 40,000 J

3. On Mars, the acceleration due to gravity is 3.8 meters per second squared. What is the weight of an 80 kilogram person on Mars?

   A) 0.05 N
   B) 21.1 N
   C) 304 N
   D) 3040 N

4. A radio transmitter emits what type of wave?

   A) mechanical
   B) electromagnetic
   C) longitudinal
   D) transverse

5. The International Space Station orbits Earth at 17,500 miles per hour. What is its speed in meters per second?

   A) 5000 m/s
   B) 7822 m/s
   C) 17,500 m/s
   D) 39,155 m/s

6. What is the gravitational potential energy stored in a 2.5 gram penny held over the edge of a building that is 400 meters tall?

   A) 9.8 J
   B) 98 J
   C) 980 J
   D) 9800 J

7. Electrons move through a conducting wire at a constant speed, producing a constant current. What type of field do they produce?

   A) electric field
   B) magnetic field
   C) gravitational field
   D) no field

8. What magnitude of force does a 1 kilogram object exert on the surface of the earth?

   A) 0.10 N
   B) 0.98 N
   C) 9.8 N
   D) 98 N

9. How much time does it take a 100 watt light bulb to do 100 joules of work?

   A) 0.01 s
   B) 1 s
   C) 100 s
   D) 1 hour

10. What is the intensity of a sound that delivers 0.5 watts of power to a square space with sides of 2 meters?

   A) 0.125 W/m²
   B) 1 W/m²
   C) 2 W/m²
   D) 12.5 W/m²

11. A water balloon is launched at 47 meters per second at an angle of 39 degrees above the horizontal. What is the vertical component of its velocity?

A) 26.5 m/s

B) 28.5 m/s

C) 29.6 m/s

D) 36.5 m/s

12. A child swings a tennis ball above her head on the end of a 1 meter rope. She lets go and it flies off at 2.5 meters per second. What was the centripetal acceleration of the tennis ball the moment before the girl let it go?

A) 2.5 m/s^2

B) 6.25 m/s^2

C) 62.5 m/s^2

D) 112.5 m/s^2

13. A force meter attached to a rope swinging an 88 gram baseball reads 0.5 newtons. If the rope is 80 centimeters long, what is the tangential velocity of the baseball?

A) 2.1 m/s

B) 4.5 m/s

C) 21 m/s

D) 45 m/s

14. Light entering a diamond from air at 30 degrees from the surface normal is refracted at 12 degrees. What is the index of refraction of the diamond?

A) 2.02

B) 2.40

C) 3.00

D) 2.42 × 10^2

15. What is the velocity of a wave with a frequency of 100 hertz and a wavelength of 400 meters?

A) 4 m/s

B) 4 × 10^4 m/s

C) 4 × 10^8 m/s

D) 3 × 10^8 m/s

16. A 17 nanocoulomb charge is placed 8 centimeters from a 22 nanocoulomb charge. What is the magnitude of the electric force between them? ($k = 9 \times 10^9$ N m^2/C^2)

A) 4.21 × 10^{-5} N

B) 5.26 × 10^{-4} N

C) 4.21 × 10^4 N

D) 5.26 × 10^4 N

17. How much resistance is required for a high-voltage power supply of 3 kilovolts to only supply 0.1 ampere?

A) 30 Ω

B) 30,000 Ω

C) 300,000 Ω

D) 30,000,000 Ω

18. Eight AA batteries of 1.5 volts are connected in series. What current flows if they are connected to a single 10 ohm resistor?

A) 0.15 A

B) 0.27 A

C) 2.7 A

D) 27 A

19. A mass triples its speed. By what factor is its kinetic energy increased?

A) $\frac{1}{3}$

B) $\frac{1}{9}$

C) 3

D) 9

20. Before being pushed across a floor, a crate is weighed on a scale as 47 kilograms. If the coefficient of friction between the crate and a rug is known to be 0.40, with what force will friction oppose the crate's motion?

A) 74 N

B) 84 N

C) 174 N

D) 184 N

21. A 0.5 kilogram ball moving at 5 meters per second bounces off a wall at 3 meters per second. What magnitude of impulse was delivered to the wall?

A) 0.75 kg m/s

B) 1 kg m/s

C) 2.25 kg m/s

D) 4 kg m/s

22. What is the magnitude of the electric field between two parallel plates separated by 2 millimeters and held at a potential difference of 30 volts?

A) 0.06 V/m

B) 6.0 V/m

C) 15 V/m

D) 15,000 V/m

23. A laser is directed at a reflective mirror 50 degrees from the normal to the mirror surface. At what angle from the normal is the beam reflected?

A) 0°

B) 40°

C) 50°

D) 90°

24. Seventeen 12 ohm resistors are connected in series. What is the total resistance of this circuit?

A) 0.71 Ω

B) 1.42 Ω

C) 194 Ω

D) 204 Ω

25. A proton in free space is being accelerated by a force of 3×10^{-9} newtons. What electric field is present?

A) 1.8×10^{10} N/C

B) 0.53×10^{10} N/C

C) 1.8×10^{19} N/C

D) 0.53×10^{19} N/C

26. Far away from any massive objects, an asteroid moves with a constant velocity of 8 kilometers per second. What is the magnitude of the force acting on the asteroid?

A) 0 N

B) 9.8 N

C) 78.4 N

D) 78,400 N

27. A charged object with a mass of 5 kilograms is placed in a vertical electric field of 4×10^4 newtons per coulomb and released. If the object remains stationary, what is the magnitude of charge on the object?

A) 1.23×10^{-9} C

B) 1.23×10^{-6} C

C) 1.23×10^{-3} C

D) 1.23 C

28. A friend is trying to spin a tennis ball on a string at 1 revolution per second, but does not want to exceed an angular acceleration of 1 radian per second squared. What is the shortest time it would take them to accomplish this?

A) 1 s

B) 3.14 s

C) 6.28 s

D) 10 s

29. Two identical waves each with an amplitude of 2 meters and a frequency of 7 hertz interfere in phase. What is the final amplitude and frequency of the resulting wave?

A) 0 m, 0 Hz

B) 2 m, 14 Hz

C) 4 m, 7 Hz

D) 4 m, 14 Hz

30. Light from air enters a material of $n = 1.5$ at an angle of 45 degrees from the normal. At what angle from the normal is the light inside the material?

A) 0.008°

B) 18.33°

C) 28.13°

D) 45°

ANSWER KEY

MATHEMATICS

1. B)

$8x + 2 = 3x + 17$

$8x = 3x + 15$

$5x = 15$

$x = 3$

2. C)

30 minutes = 0.5 hour

$\frac{13}{0.5} = \frac{x}{7}$

$0.5x = 91$

$x = 182$

3. C)

$60 \text{ in} \times \frac{2.54 \text{ cm}}{\text{in}} \times \frac{1 \text{ m}}{100 \text{ cm}} = 1.524 \text{ m}$

4. B)

$3\frac{2}{4} + 3\frac{3}{4} + 4 + 4\frac{1}{4} + 4\frac{2}{4} = 18\frac{8}{4} = 18 + 2 = 20$

5. D)

$\$75.00 - \$39.73 = \$35.27$

6. D)

$5 - 7(3^2 - 4) = 5 - 7(9 - 4)$

$= 5 - 7(5) = 5 - 35 = -30$

7. A)

$1\frac{1}{2}$ years = 18 months

$\frac{18 \times 25}{150} = 3$

8. A)

$4250 \div 125 = 34$

9. B)

$16 + 10 \div 2 = 16 + 5 = 21$

10. D)

$6.5 + 3.59 + 2 = 12.09$

11. C)

$-9b - 4 = 2b + 7 \ \rightarrow \ -9b = 2b + 11$

$-11b = 11 \ \rightarrow \ b = -1$

12. D)

$\frac{(-10)^2}{4} - 3(-10) + 4$

$\frac{100}{4} + 30 + 4$

$25 + 30 + 4 = 59$

13. B)

$7\frac{4}{8} + 2\frac{5}{8} + 7\frac{4}{8} = 16\frac{13}{8} = 16 + 1\frac{5}{8} = 17\frac{5}{8}$

14. D)

$-3\frac{1}{3} = -3.\overline{3}$

$-\frac{24}{5} = -4.8$

$-4.8 < -3.3 < 0 < 2.73$

15. C)

$0.7 = \frac{7}{10}$

16. C)

$F = 1.8C + 32$

$F = 1.8(25) + 32$

$F = 77°$

17. C)

$-7 + (-9) - (-4) = -16 + 4 = -12$

18. B)

$\text{percent} = \frac{\text{part}}{\text{whole}}$

$\frac{4}{25} = 0.16 = 16\%$

19. C)

1400 hours is 2:00 p.m. In 4 hours, it will be **6:00 p.m.**

20. B)

If the ratio of fiction to nonfiction books is 2 to 5, the ratio of fiction to the total number of books is 2 to 7.

$\frac{2}{7} = \frac{x}{735}$

$7x = 1470$

$x = 210$

21. **A)**

$\frac{1}{2.5} = \frac{x}{10}$

$2.5x = 10$

$x = 4$

22. **A)**

$26.4 \times 74 = 1953.6 \approx 1954$

23. **B)**

$110 \text{ lb} \times \frac{1 \text{ kg}}{2.2 \text{ lb}} = 50 \text{ kg}$

24. **B)**

$\$285.48 \div 6 = \$47.58$

25. **B)**

$100\% - 25\% = 75\%$

$\text{whole} = \frac{\text{part}}{\text{percent}}$

$\frac{18}{0.75} = 24$

26. **A)**

$\text{part} = \text{whole} \times \text{percent}$

$127 \times 0.23 = 29.21 \rightarrow 29 \text{ people absent}$

$127 - 29 = 98$

27. **D)**

$\frac{2}{3} \times \frac{3}{10} = \frac{1}{5}$

28. **B)**

The nurse is working an afternoon/evening shift; therefore, it is 6:45 p.m., which is **1845 in military time**.

29. **B)**

$\frac{1}{2} \div \frac{2}{3} = \frac{1}{2} \times \frac{3}{2} = \frac{3}{4}$

30. **C)**

$\text{whole} = \frac{\text{part}}{\text{percent}}$

$\frac{15}{0.94} \approx 16$

31. **B)**

$12x + 5 = 77$

$12x = 72$

$x = 6$

32. **D)**

$\frac{4x^2}{2x} + 7x = 2x + 7x = 9x$

33. **B)**

$\frac{64 \div 4}{100 \div 4} = \frac{16}{25}$

34. **A)**

$5(x + 3) - 12 = 43$

$5x + 15 - 12 = 43$

$5x + 3 = 43$

$5x = 40$

$x = 8$

35. **A)**

$7\frac{1}{3} \div \frac{4}{5} = \frac{22}{3} \div \frac{4}{5} = \frac{22}{3} \times \frac{5}{4}$

$= \frac{11}{3} \times \frac{5}{2} = \frac{55}{6} = 9\frac{1}{6}$

36. **B)**

$8 \div \frac{2}{3} = \frac{8}{1} \times \frac{3}{2} = \frac{4}{1} \times \frac{3}{1} = 12$

37. **A)**

$300 \text{ ml} \times \frac{1 \text{ L}}{1000 \text{ ml}} \times \frac{1 \text{ gal}}{3.785 \text{ L}} \times \frac{128 \text{ fl oz}}{1 \text{ gal}}$

$\approx 10.15 \text{ fl oz}$

38. **C)**

Multiply by the least common denominator to clear the fractions.

$(12)\frac{x}{4} + (12)\frac{2}{3} = (12)\frac{29}{12}$

$3x + 8 = 29$

$3x = 21$

$x = 7$

39. **D)**

48 cents = $0.48

$\$1.68 \div \$0.48 = 3.5$

40. **B)**

$\$25.44 \div 3.2 = \$7.95$

41. **C)**

$15 \text{ mL} \times \frac{0.2 \text{ tsp}}{1 \text{ mL}} = 3 \text{ tsp}$

42. B)

Distribute by multiplying coefficients and adding exponents.

$3xy(x^2 - 11xy + 10y^2) =$ **$3x^3y - 33x^2y^2 + 30xy^3$**

43. A)

Reduce coefficients, subtract exponents.

$\dfrac{10x^9y^6}{5x^3y^2} =$ **$2x^6y^4$**

44. B)

part = whole × percent

$81 \times 0.09 =$ **7.29**

45. A)

$\dfrac{4}{5} = \dfrac{x}{450} \rightarrow 5x = 1800$

$x = 360$

46. C)

$17 - 4\dfrac{3}{5} = \dfrac{85}{5} - \dfrac{23}{5} = \dfrac{62}{5} =$ **$12\dfrac{2}{5}$**

47. D)

$63 - 15.75 =$ **47.25**

48. D)

negative × negative = positive

$(-9)(-4) =$ **36**

49. B)

negative × positive = negative

$-2(11) =$ **−22**

50. B)

$8.653 + 2 + 1.06 =$ **11.713**

51. A)

$\dfrac{1}{2} + \dfrac{5}{6} - \dfrac{3}{4} = \dfrac{6}{12} + \dfrac{10}{12} - \dfrac{9}{12} =$ **$\dfrac{7}{12}$**

52. D)

$0.057(1210) + 23.50 = 68.97 + 23.50 =$ **92.47**

53. C)

$\dfrac{25}{2} = \dfrac{x}{8} \rightarrow 2x = 200$

$x = 100$

54. C)

part = whole × percent

$260 \times 0.05 = 13$

$260 - 13 =$ **247**

55. A)

11:15 a.m. is 1115 hours.

$1115 + 400 =$ **1515**

1. **A)**

   The answer provides an adequate summary of the passage overall. The other choices only provide specific details from the passage.

2. **D)**

   The primary purpose of the essay is to inform; its focus is the endocrine system's parts and functions. It is not persuasive or cautionary.

3. **A)**

   In the second paragraph, the author writes, "When the hormones reach other tissues, they catalyze certain chemical reactions, stimulating various processes or activities." The writer then goes on to describe those activities in detail, making it clear that the hormones caused those events to occur.

4. **D)**

   In the second paragraph, the author writes, "The endocrine system's function is to produce and distribute hormones."

5. **B)**

   The author writes, "Hormones are also released in humans in moments of fear or anxiety and can trigger the fight-or-flight response." There are no sentences supporting the other claims.

6. **A)**

   In the first paragraph, the author writes, "The pituitary gland serves as the 'master gland' of the endocrine system."

7. **A)**

   The passage is about how important it is for medical professionals to understand hypoglycemia, especially when it comes to patients who have diabetes. The other answer choices are details from the passage.

8. **C)**

   This detail is not found in the passage. The passage strongly focuses on patients with diabetes, but it does not state that only those patients are affected by hypoglycemia.

9. **A)**

   The text is informative, not persuasive or dramatic. It does not recount a specific event, but simply informs the audience of potential general scenarios.

10. **B)**

    In the second paragraph, the author writes, "[Y]ou will likely need to help administer glucose to them as soon as possible." In this case, administer means to give glucose to a patient.

11. **A)**

    In the second paragraph, the author states, "When a diabetic patient's blood sugar plummets, their mental state becomes altered. This can lead to unconsciousness or, in more severe cases, a diabetic coma and/or brain damage." The reader can infer from this information that diabetic comas could cause permanent brain damage.

12. **B)**

    In the third paragraph, the author writes, "A blood glucose value of less than 80 milligrams per deciliter can be considered a hypoglycemic episode."

13. **C)**

    In the second paragraph, the author writes, "Your body language speaks volumes." The writer then goes on to detail ways that body language can convey messages (with "posture, hand motions, and gestures").

14. **D)**

    In the last sentence, the author writes, "These tips will help you support people who need clarity and sensitivity."

15. **B)**

    In the first paragraph, the author writes, "Communicating with any human being in crisis—whether that crisis is physical or emotional—is going to be more difficult than normal, everyday communication."

16. **B)**

    The author writes, "In some cultures, direct eye contact can be unsettling or disrespectful." There are no sentences supporting the other claims.

17. C)

The answer provides an adequate summary of the passage overall. The other choices only provide specific details from the passage.

18. D)

The primary purpose of the essay is to advise; its focus is communication with patients in crisis. It is not persuasive or cautionary, and it does not tell a story.

19. B)

The passage is about heat exposure's causes and results. The other answer choices are details from the passage.

20. C)

The passage does not contain this detail. The passage deals with overexposure to heat, not with results of drinking too much water.

21. A)

The text is informative, not persuasive or dramatic. It does not recount a specific event, but simply informs readers about symptoms and treatment of patients experiencing overexposure to heat.

22. D)

In the first sentence, the author writes, "A variety of environmental factors can inhibit the body's ability to naturally keep itself cool." In this case, inhibit means "hinder or prevent."

23. D)

In the second paragraph, the author writes, "Excessive loss of fluids and salts can also lead to heat exhaustion, a state in which a person experiences shallow breathing, an altered mental state, unresponsiveness, dizziness or faintness, and/or moist and cool skin."

24. A)

In the first paragraph, the author states, "[E]xtremely dry heat may encourage people to push beyond their normal boundaries of exertion because they do not 'feel' the heat as much as in humid environments. Overexertion in either moist or dry heat forces the body to alter its heat-coping mechanisms, placing people at risk of experiencing heat cramps, heat exhaustion, or heat stroke. These physiological responses to heat exposure can impair important

bodily functions and can even result in death." The reader can infer from this information that ignorance about symptoms could lead people to exercise too hard in hot weather and die as a result.

25. D)

The primary purpose of the essay is to inform; its focus is on managing behavioral emergencies. It is not persuasive or cautionary. It does not deal with treating mentally ill patients.

26. B)

In the third sentence, the author writes, "Extreme cases of a behavioral emergency may result when someone's behavior is creating a danger to themselves or others."

27. A)

The author writes, "Psychological and behavioral effects can result from any number of illnesses; they can also be the result of a chemical imbalance, genetic disorder, or psychological disturbance." There are no sentences supporting the other claims.

28. C)

In the last sentence, the author states, "While medical practitioners must be trained for emergency situations that demand physical restraint, extreme cases of behavioral emergency may be directed to police for appropriate support." The reader can infer from this information that "physical restraint" means handcuffing or otherwise restraining a mentally ill patient who is violent.

29. C)

In the last sentence, the author writes, "While medical practitioners must be trained for emergency situations that demand physical restraint, extreme cases of behavioral emergency may be directed to police for appropriate support."

30. A)

The paragraph is about the thyroid gland. The other sentences give details about the main idea.

31. D)

The passage does not contain this detail. According to sentence 9, hypothyroidism causes obesity and fatigue, not hyperthyroidism.

32. **C)**

In sentences 6 – 8, the author writes, "An excess of thyroxine in the circulatory system may result in a condition known as hyperthyroidism.... A deficit of thyroxine in the circulatory system may result in a condition known as hypothyroidism." The context shows that excess and deficit are antonyms. Insufficiency, too, is an antonym for excess.

33. **A)**

The text is informative, not persuasive. It does not recount a specific event, but informs readers about the thyroid gland's function, as well as symptoms of hyper- and hypothyroidism.

34. **D)**

In sentence 10, the author writes, "Fortunately, medications are available to help patients regulate their thyroid function when they've been diagnosed with hyperthyroidism or hypothyroidism." There is no support for any of the other claims.

35. **C)**

In sentences 6 – 8, the author writes, "An excess of thyroxine in the circulatory system may result in a condition known as hyperthyroidism.... A deficit of thyroxine in the circulatory system may result in a condition known as hypothyroidism." The words excess and deficit are antonyms. The reader can infer from this information that hyper (as in hyperactive) means "too much," and that hypo (as in hypoglycemic) means the opposite: "too little" or "under the normal requirement."

36. **A)**

In the first paragraph, the author states, "Almost all sensory information the human body experiences must pass through the spinal cord in order to reach the brain." The reader can infer from this information that the spinal cord conveys to the brain sensory information such as pain, heat, coldness, and other "human body experiences."

37. **C)**

The author writes, "From top to bottom, these regions are: cervical, thoracic, lumbar, sacral, and coccygeal."

38. **B)**

In the last sentence, the author writes, "Spinal nerves 'direct' the incoming and outgoing messages of the central nervous system, making the spinal cord the main neurological conduit of the human body." In the first sentence, the author calls the spinal cord a "central messaging stem." In other words, the spinal cord channels messages from other parts of the body to the brain.

39. **B)**

The essay is about the spinal cord's function and parts. The other sentences give details about the main idea.

40. **D)**

The primary purpose of the essay is to inform; its focus is on the spinal cord's functions and parts. It is not persuasive or advisory. It does not make value judgments about body parts' comparative importance.

41. **D)**

In the second paragraph, the author writes, "Motor information, on the other hand, exits the spinal cord ventrally, meaning from the front side."

42. **B)**

In the first sentence, the author writes, "Scientists only partially understand carcinogenesis—the process by which normal cells become cancer cells."

43. **C)**

In the first two sentences, the author writes, "Scientists only partially understand carcinogenesis—the process by which normal cells become cancer cells. Yet most scientists agree that this malignant transformation results from damaged genetic material within a cell." The context shows that by "malignant transformation" the author means changing from normal cells to cancer cells.

44. **B)**

The passage is about ways that damaged genetic material can cause carcinogenesis. The first sentence introduces but does not summarize the main idea. The other two answer choices give details from the passage.

45. **C)**

The passage does not contain this detail. According to the passage, damaged genetic material—not normal DNA—causes cells to become cancerous.

46. C)

The text is informative, not persuasive or speculative. It does not recount specific events, but simply informs readers about ways that damaged DNA can cause carcinogenesis.

47. C)

In the first paragraph, the author states, "Scientists only partially understand carcinogenesis—the process by which normal cells become cancer cells. Yet most scientists agree that this malignant transformation results from damaged genetic material within a cell." During the remainder of the passage, the author does not explain how genetic material becomes damaged. The reader can infer from this information that scientists do not know exactly how such damage occurs.

48. D)

The first paragraph begins with "Most people think ...." The author goes on to describe external respiration and then asks, "Did you know there are actually two types of respiration in humans?" Finally, the author describes the other type: internal respiration. The author is probably correct in assuming that most people—excluding biologists and medical professionals—have never heard of internal respiration.

49. A)

The primary purpose of the essay is to inform; its focus is on the two types of respiration. It is not persuasive or advisory. The author is not trying to prove a point.

50. D)

In paragraph 2, the author writes, "Cells within the organs are surrounded by thousands of tiny capillaries that act as channels for the exchange of gases. Oxygen is carried through these microscopic blood vessels, moving from red blood cells to the surrounding tissue." Readers can infer from context that the phrase "these microscopic blood vessels" refers to the "thousands of tiny capillaries" in the previous sentence.

51. A)

In paragraph 2, the author writes, "Whereas external respiration centers on an exchange between the lungs and the environment, internal respiration centers on a molecular exchange between cells and capillaries."

52. C)

As the title shows, the passage is about the two types of respiration: external and internal.

53. C)

In the second paragraph, the author writes, "Additionally, built-up carbon dioxide in the tissues flows through the capillaries back to the lungs."

54. C)

In the fifth sentence in the second paragraph, the author writes, "When testosterone reaches a certain level, it inhibits the production of FSH and LH."

55. B)

The last sentence reads, "A similar but more complex feedback loop occurs in women with FSH and LH stimulating the production of estrogen, resulting in the cycle of ovulation and menstruation." Readers can infer from context that by "feedback loop," the author means the hormones FSH and LH cause a reaction that stimulates "the production of estrogen, resulting in" other reactions: "the cycle of ovulation and menstruation."

1. **A)**

   Exseption should be spelled "exception."

2. **C)**

   Precaution means "an act done in advance to ensure safety or benefit" or "protection against something or someone."

3. **C)**

   Priority means "right of precedence; order of importance."

4. **C)**

   Co-morbidity means "two disorders that occur at the same time."

5. **C)**

   Conditional means "dependent on something else."

6. **B)**

   Manifestation means "display."

7. **B)**

   Dilute means "weaken by a mixture of water or other liquid; reduce in strength."

8. **B)**

   Prone means "lying flat."

9. **D)**

   Retain means "to hold or keep in possession." Fluid retention can be a symptom of a medical condition.

10. **A)**

    Excessive means "exceeding what is normal or necessary."

11. **B)**

    Endoscopic procedures are considered minimally invasive procedures because they rely on fiberoptic tools and small incisions. *Invasive* means "intrusive."

12. **C)**

    Placment should be spelled "placement."

13. **C)**

    Predispose means "to make susceptible or to have a tendency to."

14. **B)**

    Asymmetric means "lacking symmetry or unbalanced."

15. **C)**

    A *soporific* is "a sleep-inducing drug."

16. **B)**

    Collateral means "parallel" or "secondary." Collateral blood vessels provide an alternate circulation route around injured or blocked vessels.

17. **B)**

    A *syndrome* is "a set of symptoms characteristic of a specific disease or condition."

18. **C)**

    Sublingual means "under the tongue."

19. **D)**

    Pathogenic means "causing disease." Pathogenic diseases, or infections, require protocols to prevent their spread.

20. **C)**

    A *hematologic* study examines the blood.

21. **A)**

    Pragmatic means "concerned with practical matters and results."

22. **D)**

    Ambulatory means "able to walk."

23. **B)**

    Acoustic means "of or related to sound or hearing."

24. **B)**

    Progress means "gradual betterment or improvement."

25. A)

Virulent means "severe and destructive."

26. C)

Laceration means "the tearing of soft body tissue resulting in a wound."

27. C)

Transdermal means "passing through the skin."

28. D)

Dysfunctional means "not functioning properly."

29. D)

External means "located outside of something."

30. A)

Vascular means "pertaining to bodily ducts (vessels) that convey fluids."

31. A)

Amalgam means "a mixture or blend."

32. B)

Dilate means "to widen."

33. A)

Respiration means "breathing."

34. B)

Patent means "unobstructed."

35. B)

Paroxysmal means "pertaining to a seizure, spasm, or violent outburst."

36. C)

Regress means "to move backward, often to a worse state."

37. D)

A *cannula* is "a thin tube inserted into the body to remove fluid."

38. C)

Labile means "unstable or easily changed." A patient's blood pressure may be labile.

39. B)

Something that is *obverse* is "the opposite" of something else.

40. A)

A *soporific* drug induces sleep.

41. B)

Justify means "to show to be just or right."

42. D)

Sensible means having "good sense or reason."

43. A)

Abduction means "the movement of a limb away from the body's midline."

44. A)

As used in this sentence, *superficial* means "shallow in character or attitude; on the surface." Therefore, a shallow or superficial wound does not require stitches.

45. C)

Succumb means "to yield or stop resisting."

46. A)

Resect means "to remove or cut out organs or tissue."

47. D)

Deficiency means "an amount that is lacking or inadequate."

48. A)

Superficial means "only concerned with things on the surface."

49. D)

Ossify means "to harden."

50. C)

Hydration refers to "the act of meeting body fluid demands."

51. B)

Adversely means "harmful to one's interest; unfortunate."

52. D)

Superficial means "located on the surface or not penetrating the surface."

53. C)

Subtle means "delicate or difficult to observe."

54. B)

Cardiac means "of or pertaining to the heart."

55. B)

Acuity means "mental sharpness or quickness."

1. **B)**

   Choice B correctly connects two independent clauses ("Kiana went to class" and "Lara stayed home") with a comma and the coordinating conjunction *but*. Choice A incorrectly uses a semicolon instead of a comma. Choice C is a comma splice, using a comma without a coordinating conjunction. Choice D is a run-on sentence, since it lacks a comma before the coordinating conjunction *but*.

2. **D)**

   Choice D is correct. The adverb *recently* modifies the verb *has . . . hired*. Choice A, *Our*, is a possessive pronoun; choice B, *boss*, is a common noun; and choice C, *has*, is a helping verb.

3. **C)**

   Choice C is correct. Since the bus driver and the passenger are not identified by name, using the feminine subject pronoun *she* is confusing to the reader. The reader cannot tell who spoke or who acted rudely. The whole sentence needs rewriting. For example: *After Joe, the bus driver, spoke too loudly to an elderly passenger, he realized that he might have acted rudely.*

4. **C)**

   All three words in choice C are homophones; they sound alike, and they have different spellings and meanings. In choice A, *expect* rhymes with *accept* and *except*, but expect/accept and expect/except are not homophone pairs. In choice B, the first syllable in *louder* sounds like the second syllables in *aloud* and *allowed*, but louder/aloud and louder/allowed are not homophone pairs. In choice D, *where/wear* is a homophone pair and *wear* and *weary* begin with the same four letters. However, *weary* (which rhymes with *dreary* and *theory*) does not sound like *where* and *wear*, so the three are not homophones.

5. **D)**

   Choice D correctly uses the adverb *farther*, which describes a measurable distance, such as twenty miles. In choice A, the adverb *further* describes an amount that cannot be measured in units. In choices B and C, the words *father* and *fatter* do not make logical sense—the first implies that the speaker cannot drive around any person who is a male parent, and

the second implies that the speaker cannot drive if he or she gains any more weight today.

6. **B)**

   Choice B is correct. The correct answers are a comma and a question mark. Correctly completed, the sentence looks like this: *"Jean," I asked, "Can you come over for dinner?"* Choice A is incorrect because a quotation cannot end in a colon. A colon denotes that the two sentence parts are closely related. In addition, the second half of the quotation is a question, which means an exclamation point is not the correct choice. Choice C is incorrect because a quotation cannot end in a semicolon and because a semicolon can only be used to join two complete independent clauses or items in a list. A question should not end in a period. Choice D is incorrect because a comma is used when attaching a speaker tag (*I asked*) to a quotation.

7. **B)**

   Choice B is correct. The preposition *about* is unidiomatic in the phrase "love about praise" and should be replaced with the preposition *of* to create the idiomatic phrase "love of praise."

8. **D)**

   Choice D is correct; the clause in this choice cannot stand on its own. While it contains a subject (*you*) and a verb (*are*), it begins with the subordinating conjunction *if*. It therefore cannot stand on its own and must be connected to another independent clause. Choice A has a subject (*I*) and a verb (*want*). Choice B has a subject (*we*) and a verb (*hike*). Choice C has a subject (*She*) and a verb (*drives*). Choices A, B, and C can all stand alone as full sentences and do not need to be connected to any other clauses.

9. **D)**

   The correct answers are *too* and *to*. The adverb *too* correctly modifies the adjective *busy*. *To* combined with *attend* forms the infinitive verb *to attend*.

10. **C)**

    The correct answers are *ball* and *bowl* in choice C. These two nouns make sense in the sentence. In choice A and D, *bull* is a noun that means "a male animal such as a steer or moose" and *bawl* is a verb that means "to cry." Choice B incorrectly reverses the two words *bowl* and *ball*.

11. C)

Choice C is correct. The adverb *hastily* modifies the verb "to wolf [down]," which means "to devour." *Food* is a noun, and *stomachache* is a noun.

12. B)

The correct answers are *Although* and *so* in choice B. The subordinating conjunction *although* correctly connects the opening dependent clause, "I love tomato sauces," to the middle independent clause, "I dislike the texture of raw tomatoes." It correctly implies contrast between the two clauses. The coordinating conjunction *so* correctly connects the final independent clause, "I avoid salads that contain them," to the rest of the sentence, demonstrating a cause-and-effect relationship between the first independent clause and the second. Because any of the other choices imply an incorrect relationship between the clauses, they would render the sentence nonsensical, unidiomatic, or both.

13. C)

Choice C is correct. The preposition *except* (meaning "not including") should be replaced with its homophone, the verb *accept* (which means "to agree to take [something that is offered to you]").

14. C)

Choice C is correct; the apostrophe is placed incorrectly in the contraction *Lets'*. An apostrophe only appears after a final *s* when indicating a plural possessive noun. *Let's* is a contraction of the words *let* and *us*.

15. D)

Choice D correctly matches the singular noun *cat* with the singular pronoun *its* and the singular verb *eats*; this choice also correctly matches the plural noun *dogs* with the plural pronoun *their* and the plural verb *sleep*. Choice A incorrectly matches the singular noun *cat* with the plural pronoun *their* and the plural verb *eat*; this choice also incorrectly matches the singular noun *dog* with the plural pronoun *their* and the plural verb *sleep*. Choice B incorrectly matches the plural noun *cats* with the singular possessive pronoun *its* and the singular verb *eats*; this choice also incorrectly matches the singular noun *dog* with the plural pronoun *their* and the plural verb *sleep*. In choice C, the singular

subject *cat* does not match the plural verb *eat* and the plural pronoun *their*.

16. D)

Choice D is correct. The correct answers are *There* and *there*. The word *there* is an indefinite pronoun that indicates a place, as called for in the sentence context. The contraction *they're* means "they are," and *their* is a plural possessive pronoun. Correctly completed, the sentences look like this: *There is nobody over there. Did you think you saw someone?* Each of the other choices would result in an ungrammatical sentence.

17. D)

Choice D is correct. The preposition *under* begins the prepositional phrase "under the bed," which tells where the cats hide. Choice A, *whenever*, is a conjunction; choice B, *our*, is a possessive pronoun; and choice C, *hide*, is a verb.

18. A)

Choice A is the clearest way to rewrite the sentence. The original version makes it sound as if the basketball is walking to school. Choice B makes it sound as if the gang members are walking to school (maybe they are and maybe they aren't). Choice C is too long and awkwardly phrased. Choice D leaves out important information about the people who stole the ball.

19. B)

The correct choice is B; the answers are *hole*, meaning "a hollow place in a solid body," and *whole*, meaning "complete or total." The noun *hole* makes sense in the phrase "a hole in your sock." The adjective *whole* correctly modifies the noun *day*, creating the idiomatic English phrase "to ruin your whole day." None of the other pairs of words make sense in the sentence. *Howl* is a "loud cry uttered by an animal" and *whale* is a "large marine mammal with a horizontal tailfin and blowhole."

20. B)

Choice B is correct. The adjective *four* correctly modifies *teammates*. The preposition *for* correctly completes the phrase "practicing for the big game."

21. B)

Choice B correctly pairs the plural subject "my teacher and the school principal" with the plural verb *have worked*. Choice A incorrectly pairs the plural subject "my teacher and the school principal" with the singular verb *has worked*. Choice C contains a verb error ("have been worked together"), and choice D also contains a verb error ("had working together").

22. **A)**

Choice A correctly capitalizes the proper nouns *Austin* and *Texas*. In choice B, the common nouns *weekend* and *graduation* are incorrectly capitalized. Choice C incorrectly lowercases *Austin* (in the proper noun *Austin, Texas*) and incorrectly capitalizes the common possessive noun *brother's*. Choice D incorrectly lowercases the proper noun *Texas* and incorrectly capitalizes the common noun *weekend*.

23. **D)**

Choice D is correct. *Mourning* should be replaced with its homophone, *morning*: *How are you feeling on this sunny Saturday morning?* *Mourning* is a verb that means "grieving for a loved one who has died," and *morning* is a noun that means the opposite of *evening*.

24. **A)**

Choice A correctly uses the possessive pronoun *yours* (meaning "the one that belongs to you"). Choice B misspells the possessive proper noun *Shelby's* by omitting the apostrophe. Choice C incorrectly uses *your* in place of *yours*, and choice D incorrectly uses *you* in place of *yours*.

25. **D)**

The correct answers are *brakes* and *break* in choice D. The verb *brakes* means "uses a vehicle's brakes [to stop]." The verb *break* means "to damage or ruin." Choices A, B, and C are incorrect. The noun *brain* refers to "the organ that functions as the operating center for nervous, sensational, and operating function in a vertebrate animal." The word *bray* can function as a noun or a verb and means "the loud harsh cry of a donkey or mule" or the action of uttering that sound.

26. **C)**

Choice C is correct. The common noun *summer*, the name of a season, should not be capitalized. Months' names (like *October*) are proper nouns, but seasons' names (*spring, summer, fall,* and *winter*) are common nouns.

27. **A)**

Choice A is correct. The subordinating conjunction *because* joins a dependent clause to an independent

one. Choice B, *love,* is a verb; choice C, *family,* is a noun; and choice D, *and,* is a coordinating conjunction.

28. **B)**

Choice B has two independent clauses joined by the coordinating conjunction *and,* making it a compound sentence. Choice A is a simple sentence with one subject (*ride*) and one verb (*does [not] take*). Choice C is a complex sentence (one dependent clause and one independent one, joined by the subordinating conjunction *although*). Choice D is a compound-complex sentence: it has one dependent clause ("If you . . . Bay Bridge") and two independent clauses ("it will . . . longer" and "you will . . . traffic").

29. **B)**

Choice B is correct. *Rite* (a noun meaning "a religious practice or custom") should be replaced with its homophone, *right*: *You're right: the best time to write . . . Right* can be an adjective that means "correct." When it appears later in the sentence, it acts as an intensifier and means "immediately or close to." The word *write* means to "mark on a surface" and is used correctly.

30. **C)**

Choice C uses the following punctuation marks correctly: an apostrophe in *isn't*, a colon, an apostrophe in *there's*, a comma, another comma, and a period. In choice A, the comma after *home* should be changed to a semicolon or a colon. In choice B, an apostrophe is missing from the contraction *isn't* and from the contraction *there's*. In choice D, the apostrophe in the word *isn't* is misplaced (it is at the end of the word). Also, the question mark after *home* should be changed to a period; the clause "My cat . . . home" forms a statement, not a question.

31. **A)**

Choice A is correct. The past-tense verbs *rained* and *reined* sound alike, but have different spellings and meanings. None of the other choices contain a homophone pair.

32. **C)**

Choice C correctly uses the present-tense verb *bear*, which means "tolerate" or "endure." Choice A incorrectly uses *bare*, an adjective meaning "naked," in place of its homophone *bear*. Choice B incorrectly uses the past-tense verb *bore* in place of its present-tense form *bear*. Choice D incorrectly uses *burn*, meaning "cause to catch fire," in place of *bear*.

33. D)

Choice D correctly pairs the singular subject *no one* with the singular verb *wants*. Choice A incorrectly pairs the singular subject *one* with the plural verb *hope*. Choice B incorrectly pairs the plural subject *two* with the singular verb *hopes*. Choice C incorrectly pairs the plural subject *all* with the singular verb *hopes*.

34. D)

Choice D is correct. *Yours* is a possessive pronoun that means "the one that belongs to you." Choices A, B, and C contain the pronouns *I*, *they*, and *it*, but they are not possessive.

35. B)

Choice B is correct. The verb *affect* means "to have an impact on [someone or something]." The noun *effect* means "result" or "impact." Choice A is incorrect. These words are commonly confused. *Effect* can be used as a verb, meaning "to make something happen" (for instance, "to effect change"). Likewise, *affect* can be used as a noun, most commonly in psychological contexts describing someone's demeanor: "the patient had a flat affect." These uses are far less common. It makes more sense for a medication to have an impact on a person, and a medication cannot have a demeanor, so choice B is a better choice than A. Choice C incorrectly uses the verb *effected*, and choice D incorrectly uses the noun *affect*.

36. B)

Choice B correctly compares three or more items using the suffix *–est*. Choice A incorrectly uses *most* with a one-syllable adjective, *soft*. Choice C incorrectly compares six items (more than two) using the suffix *–er*. Choice D incorrectly pairs *most* with the comparative adjective *softest*.

37. A)

Choice A is correct. The word *summer* should be lowercased—it is a common noun. So are the words *spring*, *fall*, and *winter*. The names of months are always capitalized, but the names of seasons are not.

38. B)

Choice B, *went*, is the correct answer. It should be replaced with *gone*, the past participle of *to go*.

39. A)

The correct answers are *mortal* and *mourning* in choice A. The adjective *mortal* (meaning "deadly") correctly modifies *wound*. To be "in mourning" means "to mourn or grieve for a loved one who has died." The verb *mooring* means "securing [a boat or aircraft] with lines or anchors." The word *morning* is "the earliest part of the day, after the sun has risen but before noon." None of these other pairs of words make sense in the sentence.

40. D)

Choice D is correct. *Sweet* should be replaced with its homophone, *suite*: *There are two bedrooms, a bathroom, and a sitting room in our hotel suite.* *Sweet* is an adjective that means "sugary." *Suite* is a noun that means "a group of connected rooms."

41. A)

Choice A is correct: *I* and *she* are subject pronouns, and *her* is an object pronoun. In choice B, the three words are verbs. Choice C includes an infinitive (*to*), a preposition (*for*), a conjunction (*but*), and a verb of being (*was*). Choice D includes a noun (*test*), an adverb (*too*), and an adjective (*busy*).

42. A)

Choice A is correct. The plural verb *were* agrees with the plural subject pronoun *we*. Choices B, C, and D are all ungrammatical. Choice B is a singular verb. Choice C is past-perfect progressive, which indicates that the action was ongoing in the past, but before the other action—it is awkward and goes too far into the past. Choice D is past progressive, which also indicates an ongoing action in the past.

43. B)

Choice B is correct. The verb *bring* should be replaced with *take*: *Please take that unsafe toy away from your little brother.* *Bring* means "to carry [something] from one place to another," and *take* means "to remove [something] from someone or move it from one place to another."

44. D)

Choice D correctly uses the verb *affect*, which means "to cause a change." Choice A incorrectly uses *effect*, which is a noun that means "a result of a cause." Choice B incorrectly uses the verb *infect*, which means "to transmit a disease to [someone]." Choice C incorrectly uses the verb *inspect*, which means "to examine or study."

45. A)

Choice A is correct. *New* and *knew* sound alike but have different spellings and meanings, which makes them a homophone pair. Choices B (*royal/rayon*), C (*sweet/sweat*), and D (*manner/manure*) are not homophone pairs because they do not sound enough alike.

46. D)

The correct answers are *am* and *are* in choice D. The singular first-person subject pronoun *I* matches *am*, the singular first-person form of the verb *to be*. The plural third-person subject *my brothers* matches *are*, the plural third-person form of the verb *to be*.

47. C)

Choice C is correct. *Principle's* should be replaced with its homophone, *principal's*: *My elementary school principal's name was Mrs. Woodnancy.* *Principle* is a synonym for *belief, value,* and *rule*. *Principal* means "leader or head [of a school]."

48. C)

The interjection *hey* interrupts the sentence's flow as a new idea occurs to the speaker. Choice A, *considering*, is a verb; choice B, *English*, is a proper noun; and choice D, *biology*, is a common noun.

49. A)

Choice A correctly connects two independent clauses, "DeQuan loves eating pizza" and "meat toppings make him feel queasy," using a comma and the coordinating conjunction *but*. Choice B has a misplaced modifier: the dependent clause "[t]hough he avoids meat toppings." That clause incorrectly modifies *pizza* when it should modify *DeQuan*. In choice C, the verb *makes* is incorrectly conjugated: it should be plural to match the plural subject *toppings*. Choice D is a run-on sentence; it lacks a comma before *but*.

50. D)

Choice D is correct. The correct answers are *principal* and *principle*. A *principal* is the head of a school, and a *principle* is a value or maxim. In choice B, the masculine noun *prince* does not agree with the feminine pronoun *she*. In choice C, the adjective *invincible* (meaning "unbeatable") does not make sense in the sentence.

51. D)

Choice D uses the following punctuation marks correctly: an opening quotation mark, an apostrophe in the contraction *I'm*, an exclamation point, a closing quotation mark, and a period. Choice A incorrectly omits the apostrophe in the contraction *I'm*. Choice B incorrectly omits a closing quotation mark following *over!* Choice C incorrectly uses a question mark instead of an exclamation point to end the direct quotation, which is not a question.

52. C)

Choice C is correct. *You're* (a contraction meaning "you are") should be replaced with its homophone, *your*: *Hundreds of years ago (in days of yore), if you were female, your destiny was not yours to decide . . . Your* is a second-person possessive pronoun that means "belonging to you" or "owned by you." The noun *yore* is used correctly in the sentence; it means "long ago" or "former times."

53. A)

Choice A is correct. *Flour* is an ingredient in many recipes, and some bakers decorate cakes with fresh flowers or flowers made from icing. Choice B reverses the two homophones so that each is used incorrectly in the place of the other. Choice C uses *fleer*, which is not an English word, and *flowing* (meaning "moving freely") does not fit the sentence. Choice D misuses the word *flair*, which means "style," and incorrectly adds an –s to the word *flour*.

54. D)

Choice D is correct. A *metal* is an element like gold or silver. *Metal* also refers colloquially to many hard substances. The verb *meddle* means "to interfere with [something]." A *medal* is an award. Gold might be used to make a medal, but it is not a medal by itself. The noun *mettle* refers to a person's grit or determination. None of these answer choices make sense in the context of the sentence.

55. D)

Choice D has one dependent clause ("Because . . . awake") and two independent clauses ("I can't . . . evening" and "I need . . . morning"), so it is a compound-complex sentence. Choice A is a simple sentence with one subject (*mug*) and one main verb (*is*). Choice B is a compound sentence: two independent clauses joined by the coordinating conjunction *and*. Choice C has one dependent clause and one independent one, joined by the subordinating conjunction *although*, so it is a complex sentence.

1. **D)**

   The electrons in a water molecule are more attracted to the oxygen atom, which gives the oxygen atom a negative charge and the hydrogen atoms a positive charge.

2. **B)**

   The fatty acid tails of phospholipids are nonpolar, and nonpolar molecules are repelled by water and other polar molecules.

3. **A)**

   Both plant and animal cells have carbohydrates, nucleic acids, proteins, and lipids. Plants and animals have similar organelles, including the Golgi apparatus. However, plant cells have a cell wall, whereas animal cells do not.

4. **C)**

   In a frameshift mutation, insertions of nucleotides in numbers other than three will shift all the following codons read by the tRNA, producing a dysfunctional protein.

5. **C)**

   Oxygen acts as the final electron acceptor during the electron transport chain. In the process of making energy (ATP), ATP synthase passes electrons on to oxygen.

6. **A)**

   DNA is organized into chromosomes using histone proteins. First, DNA is wound into nucleosomes by histones. Next, the nucleosomes are wound into chromatin, which is wound even tighter to form chromosomes.

7. **D)**

   During prophase, the nuclear envelope disappears and the chromosomes begin to condense into chromatin, which makes them visible using a light microscope.

8. **B)**

   Transcription is the process of converting DNA into mRNA so that the genetic code (DNA) can be translated into protein on ribosomes.

9. **C)**

   Egg cells have a haploid (1n) number of chromosomes. A skin cell would have a diploid (2n) number, so the skin cell would have 14 × 2 = 28 chromosomes.

10. **B)**

    The oxygen and hydrogen in a water molecule share electrons, creating a covalent bond.

11. **C)**

    There is a 50 percent chance that their child will have red-green color blindness. The children with the phenotypes XcXc and XcY would be color blind. The children with the phenotypes XcX and XY would not.

    Mother

		Xc	X
Father	Xc	XcXc	XcX
	Y	XcY	XY

12. **A)**

    Organic compounds must contain carbon. They may contain other elements, including phosphorous, nitrogen, or oxygen.

13. **B)**

    The light reactions of photosynthesis occur in the chloroplast. Each chloroplast has stacks of membranes called thylakoids where enzymes convert light energy into chemical energy.

14. **B)**

    The Calvin cycle is the part of photosynthesis where ATP is used to convert CO_2 and water to sugar.

15. **A)**

    New nucleotides are added in the 5' to 3' direction. In order to add a new nucleotide, there has to be a free 3' end. The leading strand is synthesized continuously because the 3' end is always free. The lagging strand is synthesized, and it fragments as the DNA strands are unwound.

16. **D)**

    Meiosis produces gametes.

17. B)

Each tRNA molecule has an anticodon that is complementary to the codon on the mRNA strand. Once the mRNA strand is correctly aligned on the ribosome, the tRNA binds and the appropriate amino acid is added to the protein.

18. A)

Because cystic fibrosis is a recessive trait, the offspring would have to inherit two recessive alleles in order to have the disorder. Since the mother can only pass on dominant alleles, all of the children will have at least one dominant allele and thus will not have cystic fibrosis.

		Mother	
		C	C
Father	C	CC	CC
	c	Cc	Cc

19. C)

Carbohydrates, such as fructose, are sugars. DNA polymerase is a protein, vegetable oil is a lipid, and mRNA is a nucleic acid.

20. A)

Mitochondria produce energy for cells in the form of ATP. The electron transport chain, which is responsible for most of the ATP produced during respiration, occurs across the membranes of the mitochondria.

21. B)

ATP is unstable: when a phosphate group is removed from the molecule, energy is released.

22. A)

Telomeres are the ends of chromosomes. An easy way to distinguish *telomere* and *centromere* is that "telo" means terminal, and telomeres are at the terminus, or end, of chromosomes.

23. D)

At the beginning of telophase I, homologous chromosomes are located at opposite ends of the cell. As telophase I progresses, the 2n cell divides into two cells with a reduced number (1n) of chromosomes.

24. C)

Ribosomes are the small organelles that synthesize proteins.

25. A)

Each codon contains three nucleotides.

26. A)

NADH is one of the molecules used to carry electrons within cells.

27. C)

Each tRNA molecule has an anticodon that binds to the complementary codon on the mRNA strand. A bonds with U (not T, as in DNA), U bonds with A, and G bonds with C.

28. B)

If an organism has 8 pairs of chromosomes, it would have a diploid number (2n) of 16. The haploid number (1n) would be 8.

29. B)

DNA is replicated during the S, or synthesis, phase of the cell cycle.

30. C)

When incomplete dominance occurs, neither allele is dominant, and the offspring will have a phenotype that is a blend of the two alleles.

CHEMISTRY

1. B)

Br^- is element number 35, which means it has thirty-five protons. Mg^{2+} has twelve, Na^+ has eleven, and N^{3-} has seven.

2. D)

Both Se and O are found in group 16, so they have six electrons in their valence shell. They will add two electrons to fill the shell, resulting in a charge of −2.

3. A)

Ionic bonds contain an atom that has lost electrons to the other atom, which results in a positive charge on one atom and a negative charge on the other atom.

4. C)

An unsaturated solution is when a solution contains less than the amount of possible dissolvable solute.

5. D)

Electronegativity increases from left to right and bottom to top on the periodic table, with fluorine (F) being the most electronegative element.

6. C)

Toxicity is a chemical property: measuring the toxicity of a material will change its chemical identity.

7. A)

The balanced equation is $Pb(NO_3)_2 + K_2CrO_4 \rightarrow PbCrO_4 + 2KNO_3$, showing 1 Pb, 2 NO_3, 2K, and 1 CrO_4 on each side of the arrow. The answer choice is 1, 1, 1, 2.

8. A)

$Ba(OH)_2$ is a base; bases usually include a hydroxide ion (OH).

9. D)

The answer is 20 moles of KNO_3. Set up railroad tracks using the conversion factor given by the chemical equation.

10 mol Pb $(NO_3)_2$	2 mol KNO_3	= **20 mol KNO³**
	1 mole $Pb(NO_3)_2$	

10. D)

After twenty days, there will be 100 × ½ = 50 g left. After the next twenty days there will be 50 × ½ = 25 g left.

11. B)

The half-life is the amount of time it takes for half of a radioactive sample to decay. After one half-life of four days, the sample would include 100 g ÷ 2 = 50 g.

12. C)

The number of protons determines which element it is.

13. D)

Both Mg and Ca are found in group 2, so they have two electrons in their valence shell. They will lose those two electrons in order to have a full valence shell, resulting in a charge of +2.

14. B)

Covalent bonds occur when two atoms share electrons.

15. D)

atomic mass − atomic number = number of neutrons

16. A)

A solid has a definite shape and definite volume.

17. A)

Solutions that have a sour taste and react strongly with metals are acidic.

18. A)

The joining of two reactants ($2Li + Cl_2$) to form one product (2LiCl) is a synthesis reaction.

19. D)

Electrons are negatively charged subatomic particles.

20. A)

Group 17, called the halogens, have seven electrons in their valence shell and need one electron to complete the shell.

21. A)

The London dispersion force is a temporary force that occurs when electrons in two adjacent atoms form spontaneous, temporary dipoles.

22. D)

The answer is 30 moles of O_2. Set up railroad tracks using the conversion factor given by the chemical equation.

20 mol $KClO_3$	3 mol O_2	= **30 mol O_2**
	2 moles $KClO_3$	

23. A)

Condensation occurs when a substance goes from gas to liquid.

24. D)

Cereal in milk is a heterogeneous mixture because the elements are not evenly distributed.

25. B)

The breaking down of one reactant ($2H_2O_2$) into two products ($2H_2O + O_2$) is a decomposition reaction.

26. C)

The elements F, Cl, and Br are halogens in group 17, and thus have seven electrons in their valence shells.

27. B)

The reaction is a synthesis reaction that has the form A + B → C. Potassium (K) and chlorine gas (Cl_2) combine to form potassium chloride (KCl).

28. A)

The valence shell of the noble gases, group 18, is full, so they do not need any electrons to complete them.

29. D)

Deposition is the phase transition that occurs when a gas becomes a solid.

30. C)

The zinc and copper reactants switch places with each other on the product side, so this is a single displacement reaction.

1. **C)**

The pulmonary valve directs blood flow into the pulmonary arteries and prevents blood from going back to the right ventricle.

2. **A)**

Nerve endings, blood vessels, and nervous tissue are found in the periosteum.

3. **B)**

The appendix is attached to the cecum.

4. **D)**

The urethral meatus is toward the front, or anterior, relative to the anus.

5. **D)**

The left subclavian artery branches off directly from the aortic arch.

6. **D)**

Afferent neurons receive information from the sensory organs, like the skin.

7. **B)**

Inflammation increases the blood flow to the damaged area, increasing its temperature and bringing white blood cells to the site.

8. **B)**

The dermis is the layer of the skin where blood vessels, hair follicles, and glands are found.

9. **C)**

Calcium is released as bones are degraded, which helps balance the calcium level in the body.

10. **A)**

The soma houses the cellular organelles.

11. **D)**

Melatonin is produced by the pineal gland and causes drowsiness.

12. **A)**

Apocrine glands are located in the armpit and also in the groin.

13. **B)**

The A-band has thick myosin filaments that do not shorten with muscular contraction.

14. **B)**

The corpus luteum, which remains in the ovary after the egg is released, produces progesterone and estradiol after the egg is fertilized in the fallopian tube.

15. **D)**

The large intestine absorbs water and electrolytes before waste is moved to the rectum to be expelled.

16. **C)**

The cerebrum is the largest and outermost part of the brain.

17. **A)**

Costal cartilage connects the ribs to the sternum.

18. **B)**

The lungs will never be absent of air, even during expiration.

19. **A)**

The eight carpal bones are in the wrist and connect the bones of the forearm (ulna and radius) to the hand.

20. **C)**

Myoglobin stores oxygen to allow aerobic respiration to occur when there is no blood coming to the muscles.

21. **B)**

Mitochondria are present in muscle fibers to provide the energy needed to contract the muscle.

22. **A)**

The corpus callosum is a bundle of white matter that joins the two hemispheres of the cerebrum.

23. C)

Platelets, also known as thrombocytes, play an important role in blood clotting.

24. D)

Lumbar vertebrae are also called the lower back vertebrae.

25. A)

The triceps is the agonist; it contracts to extend the elbow.

26. B)

Dura mater is the outermost layer of the meninges, which protect the spinal cord and brain.

27. B)

The bladder's external sphincter is mostly made of smooth voluntary muscle. The internal sphincter is made of involuntary muscle.

28. A)

The liver produces bile, which is needed for the digestion of fats.

29. A)

Neutrophils are a type of leukocyte, or white blood cell, whose role is to digest bacteria.

30. C)

The thyroid gland controls the use of energy by the body.

1. **A)**

Convert 60 miles per hour to meters per second.

$$\frac{60 \text{ mi}}{\text{hr}} \times \frac{1609 \text{ m}}{1 \text{ mi}} \times \frac{1 \text{ hr}}{3600 \text{ sec}} = 26.8 \text{ m/s}$$

Plug the variables into the appropriate formula and solve for acceleration.

$v_f = v_i + at$

$26.8 \text{ m/s} = 0 + a(4 \text{ s})$

$a = \frac{26.8 \text{ m/s}}{4 \text{ s}}$

$a = 6.7 \text{ m/s}^2$

2. **C)**

Plug the variables into the appropriate formula and solve.

$W = Fd$

$W = (400 \text{ N})(10 \text{ m}) = \textbf{4000 J}$

3. **C)**

Plug the variables into the appropriate formula and solve.

$F_g = mg$

$F_g = 80 \text{ kg}(3.8 \text{ m/s}^2) = \textbf{304 N}$

4. **B)**

Radio waves are **electromagnetic waves**.

5. **B)**

Convert 17,500 miles per hour to meters per second.

$$\frac{17{,}500 \text{ mi}}{\text{hr}} \times \frac{1609 \text{ m}}{\text{mi}} \times \frac{1 \text{ hr}}{3600 \text{ s}} = \textbf{7822 m/s}$$

6. **A)**

Plug the variables into the appropriate formula and solve.

$PE_g = mgh$

$PE_g = (0.0025 \text{ kg})(9.8 \text{ m/s}^2)(400 \text{ m}) = \textbf{9.8 J}$

7. **B)**

Moving charged particles produce a **magnetic field**. A changing current produces an electric field.

8. **C)**

Plug the variables into the appropriate formula and solve.

$F_g = mg$

$F_g = 1 \text{ kg}(9.8 \text{ m/s}^2) = \textbf{9.8 N}$

9. **B)**

Plug the variables into the appropriate formula and solve.

$P = \frac{W}{t}$

$t = \frac{W}{P} = \frac{100 \text{ J}}{100 \text{ W}} = \textbf{1 s}$

10. **A)**

Plug the variables into the appropriate formula and solve.

$I = \frac{P}{A}$

$I = \frac{P}{s^2}$

$I = \frac{0.5 \text{ W}}{(2 \text{ m})^2} = \textbf{0.125} \frac{\textbf{W}}{\textbf{m}^2}$

11. **C)**

Plug the variables into the appropriate formula and solve.

$v_y = v \sin\theta$

$v_y = 47 \sin 39 = \textbf{29.6 m/s}$

12. **B)**

Plug the variables into the appropriate formula and solve.

$a_{rad} = \frac{v^2}{r}$

$a_{rad} = \frac{(2.5 \text{ m/s})^2}{1 \text{ m}} = \textbf{6.25} \frac{\textbf{m}}{\textbf{s}^2}$

13. **A)**

Plug the variables into the appropriate formula and solve.

$F_c = m \left(\frac{v^2}{r} \right)$

$v = \sqrt{\frac{rF_c}{m}}$

$v = \sqrt{\frac{(0.80 \text{ m})(0.5 \text{ N})}{0.088 \text{ kg}}} = \textbf{2.1 m/s}$

14. **B)**

Plug the variables into the appropriate formula and solve.

$n_1 \sin\theta_1 = n_2 \sin\theta_2$

$n_2 = n_1 \left(\frac{\sin\theta_1}{\sin\theta_2} \right)$

$$n_2 = 1.00 \left(\frac{\sin 30°}{\sin 12°} \right) = \textbf{2.40}$$

15. B)

Plug the variables into the appropriate formula and solve.

$v = \lambda f$

$v = (100 \text{ Hz})(400 \text{ m}) = \textbf{4} \times \textbf{10}^4 \textbf{ m/s}$

16. B)

Plug the variables into the appropriate formula and solve.

$N = \dfrac{Q_{TOT}}{q}$

$F = 9 \times 10^9 \left(\dfrac{(17 \times 10^{-9})(22 \times 10^{-9})}{(0.08)^2} \right)$

$= \textbf{5.26} \times \textbf{10}^{-4} \textbf{ N}$

17. B)

Plug the variables into the appropriate formula and solve.

$V = IR$

$R = \dfrac{V}{I}$

$R = \dfrac{3000 \text{ V}}{0.1 \text{ A}} = \textbf{30,000 } \Omega$

18. C)

Plug the variables into the appropriate formula and solve.

$V_t = V_1 + V_2 + \ldots = 18 \times 1.5 \text{ V} = 27 \text{ V}$

$V = IR$

$I = \dfrac{V}{R} = \dfrac{27 \text{ V}}{10 \, \Omega} = \textbf{2.7 A}$

19. D)

Plug the variables into the appropriate formula and solve.

$KE = \dfrac{1}{2} mv^2$

$KE = \dfrac{1}{2} m(3v)^2 = 9 \dfrac{1}{2} m(v)^2 = \textbf{9KE}$

20. D)

Plug the variables into the appropriate formula and solve.

$F_f = \mu_k N = \mu mg$

$F_f = 0.40(47 \text{ kg})(9.8 \text{ m/s}^2) = \textbf{184 N}$

21. D)

Plug the variables into the appropriate formula and solve.

$J = \Delta p = p_2 - p_1$

$J = mv_2 - mv_1 = m(v_2 - v_1)$

$J = 0.5 \text{ kg}(5 \text{ m/s} - (-3 \text{ m/s})) = \textbf{4 kg m/s}$

22. D)

Plug the variables into the appropriate formula and solve.

$\Delta V = Ed$

$E = \dfrac{\Delta V}{d}$

$E = \dfrac{30 \text{ V}}{0.002 \text{ m}} = \textbf{15,000 V/m}$

23. C)

The normal angles of incident and reflected light rays are always identical.

24. D)

Plug the variables into the appropriate formula and solve.

$R_t = R_1 + R_2 + R_3 + \ldots$

$R_t = 17(12 \, \Omega) = \textbf{204 } \Omega$

25. A)

Plug the variables into the appropriate formula and solve.

$F = qE$

$E = \dfrac{F}{q}$

$E = \dfrac{3 \times 10^{-9} \text{ N}}{1.602 \times 10^{-19} \text{ C}} = \textbf{1.8} \times \textbf{10}^{10} \textbf{ N/C}$

26. A)

The asteroid is moving at a constant velocity, so the acceleration is **zero**.

27. C)

Plug the variables into the appropriate formula and solve.

$F = qE$

$q = \dfrac{mg}{E}$

$q = \dfrac{(5 \text{ kg})(9.8 \text{ m/s}^2)}{(4 \times 10^4 \text{ N/C})} = 0.00123 \text{ C}$

$= \textbf{1.23} \times \textbf{10}^{-3} \textbf{ C}$

28. C)

Convert 1 revolution to radians.

1 rev = 2π rad

Plug the variables into the appropriate formula and solve.

$\omega_f = \omega_i + at$

$\omega_f = \omega_i + at$

$t = \dfrac{2\pi \text{ rad/s} - 0 \text{ rad/s}}{1 \text{ rad/s}^2} = 2\pi \text{ s} = \textbf{6.28 s}$

29. C)

Constructive interference of two identical waves in phase will double the amplitude but leave the frequency unchanged.

30. C)

Plug the variables into the appropriate formula and solve.

$n_1 \sin\theta_1 = n_2 \sin\theta_2$

$\theta_2 = \sin^{-1}\left(\dfrac{n_1}{n_2}\sin\theta_1\right)$

$\theta_2 = \sin^{-1}\left(\dfrac{1}{1.5}\left(\sin 45°\right)\right) = \textbf{28.13°}$

Follow the link below to take your second HESI A² practice test and to access other online study resources:

https://www.ascenciatestprep.com/hesi-a2-online-resources

TWO: PRACTICE TEST TWO

Mathematics

Directions: Work the problem carefully, and choose the best answer.

1. A skateboarder is moving down the sidewalk at 15 feet per second. What is his approximate speed in miles per hour?

A) 30.7 mph

B) 22 mph

C) 15.9 mph

D) 10.2 mph

2. Evaluate the following expression for $x = 2$, $y = -1$, and $z = 5$: $xyz - (y + z)^2$

A) -26

B) 6

C) 26

D) -6

3. $\frac{4}{5} - \frac{1}{3} =$

A) $\frac{3}{8}$

B) $\frac{3}{2}$

C) $1\frac{2}{15}$

D) $\frac{7}{15}$

4. When Darlene left the house on Monday morning, the odometer in her car read 66,284.8. After work on Friday, it read 66,653.2. How many miles did she drive that week?

A) 368.4 mi

B) 431.6 mi

C) 36.84 mi

D) 479.5 mi

5. Simplify the following expression: $9^2 + 2(7^2 - 1)$

A) 3984

B) 44

C) 177

D) 260

6. Convert 1315 hours to standard time.

A) 3:15 a.m.

B) 3:15 p.m.

C) 1:15 p.m.

D) 1:15 a.m.

7. Simplify the following expression:

$(5 + 1)^2 \div 4 + 1$

A) 4

B) 10

C) 7.2

D) 2

8. $8.7 - 4.243 =$

A) 4.156

B) 4.457

C) 4.543

D) 3.373

9. $8\frac{1}{4} - 5\frac{4}{5} =$

A) $2\frac{9}{20}$

B) $3\frac{11}{20}$

C) $3\frac{1}{3}$

D) $2\frac{1}{2}$

10. A company's yearly profits can be predicted by the equation $P = 6.25x - 19,000$, where x represents the number of products sold. What is the company's profit for a year in which they sell 25,000 units?

A) $156,250

B) $6,000

C) $37,000

D) $137,250

11. The recommended dosage of a particular medication is 4 milliliters per 50 pounds of body weight. What is the recommended dosage for a person who weighs 175 pounds?

A) 25 ml

B) 140 ml

C) 14 ml

D) 28 ml

12. What is 40% of 124?

A) 310

B) 4.96

C) 49.6

D) 31

13. Dave has $\frac{2}{5}$ pounds of walnuts, Zack has 0.45 pounds, Randy has $\frac{1}{3}$ pound, and Misty has 0.4 pounds. Who has the most walnuts?

A) Dave

B) Zack

C) Randy

D) Misty

14. $4.368 \div 2.8 =$

A) 1.56

B) 0.156

C) 15.6

D) 156

15. Joe's doctor has directed him to take 5 units of insulin before breakfast and 10 units of insulin before dinner each day. How many units of insulin will he need for a 30-day supply?

A) 450 units

B) 15 units

C) 300 units

D) 150 units

16. A dietitian has directed an underweight patient to increase her calorie intake by 675 calories per day. If the patient was eating an average of 1250 calories per day, what should her new daily calorie target be?

A) 1875 cal

B) 2000 cal

C) 1925 cal

D) 2200 cal

17. Find the product of 2.7 and 9.6.

A) 12.5

B) 259.2

C) 6.9

D) 25.92

18. What fraction is equivalent to 0.375?

A) $\frac{37}{100}$

B) $\frac{3}{8}$

C) $\frac{2}{5}$

D) $3\frac{3}{4}$

19. Put the following numbers in order from least to greatest: $\frac{7}{10}, \frac{3}{5}, 0.613, 0.65$

A) $\frac{3}{5}, \frac{7}{10}, 0.65, 0.613$

B) $\frac{3}{5}, 0.613, 0.65, \frac{7}{10}$

C) $\frac{7}{10}, 0.65, 0.613, \frac{3}{5}$

D) $0.613, \frac{7}{10}, 0.65, \frac{3}{5}$

20. Convert 6:00 a.m. to military time.

A) 1600

B) 1200

C) 1800

D) 0600

21. A half-cup serving of sliced peaches has 18 grams of sugar. How many grams of sugar are in 2 cups of sliced peaches?

A) 18 g

B) 72 g

C) 36 g

D) 9 g

22. 33 is 15% of what number?

A) 33.15

B) 165

C) 220

D) 48

23. Normal body temperature is 98.6°F. Convert the temperature to Celsius.

A) 37°C

B) 54.8°C

C) 66.6°C

D) 47°C

24. Solve: $2(3x + 1) - 3 = 4x + 3$

A) 2

B) 4

C) 1

D) −1

25. $5\frac{2}{3} \times 2\frac{8}{17} =$

A) $10\frac{16}{51}$

B) $11\frac{1}{3}$

C) 7

D) 14

26. $5\frac{2}{3} \div 1\frac{1}{2} =$

A) $3\frac{7}{9}$

B) $8\frac{1}{2}$

C) $\frac{9}{34}$

D) $5\frac{1}{3}$

27. A local supermarket is sponsoring a 10k (10 kilometer) run for charity. How many miles is the run?

A) 16.1 mi

B) 10 mi

C) 5 mi

D) 6.2 mi

28. Solve: $7x - 2(3x + 7) = 2x + 1$

A) -13

B) 13

C) -15

D) 5

29. 85 is 17% of what number?

A) 150

B) 415

C) 500

D) 14.45

30. Write $\frac{4}{5}$ as a decimal number.

A) 0.8

B) 0.08

C) 0.45

D) 0.045

31. Beth spends $550 per month on rent, which is 25% of her budget. What is Beth's total budget?

A) $1375

B) $2500

C) $1650

D) $2200

32. Solve: $\frac{x}{4} - \frac{1}{3} = \frac{7x}{12} + \frac{5}{6}$

A) $\frac{3}{2}$

B) $-\frac{7}{2}$

C) -3

D) $\frac{7}{2}$

33. A bottle contains 712 milliliters of cleaning fluid. Convert the volume to liters.

A) 71.2 L

B) 71,200 L

C) 7.12 L

D) 0.712 L

34. Simplify the following expression:
$4x - 3y + 12z + 2x - 7y - 10z$

A) $2x - 4y$

B) $6x - 10y + 2z$

C) $6x - 4y - 2z$

D) $-2xyz$

35. The budget for hospital renovations is $2\frac{1}{2}$ billion. The hospital will receive $\frac{2}{5}$ of the funding from a local charity. How much will be donated by the charity?

A) $1 million

B) $1\frac{1}{5}$ million

C) $1\frac{1}{2}$ million

D) $2 million

36. $3\frac{3}{8} \div 9 =$

A) $30\frac{3}{8}$

B) $1\frac{1}{8}$

C) $1\frac{5}{8}$

D) $\frac{3}{8}$

37. Simplify the following expression:
$2x^2(4x^2 + 2xy - 3y^2)$

A) $12x^5y^3$

B) $6x^4 + 4x^3y - 5x^2y^2$

C) $8x^4 + 4x^3y - 6x^2y^2$

D) $6x^9y^3$

38. Marty pays $0.187 per kilowatt-hour for electricity at his business. Find the cost of electricity for a month in which the business uses 927 kilowatt-hours.

A) $111.40

B) $741.00

C) $495.72

D) $173.35

39. A box of books weighs 6.3 pounds. If there are 18 books in the box, how much does each book weigh?

A) 1.134 lb

B) 11.7 lb

C) 0.35 lb

D) 3.5 lb

40. A tablet contains 0.52 grams of vitamin A. Convert the amount of vitamin A in the tablet to milligrams.

A) 520 mg

B) 52 mg

C) 5200 mg

D) 5.2 mg

41. Simplify the following expression:
$4x - 3(y - 2x)$

A) $2x - 3y$

B) $-2x + 3y$

C) $3y - 10x$

D) $10x - 3y$

42. The price of a movie ticket increased from $9.75 to $11.50. Find the percent increase. Round your answer to the nearest tenth of a percent.

A) 84.8%

B) 22%

C) 17.9%

D) 15.2%

43. Simplify the following expression:
$\dfrac{9a^7b^3}{18a^2b^5}$

A) $2a^5b^2$

B) $\dfrac{a^5}{9b^2}$

C) $\dfrac{a^5}{2b^2}$

D) $2a^9b^8$

44. If 2 tablets contain 600 milligrams of medicine, how much medicine is in half a tablet?

A) 300 mg

B) 150 mg

C) 120 mg

D) 1200 mg

45. Find 90% of 62.

A) 55.8

B) 7.2

C) 5.58

D) 0.72

46. $\dfrac{2}{5} - \dfrac{1}{3} =$

A) $\dfrac{1}{2}$

B) $\dfrac{1}{15}$

C) $\dfrac{11}{15}$

D) $\dfrac{1}{30}$

47. $65 - 14.46 + 5.8 =$

   A) 14.53
   B) 15.69
   C) 56.34
   D) 73.66

48. $-48 \div (-6) =$

   A) −8
   B) 8
   C) 7
   D) 6

49. Chris makes $13.50 an hour. How much will he earn in a 7.5-hour day?

   A) $101.25
   B) $1012.50
   C) $20.75
   D) $91.00

50. Joan has 5 yards of fabric. If she uses $3\frac{1}{3}$ yards to make a dress, how much fabric does she have left?

   A) $2\frac{2}{3}$ yd
   B) $2\frac{1}{3}$ yd
   C) $1\frac{1}{2}$ yd
   D) $1\frac{2}{3}$ yd

51. On a map, 1 inch represents 22 miles. If 2 towns are 4.5 inches apart on the map, what is the actual distance between them?

   A) 50 mi
   B) 44 mi
   C) 90 mi
   D) 99 mi

52. A pregnant woman arrives at the hospital at 1:00 p.m. After five and a half hours, she delivers a healthy baby boy. What time of birth will be recorded in the chart?

   A) 0630
   B) 1230
   C) 1630
   D) 1830

53. 140 is 35% of what number?

   A) 260
   B) 400
   C) 175
   D) 500

54. $-2 - 10 =$

   A) −12
   B) 12
   C) 8
   D) −8

55. Solve: $\frac{x}{4} = \frac{x+2}{2}$

   A) 2
   B) −4
   C) 1
   D) −1

Reading

Directions: Read the passage carefully, and then read the questions that follow and choose the most correct answer.

There is a cultural myth that pervades discussions surrounding the common cold. According to this myth, exposure to cold temperatures causes people to catch a cold. This, however, is simply not true. The common cold is caused by viruses, not cold weather; low temperatures alone will not leave us sneezing.

This persistent myth is one part personal observation, two parts flawed assumption. Cases of the cold definitely tend to skyrocket when it is coldest and wettest outside—namely, winter. But the cause is not the snow and ice outside; it's the pathogens and crowded spaces inside. Cold weather forces humans to "hibernate" within the warmth of their homes and workplaces, where they cannot escape the coughs, sneezes, and contaminated handshakes of their sick coworkers, family members, and fellow commuters. This increases the chance of catching a cold. In fact, it is hand-shakes, not snowfalls, that put us at the greatest risk of acquiring cold viruses; there are simply more contaminated surfaces that we cannot avoid touching. This is why good hand-washing hygiene, not cozier sweaters, is our best defense from the common cold.

1. Which of the following statements can the reader infer from the passage?

    A) Becoming cold and wet cannot make a sick person even sicker.

    B) Washing your hands several times a day can reduce your chances of catching a cold.

    C) Washing your hands several times a day guarantees that you will not catch a cold.

    D) Refusing to shake hands with others ensures that you will not catch a cold.

2. What is the author's primary purpose in writing this paragraph?

    A) to dispel a myth that shaking hands can pass cold viruses

    B) to dispel a myth that cold weather causes the common cold

    C) to advise readers about ways to treat patients' cold symptoms

    D) to inform readers about proven cures for the common cold

3. According to the passage, what is true of winter?

    A) Very few people catch colds during this season.

    B) Many people catch colds during this season.

    C) Due to cold weather during winter, colds are more severe.

    D) In winter, below-freezing temperatures kill cold viruses.

4. Which of the following statements can be considered a statement of FACT according to the content offered in the passage above?

    A) People who do not question cultural myths are foolish.

    B) It is always a bad idea to shake hands with other people.

    C) Viruses, not cold weather, cause the common cold.

    D) Pneumonia is an extreme form of the common cold.

5. According to the passage, what should people do to avoid catching colds?

    A) wear warmer clothing

    B) get eight hours of sleep each night

    C) wash their hands well and often

    D) rest and drink plenty of clear liquids

When a medical professional is taking your blood pressure, they are trying to measure how hard your bloodstream is pushing against the walls of your arteries as it exits the heart. The heart acts as the body's pump, pushing blood through the circulatory system. The arteries and veins are like the body's "pipes"—they capture the blood flow from the heart, deliver it to the rest of the body, and bring it back to the heart. Blood pressure provides doctors with information that might help them diagnose potential issues with the relationship between the heart and the rest of the circulatory system.

Generally, blood pressure varies throughout the day according to activity, posture, and stress. But consistently high or low blood pressure can be a sign of illness. Chronically high blood pressure is known as hypertension. Risk factors for hypertension include a family history, age, lack of exercise, smoking, being overweight, and stress. Persistent hypertension can lead to a number of health conditions, including stroke and heart disease, which are leading causes of often preventable deaths in the United States each year. It is important to visit your doctor regularly to monitor your blood pressure and take steps to keep it under control.

6. Which of the following statements can the reader infer from the passage?

    A) Hypertension is a more dangerous condition than low blood pressure.

    B) Low blood pressure may show a problem with the patient's heart or circulation.

    C) Low blood pressure is a more serious condition than high blood pressure.

    D) If a medical professional says you have low blood pressure, you should not worry.

7. What is the author's primary purpose in writing this essay?

    A) to advise readers about ways to treat patients with low blood pressure

    B) to provide details about hypertension and low blood pressure

    C) to persuade readers to stop smoking and to exercise regularly

    D) to inform readers about blood pressure: normal, high, and low

8. Which sentence best summarizes the passage's main idea?

    A) The term "blood pressure" means how hard your bloodstream is pushing against the walls of your arteries as it leaves your heart.

    B) Doctors use blood pressure to diagnose heart trouble and other problems with patients' circulatory systems.

    C) Lack of exercise, old age, smoking, obesity, and stress can cause hypertension, or the patient may simply have a family history of high blood pressure.

    D) It is wise to have your blood pressure checked at least once every six months.

9. In the last sentence, what does the word *monitor* mean?

    A) supervisor or overseer

    B) to observe regularly

    C) computer screen

    D) to inspect precisely

10. According to the passage, what causes low blood pressure?

    A) The author does not explain what causes low blood pressure.

    B) It is most often caused by a family history of this condition.

    C) It can be caused by stress, lack of exercise, and/or being overweight.

    D) It is caused by heart disease, strokes, or hypertension.

11. Which words or phrases in the second paragraph provide clues to the meaning of the word *chronically*?

    A) *generally* and *regularly*

    B) *lead to* and *causes of*

    C) *consistently* and *persistent*

    D) *preventable* and *under control*

Water accounts for roughly 60 percent of an adult human's body weight and is essential for most bodily functions. Dehydration is a deficit of water in the body. It can be caused by illness, exercise, heat, stress, or lack of self-care, and its effects range from a simple headache to cardiac arrest.

Throughout the day, humans continuously lose water through urine, feces, breath, and skin. If you are waiting until you are thirsty to drink something, then you are already dehydrated; our thirst mechanism fails to "notify" our body of dehydration in time. Mild dehydration is easily remedied, but dehydration can affect brain capacity, motor skills, and attention. Severe or chronic cases of dehydration have more dramatic effects. It can damage your kidneys, increase your heart rate to the point of cardiac arrest, cause you to collapse or faint, or force your body into a state of hyperthermia.

Under normal circumstances, all of this can be prevented by replenishing fluids throughout the day. The amount of water an individual needs varies based on such factors as metabolism or diet, but conventional wisdom is that humans should take in anywhere between 2.7 and 3.7 liters of water each day. This intake can come from various sources, including juices and foods with high water content, such as fruits and vegetables.

12. In the third paragraph, what does the phrase "conventional wisdom" mean?

    A) conservative thinking

    B) unadventurous precautions

    C) standard guidelines

    D) casual suggestions

13. According to the passage, what causes dehydration?

    A) illness, exercise, heat, stress, or lack of self-care

    B) urine, feces, breath, and skin

    C) kidney damage, cardiac arrest, fainting, or hyperthermia

    D) juices, fruits, and vegetables

14. Which of the following statements can the reader infer from the passage?

    A) Most headaches are a result of dehydration.

    B) The human body does not "notify" us when it is dehydrated.

    C) Dehydration is a medical problem, but it is not life threatening.

    D) Doctors say we should drink eight full glasses of water each day.

15. In the first sentence, what does the word *essential* mean?

    A) basic

    B) helpful

    C) crucial

    D) preferred

16. What is the author's primary purpose in writing this essay?

A) to advise readers on ways to treat patients with severe dehydration

B) to warn readers that dehydration can kill patients

C) to explain what dehydration is and how it can be prevented

D) to tell a story about someone who was successfully treated for dehydration

17. Which sentence best summarizes the passage's main idea?

A) An adult human's body is 60 percent water.

B) Severe dehydration can cause kidney damage, cardiac arrest, fainting, or hyperthermia.

C) Every person needs to drink between 2.7 and 3.7 liters of water each day.

D) Dehydration has a variety of causes and a range of effects, from mild to severe.

E-cigarettes have only been around for about fifteen years, but they are a booming business. E-cigarettes do not contain tobacco; instead, they contain a liquid that is heated to produce an aerosol that is then inhaled. The liquid usually contains nicotine, the primary addictive substance in tobacco. Some political officials and health professionals are likening e-cigarettes—in spite of their modern electronic disguise—to their tobacco-laden predecessors, questioning the health effects of inhaling some of the liquid's other ingredients. Consequently, debates over e-cigarettes are currently being waged in schools, households, legislatures, and science labs across the globe.

Politicians and health experts are pressing governments to regulate e-cigarettes because they believe their popularity will undermine public health gains made in the decades-long war on traditional smoking. Other medical professionals believe e-cigarettes may, in fact, help this war by providing smokers with an alternative to smoking tobacco, which, in addition to nicotine, contains many harmful substances and is unequivocally linked with multiple types of cancer.

Scientists have been researching the health effects of e-cigarettes. Recent studies, unfortunately, have created more questions than answers. While one trial showed that e-cigarettes may be as effective as nicotine patches in helping people quit smoking, another showed that e-cigarette vapor may contain metal that could cause "popcorn lung." As we await answers, the growth of the e-cigarette industry looks like it is not going to slow in the near future: e-cigarettes manufacturing and sales is a multibillion-dollar industry that is likely going to continue stirring debate in the decades to come.

18. Readers can infer from reading this passage that smoking e-cigarettes _____.

A) probably causes cancer

B) is no less harmful than smoking tobacco

C) is usually addictive

D) is as pleasurable as smoking tobacco

19. What is the meaning of the word *booming* in the first paragraph?

A) loud

B) bellowing

C) successful

D) selling

20. Which of the following statements can the reader infer from the passage?

A) The author thinks it is very wrong to make and sell e-cigarettes.

B) The author believes quitting tobacco smoking is a positive step.

C) In the author's opinion, e-cigarettes are just as harmful as cigarettes made with tobacco.

D) The author has no opinions about any of the content in the passage.

21. Which of the following is NOT listed as a detail in the passage?

A) Instead of tobacco, e-cigarettes contain a liquid; the liquid is heated to produce an aerosol that the e-cigarette user inhales.

B) Like cigarettes made from tobacco, e-cigarettes contain nicotine, which is addictive.

C) Studies have shown that like cigarettes made from tobacco, e-cigarettes cause lung cancer.

D) One study showed that e-cigarettes can help people quit smoking cigarettes containing tobacco.

22. What is the author's primary purpose in writing this essay?

A) to reassure readers that it is safe to smoke e-cigarettes

B) to inform readers that scientists do not yet know all the effects of e-cigarette smoking

C) to warn readers about cause-effect relationships between e-cigarette smoking and cancer

D) to persuade readers to quit smoking tobacco and start "vaping" e-cigarettes

23. Which sentence best summarizes the passage's main idea?

A) "E-cigarettes do not contain tobacco; instead, they contain a liquid that is heated to produce an aerosol that is then inhaled."

B) "Some political officials and health professionals are likening e-cigarettes—in spite of their modern electronic disguise—to their tobacco-laden predecessors, questioning the health effects of inhaling some of the liquid's other ingredients."

C) "Other medical professionals believe e-cigarettes may, in fact, help this war by providing smokers with an alternative to smoking tobacco, which, in addition to nicotine, contains many harmful substances and is unequivocally linked with multiple types of cancer."

D) "As we await answers, the growth of the e-cigarette industry looks like it is not going to slow in the near future: e-cigarettes manufacturing and sales is a multibillion-dollar industry that is likely going to continue stirring debate in the decades to come."

If you frequent your local Whole Foods, you will likely come across a popular international spice: turmeric. Turmeric comes from the bulbous root of a plant known as *Curcuma longa*. It is related to ginger, but the fleshy inside of the root is a deep yellow. Once the root is boiled, dried, and ground, it creates a bitter yellow powdered spice that gives Indian curry its distinctive color. Turmeric has been used medicinally—as well as in cooking, as a dye, and in religious rituals—in India and Southeast Asia for millennia. Its anti-inflammatory properties have gained the adoration of Western health and wellness gurus in recent years.

Today, many Americans are touting turmeric as a holistic medicinal replacement for anti-inflammatory drugs. Small-scale studies have shown that curcumin, a key compound found in turmeric, can help with both skin inflammation and joint inflammation. Companies are adding turmeric to topical creams for skin care, and patients with rheumatoid arthritis are taking their daily dose of turmeric pills to help decrease pain and stiffness in their joints. Larger-scale clinical studies have not provided conclusive evidence for these benefits.

Regardless of its true health benefits, expect to see turmeric continue to impact the health food and holistic medicine industries in the near future. It is hard to walk through any upscale health food store without seeing the buzzword *turmeric* plastered on trendy juices and vegan powder canisters.

24. Readers can infer from the passage that the author _____.

   A) believes in turmeric's anti-inflammatory health properties

   B) is not sure that turmeric is an effective anti-inflammatory aid

   C) uses turmeric at home to add spice to Indian cuisine

   D) has used turmeric to dye cloth a deep yellow

25. In paragraph 1, what does the word *distinctive* mean?

   A) deep yellow

   B) characteristic

   C) fluorescent

   D) bright

26. Which sentence best summarizes the passage's main idea?

   A) "Turmeric comes from the bulbous root of a plant known as *Curcuma longa.*"

   B) "Once the root is boiled, dried, and ground, it creates a bitter yellow powdered spice that gives Indian curry its distinctive color."

   C) "Small-scale studies have shown that curcumin, a key compound found in turmeric, can help with both skin inflammation and joint inflammation."

   D) "Regardless of its true health benefits, expect to see turmeric continue to impact the health food and holistic medicine industries in the near future."

27. What is the author's primary purpose in writing this essay?

   A) to persuade readers with arthritis to buy turmeric

   B) to criticize health food businesses for selling turmeric

   C) to explain what turmeric is and why it has become popular

   D) to warn consumers not to be gullible enough to buy turmeric

28. According to the passage, when did people first begin to use turmeric medicinally?

   A) hundreds of years ago

   B) in the mid-1900s

   C) in the early 2000s

   D) a few years ago

29. According to the passage, which types of studies have shown that turmeric is an effective medicine?

   A) studies run by wellness gurus

   B) small-scale studies

   C) larger-scale clinical studies

   D) studies run by the health food and holistic medicine industries

New studies indicate that the impact of a single concussion, even if it is a person's first, can cause longer-lasting neurological damage than we previously knew—possibly even permanent. This changes the ways school districts and medical professionals are treating high school students who experience concussions. Many high school athletes return to their respective sports just one or two weeks after sustaining a concussion, but research shows that clinical symptoms of a concussion can continue for up to six months after the initial injury.

Even more troubling is the evidence that damage caused by a concussion may be permanent. The brain is commonly known for its fragility; ironically, it may be its resiliency that is hiding the long-term effects of concussions. A concussion is a mild traumatic brain injury. The brain is tremendously resilient in how it deals with the damage: it can "rewire" around the area of trauma and make new neurological connections. The consequence of this "rewiring" is that we may not recognize the extent of a brain injury. If students return to play too soon, they can exacerbate the initial damage or prolong the side effects.

30. Which sentence best summarizes the passage's main idea?

A) Due to new studies, school districts are now requiring injured athletes to wait for six months before returning to play.

B) Following a concussion, it is probably advisable for a student athlete to wait up to six months before returning to play.

C) The human brain is so resilient that it can heal from a concussion by "rewiring" around the traumatized area.

D) The human brain is too fragile to heal from even a mild concussion within two weeks.

31. What is the meaning of the word *resiliency* in the second paragraph?

A) deceitfulness

B) ability to heal quickly

C) ability to quietly endure

D) mild sarcasm

32. Which of the following is NOT listed as a detail in the passage?

A) New studies show that permanent brain damage can possibly result from a concussion.

B) In the past, school coaches have insisted that injured athletes resume playing too soon.

C) After sustaining concussions, many high school athletes begin playing again after two weeks.

D) The brain can "rewire" around an injured area and make new neurological connections.

33. What is the author's primary purpose in writing this essay?

A) to reassure readers that teenagers' brains can quickly heal following concussions

B) to suggest that, following a concussion, a student athlete should take several months off to heal

C) to scare readers about cause-effect relationships between sports injuries and permanent brain damage

D) to persuade readers not to allow their children to play high-school sports such as football

34. Readers can infer from reading this passage that concussions are _____.

A) more harmful than researchers knew in the past

B) less harmful than researchers thought in the past

C) not serious due to the brain's remarkable resiliency

D) uncommon among high school and college athletes

35. In the first sentence, what does the word *neurological* mean?

A) physical

B) psychological

C) having to do with the brain

D) having to do with athletic injuries

Have you ever devoured a tasty snow cone only to experience the agony of "brain freeze"? Have you ever wondered why or how that happens? Well, scientists now believe they understand the mechanism of these so-called ice cream headaches.

It begins with the icy temperature of the snow cone (or any cold food, or sometimes even exposure to cold air). When a cold substance (delicious or otherwise) presses against the roof of your mouth, it causes blood vessels there to begin to constrict, and your body starts to sense that something is awry. In response, blood is pumped to the affected region to try to warm it up, causing rapid dilation of the same vessels. This causes the neighboring trigeminal nerve to send rapid signals to your brain. Because the trigeminal nerve also serves the face, the brain misinterprets these signals as coming from your forehead. The duration of the pain varies from a few seconds up to about a minute.

Regardless of the time spent wincing, the danger of the ice cream headache certainly will not stop people for screaming for their favorite frozen treat in the future.

36. Readers can infer from the passage that the author is trying to _____ us.

    A) inform and persuade

    B) inform and entertain

    C) warn and persuade

    D) amuse and entertain

37. Why does the author use the word *screaming* in the last sentence?

    A) to show how painful "brain freeze" can be

    B) to show that ice cream headaches are dangerous

    C) to jokingly refer to a play on words: "I scream for ice cream"

    D) to rhyme with the word *creaming* in a traditional poem

38. According to the passage, what happens immediately after the roof of the mouth grows cold?

    A) Blood vessels on the roof of the mouth begin to expand.

    B) The body pumps blood to the roof of the mouth to warm it up.

    C) The trigeminal nerve sends rapid signals to the brain.

    D) Blood vessels on the roof of the mouth begin to narrow.

39. Which sentence best summarizes the passage's main idea?

    A) "Have you ever devoured a tasty snow cone only to experience the agony of 'brain freeze'?"

    B) "Well, scientists now believe they understand the mechanism of these so-called ice cream headaches."

    C) "When a cold substance (delicious or otherwise) presses against the roof of your mouth, it causes blood vessels there to begin to constrict, and your body starts to sense that something is awry."

    D) "Because the trigeminal nerve also serves the face, the brain misinterprets these signals as coming from your forehead."

40. Which body part is NOT mentioned in the passage?

    A) the roof of the mouth

    B) the tongue

    C) the face

    D) the forehead

41. In the last sentence of the second paragraph, what does the word *duration* mean?

    A) time period

    B) skin surface

    C) intensity

    D) strength

Many snakes produce a toxic fluid in their salivary glands called venom. The two key ingredients in all snake venoms are enzymes and polypeptides. Some enzymes help the snake disable its prey, and others help the snake digest its prey. The victim of the snakebite has a much less beneficial experience with these enzymes: snake venoms can speed up chemical reactions that lower blood pressure, paralyze muscles, destroy tissues, deconstruct red blood cells, or cause internal bleeding.

There are many different types of snake venom, composed of various combinations of toxic and nontoxic substances. Toxins in snake venom are often divided into three categories: hemotoxins, neurotoxins, and cytotoxins. Hemotoxins affect the blood by interfering with the process of blood coagulation. In some cases, hemotoxins inhibit the process of blood clotting, and in other cases they cause excessive clotting. Neurotoxins target the nervous system rather than body tissues; they disrupt the messages sent by neurotransmitter production and reception throughout the body. Neurotoxins can paralyze muscles, causing respiratory failure and possibly death. Cytotoxins cause liquefactive necrosis of body cells; they dissolve cells, leading to the death of tissues or organs. Some cytotoxins target specific types of cells—myotoxins affect muscles, cardiotoxins attack the heart, and nephrotoxins damage the kidneys.

In addition to research on various antivenoms to combat the potentially deadly effects of snake venom, scientists have also been looking at the venom itself as a possible source of medical benefits. Researchers have been studying the chemical compositions of these venoms and have been making strides in using the science behind the toxins to combat major diseases such as cancer, heart disease, and Alzheimer's. For instance, a drug called captopril, used to treat hypertension, is based on a toxin in the venom of a pit viper found in Brazil.

42. Which sentence best summarizes the passage's main idea?

   A) "Many snakes produce a toxic fluid in their salivary glands called venom."

   B) "There are many different types of snake venom, composed of various combinations of toxic and nontoxic substances."

   C) "Some cytotoxins target specific types of cells—myotoxins affect muscles, cardiotoxins attack the heart, and nephrotoxins damage the kidneys."

   D) "Researchers have been studying the chemical compositions of these venoms and have been making strides in using the science behind the toxins to combat major diseases such as cancer, heart disease, and Alzheimer's."

43. In the last paragraph, what does the word *strides* mean?

   A) long steps

   B) heavy stomping

   C) improvements

   D) experiments

44. According to the passage, how does venom benefit snakes, besides the fact that this fluid allows snakes to kill their prey?

   A) It helps snakes to disable and digest their prey.

   B) It can heal snakes' diseases such as cancer and Alzheimer's.

   C) It terrifies snakes' prey, momentarily paralyzing these creatures.

   D) It discourages other predators from pursuing and eating snakes.

45. What is the author's primary purpose in writing this essay?

   A) to advise readers on ways to treat patients with snakebites

   B) to warn readers that most snakes are venomous

   C) to inform readers about the contents of snake venom

   D) to tell a story about a scientist who used venom as a medicine

46. Which of the following statements can the reader infer from the passage?

   A) All snakes produce venom.

   B) Some snakes are not venomous.

   C) A venomous snake never bites other members of its own species.

   D) A Brazilian pit viper's venom is not poisonous to humans.

47. In the last sentence in the second paragraph, what does the word part *nephro* in the word *nephrotoxins* probably mean?

   A) poison

   B) heart

   C) muscle

   D) kidney

The history of vaccines dates back further than one might imagine—all the way to tenth-century China, where smallpox scabs were ground up and blown into a person's nostrils. However, what we recognize as the precursor to the modern vaccine came in 1796. English surgeon Edward Jenner built on the knowledge that people who worked with cows and had been exposed to cowpox, which has a mild effect on humans, did not catch smallpox. Jenner deliberately exposed a child to cowpox by taking some of the serum from a pustule on the hand of a milkmaid and scratching it into the child's skin. Six weeks later, he exposed the child to smallpox—and the child remained healthy.

Vaccines work by stimulating the immune system to produce antibodies against a particular disease. How does this happen? A minute amount of the disease-producing pathogen is injected into the bloodstream (although some vaccines can be taken orally or even as a nasal spray). The pathogen is either present in such a small amount that it will not cause illness or the pathogen is "dead." Either way, you cannot get sick, but your immune system will ramp up to repel the invaders. Your immune system hangs on to the antibodies it creates; if you are exposed to the pathogen in the future, your body is ready to fight it off.

Vaccines have been a crucial component in the long history of public health efforts in the United States—they have helped eradicate or almost eradicate previously widespread diseases such as whooping cough, polio, rubella, tetanus, tuberculosis, smallpox, diphtheria, and measles. The creation of the National Vaccine Agency in 1813 encouraged many states to adopt mandatory immunizations for schoolchildren for the first time. Today, every state requires some immunizations for children entering public schools, though all allow medical exemptions and most allow exemptions on religious or philosophical grounds.

48. What does the first paragraph mainly concern?

   A) smallpox vaccines in tenth-century China

   B) Jenner's smallpox vaccine in 1796

   C) a cure for cowpox in the late 1700s

   D) wiping out widespread diseases in the United States

49. What is the meaning of the word *immunizations* in the last paragraph?

   A) immune systems

   B) pathogens

   C) pustules

   D) vaccinations

50. Which of the following statements can be considered a statement of FACT according to the content offered in the paragraphs above?

   A) Chinese doctors were the first to successfully cure smallpox.

   B) A vaccine works with the body's immune system to prevent someone from getting a disease.

   C) Thanks to Edward Jenner, diseases such as whooping cough and polio no longer exist.

   D) Thanks to worldwide vaccination programs, most infectious diseases will soon be eradicated.

51. According to the passage, what is true about state laws on vaccinating schoolchildren?

    A) There are no exceptions to these requirements.

    B) The only exceptions to these laws are for medical reasons.

    C) Everyone should obey these laws, because diseases are infectious.

    D) Most states have religious and philosophical exemptions to these laws.

52. Readers can infer that neither _____ nor the common cold have been eradicated or close to eradicated in the United States.

    A) all flu viruses

    B) the measles

    C) tetanus

    D) tuberculosis

53. What is the author's primary purpose in writing this essay?

    A) to warn parents about possible side effects of vaccines

    B) to persuade parents to have their children vaccinated

    C) to advise people about different treatments for infectious diseases

    D) to inform readers about the history of vaccines, including how they work

Sweat glands can be found all over the body. They lie beneath the skin and help regulate body temperature by transporting water to the skin's surface. The most common type of sweat glands are eccrine glands. They are tiny, coiled glands and are concentrated on the palm of your hand and the sole of your foot. There are about two million to five million eccrine glands in the body, with about four hundred to five hundred per square centimeter in the palm of your hand. These glands are controlled by the sympathetic nervous system, which stimulates perspiration. The sweat that pours out of these glands is normally colorless and odorless.

Body odor tends to form around a special type of sweat gland—the apocrine glands—which develop in human beings during puberty. They are located in the armpits and in the groin. They, too, emit odorless perspiration, but bacteria in these areas mix with the apocrine secretions to create body odor.

Mammary glands are specialized examples of apocrine glands. Mammary glands produce milk following the birth of a child. Thus, sweat glands are not only associated with perspiration, but also lactation.

54. What is the author's primary purpose in writing these paragraphs?

    A) to define the word *sweat*

    B) to persuade readers to practice good hygiene

    C) to inform readers about the sympathetic nervous system

    D) to inform readers about types and functions of sweat glands

55. According to the passage, what is one specialized type of apocrine gland?

    A) sweat glands

    B) glands in the hands and feet

    C) mammary glands

    D) endocrine glands

Vocabulary

Directions: Read the question and then choose the most correct answer.

1. Select the meaning of the underlined word in the sentence.

   To <u>triage</u> patients, nurses must be able to quickly judge how severe a patient's condition is.

   A) sort
   B) identify
   C) treat
   D) document

2. Which word is not spelled correctly in the context of this sentence?

   Diets containing too many vitamin supplements can harm a patience health.

   A) too
   B) vitamin
   C) supplements
   D) patience

3. Select the word that means "to a great degree."

   The laceration required immediate medical attention to prevent severe blood loss.

   A) immediate
   B) attention
   C) severe
   D) loss

4. Select the meaning of the underlined word in the sentence.

   The intermittent and <u>transient</u> nature of her symptoms left the medical team puzzled.

   A) repetitive
   B) severe
   C) extreme
   D) temporary

5. A diagnosis of enteral bleeding suggests that the patient has bleeding in the

   A) small intestine.
   B) kidneys.
   C) uterus.
   D) liver.

6. Select the meaning of the underlined word in the sentence.

   Failure to take all prescribed antibiotic medicines results in the <u>recurrence</u> of the illness.

   A) cure
   B) return
   C) resolution
   D) suppression

7. Select the word that best completes the sentence.

   _____ disorders affect the blood vessels, sometimes causing strokes and aneurysms.

   A) Hematologic
   B) Renal
   C) Neurovascular
   D) Paroxysmal

8. A change in the symmetry of a tumor means that it

   A) has changed in shape and size.
   B) has changed in color.
   C) shows no signs of growth.
   D) is benign.

9. Which word means "enough to meet a need"?

   A) sufficient

   B) virulent

   C) latent

   D) secondary

10. Select the meaning of the underlined word in the sentence.

   The child's fever and swelling subsided after an <u>analgesic</u> was administered.

   A) compress

   B) soporific

   C) pain reliever

   D) antiseptic

11. Select the meaning of the underlined word in the sentence.

   To the relief of all, his <u>status</u> was updated from critical to stable.

   A) prescription

   B) condition

   C) vitals

   D) chart

12. Select the meaning of the underlined word in the sentence.

   Managers must be willing to <u>initiate</u> conversations about performance improvement.

   A) stop

   B) begin

   C) continue

   D) understand

13. What best describes the term *transdermal*?

   A) moving from one place on the body to another

   B) able to pass through the skin

   C) the administration of medication by syringe

   D) the transmission of pathogens

14. Select the meaning of the underlined word in the sentence.

   Co-workers who are <u>incompatible</u> may need assistance resolving differences.

   A) friendly

   B) cooperative

   C) mismatched

   D) talkative

15. Which word is not spelled correctly in the context of this sentence?

   Eating a diet that is high in carbohydrates can place you at a higher risk for diabeetes.

   A) diet

   B) carbohydrates

   C) higher

   D) diabeetes

16. Select the meaning of the underlined word in the sentence.

   Analgesics are prescribed to help <u>diminish</u> pain.

   A) identify

   B) decrease

   C) stop

   D) intensify

17. Select the word that means "expand; make larger."

   Cervical dilation begins several days before labor and is complete when the cervix reaches 10 cm.

   A) dilation

   B) labor

   C) complete

   D) reaches

18. Select the meaning of the underlined word in the sentence.

The physician stated a <u>shunt</u> would be required to drain the excess fluid.

A) tube

B) needle

C) dressing

D) suture

19. A musculoskeletal disorder such as osteoarthritis affects

A) the nervous system.

B) the muscles.

C) the skeleton.

D) both the muscles and the skeleton.

20. Select the meaning of the underlined word in the sentence.

The coach gave a <u>jerk</u> of his head to the left to indicate to the batter the direction he should hit the ball.

A) unexpected response

B) delicate turn

C) slow nod

D) sudden movement

21. Select the word that best completes the sentence.

The patient's severe blood loss led to _____ shock.

A) anaphylactic

B) septic

C) neurological

D) hypovolemic

22. Which word means "free from bacteria"?

A) acute

B) aseptic

C) analgesic

D) asymptomatic

23. Select the meaning of the underlined word in the sentence.

After her first infusion of chemotherapy, the woman experienced a fever and feeling of <u>malaise</u>.

A) nausea

B) headache

C) unease

D) vomiting

24. Select the meaning of the underlined word in the sentence.

The elderly woman had restricted mobility, so the caretaker helped with her <u>hygiene</u>.

A) feeding

B) exercise

C) cleanliness

D) clothing

25. Select the word that means "a temporary pause in breathing."

Her nighttime apnea left her feeling lethargic and disoriented in the morning.

A) nighttime

B) apnea

C) lethargic

D) disoriented

26. Select the meaning of the underlined word in the sentence.

Overexertion without hydration results in <u>fatigue</u>.

A) weariness

B) stress

C) pain

D) lightheadedness

27. Select the word that best completes the sentence.

The _____ co-workers could not work together and were separated by their boss.

A) friendly

B) incompatible

C) potential

D) ambivalent

28. Select the meaning of the underlined word in the sentence.

The ability to demonstrate empathy is considered a type of emotional intelligence.

A) gentleness

B) kindness

C) charity

D) understanding

29. Which word means "discontinue"?

A) cease

B) yield

C) propel

D) extend

30. Select the meaning of the underlined word in the sentence.

The aging process is responsible for the loss of endogenous antioxidants in the body.

A) produced internally

B) produced externally

C) ingested

D) expressed

31. What best describes the term *vital*?

A) exposed to the environment

B) unable to move

C) essential to health

D) exceeding expectations

32. The offer to buy the house was contingent on it passing inspection.

A) independent of

B) consistent with

C) dependent on

D) compromised by

33. Select the word that means "to be open; to have a break in continuity."

No patient enjoys a gaping gown, so act with empathy to help ensure patients' privacy.

A) patient

B) gaping

C) empathy

D) privacy

34. Select the meaning of the underlined word in the sentence.

Practice will improve your consistency when performing specific skills.

A) irregularity

B) precision

C) mistakes

D) uniformity

35. Select the word that best completes the sentence.

The patient's _____ movements were a result of her long and wearying illness.

A) occluded

B) overt

C) rapid

D) languid

36. Which word means "abundant and plentiful"?

A) platitude

B) copious

C) dearth

D) prodigious

37. Select the meaning of the underlined word in the sentence.

Smoking and immoderate drinking usually prove <u>deleterious</u> to a person's health.

A) helpful

B) harmful

C) gentle

D) constructive

38. Select the meaning of the underlined word in the sentence.

The runner suffered a <u>bilateral</u> tendon rupture requiring immediate surgery.

A) two-sided

B) split

C) lacerated

D) complete

39. What is the best description of the term *systemic*?

A) affecting the entire body

B) causing internal bleeding

C) an infection of the hepatic system

D) a normal body temperature

40. Select the meaning of the underlined word in the sentence.

I felt enormous relief when the tissue sample was pronounced <u>benign</u>.

A) symptomatic

B) harmful

C) harmless

D) detrimental

41. A patient who shows resilience after a setback

A) suffers embarrassment.

B) returns to the hospital.

C) recovers quickly.

D) improves his or her efficiency.

42. Select the meaning of the underlined word in the sentence.

Medical personnel must <u>adhere</u> to the Health Insurance Portability and Accountability Act (HIPAA) to protect patient privacy.

A) follow

B) reject

C) uphold

D) interpret

43. Select the word that best completes the sentence.

Anyone who has experienced shingles hopes that the disease will not _____ .

A) regress

B) recur

C) delay

D) abate

44. Which word means "harmful or deadly"?

A) attenuate

B) external

C) deleterious

D) imminent

45. Select the meaning of the underlined word in the sentence.

In order to complete the research, the US scientists <u>collaborated with</u> peers from the Netherlands.

A) debated with

B) worked with

C) talked to

D) discussed with

46. What best describes the term *deter*?

A) to encourage

B) to prevent

C) to escalate

D) to open

47. Select the meaning of the underlined word in the sentence.

My cohort was the first to earn the certificate of achievement.

A) colleague

B) acquaintance

C) group

D) associate

48. Select the meaning of the underlined word in the sentence.

You will need to wear the assigned badge to access that elevator.

A) enter

B) exit

C) escape

D) find

49. Pragmatic decisions are ones that

A) show little thought.

B) emphasize logic.

C) are concerned with practical matters.

D) demonstrate cooperation.

50. Select the meaning of the underlined word in the sentence.

Surgery patients must abstain from food and drink for twelve hours prior to their procedure.

A) ingest

B) resist

C) refrain

D) intake

51. What best describes the term flushed?

A) red in appearance

B) overly excited

C) dipped in water

D) speaking quietly

52. Select the meaning of the underlined word in the sentence.

Please abbreviate commonly used words in your writing.

A) lengthen

B) avoid

C) extend

D) shorten

53. An operation requiring a resection

A) involves removal of tissue.

B) requires general anesthesia.

C) involves repair of an organ.

D) will be performed laparoscopically.

54. Select the meaning of the underlined word in the sentence.

Under pressure, it can be difficult to absorb and execute complex directions.

A) respond to

B) take in

C) forget about

D) add to

55. What best describes the term excess?

A) a dearth

B) a surplus

C) absence of necessities

D) an unexpected amount

Grammar

Directions: Read the question and then choose the most correct answer.

1. Which of the following sentences is grammatically correct?

   A) You can take either the bus nor the subway.

   B) You can't take neither the bus nor the subway.

   C) You can take either the bus or the subway.

   D) You can taking either the bus or the subway.

2. Which word is used incorrectly in the following sentence?

   The members of the orchestra played good last night, so they received a standing ovation.

   A) played

   B) good

   C) received

   D) ovation

3. Select the best punctuation mark for the blank in the following sentence.

   "I wish we could go to Hawaii_____" Adelaide said.

   A) ?

   B) .

   C) ,

   D) ;

4. Which of the following sentences is grammatically correct?

   A) If your going to be on time, you will have to leave right now.

   B) If you are going to be on time, youll have to leave right now.

   C) If you're going to be on time, you'll have to leave rightly now.

   D) If you're going to be on time, you'll have to leave right now.

5. Select the best word for the blank in the following sentence.

   I can't go with you to the meeting tonight _____ I have too much work to complete for class.

   A) yet

   B) nor

   C) because

   D) although

6. Which word is used incorrectly in the following sentence?

   The cats sleeps on the living-room sofa while the dog drinks water from her bowl in the kitchen.

   A) sleeps

   B) living-room

   C) drinks

   D) kitchen

7. Which of the following sentences contains <u>two</u> adverbs?

   A) Austin can be so amazingly hot in springtime.

   B) Austin can be amazingly hot in springtime.

   C) I think one hundred degrees is too hot for May.

   D) One hundred degrees is quite hot for May, don't you think?

8. Which word is incorrectly capitalized or lowercased in the following sentence?

   let's go to the movies on Saturday, OK?

   A) let's

   B) movies

   C) Saturday

   D) OK

9. Select the best words for the blanks in the following sentence.

After I _____ taking ice-skating lessons for two years, my coach _____ I was ready to move up into the next level, the Advanced Beginners.

A) might have been; had said

B) should have been; will say

C) will have been; says

D) had been; said

10. Which of the following sentences is grammatically correct?

A) Meet me at Britt-Marie's Restaurant; I love the way they cook meat there.

B) Meat me at Britt-Marie's Restaurant; I love the way they cook meet there.

C) Mate me at Britt-Marie's Restaurant; I love the way they cook mead there.

D) Moot me at Britt-Marie's Restaurant; I love the way they cook might there.

11. Which word is used incorrectly in the following sentence?

Max left home early on Thursday morning, for he was still late for work.

A) home

B) Thursday

C) for

D) late

12. Select the best word for the blank in the following sentence.

His love _____ espresso drinks kept him coming back to the coffee bar every morning.

A) about

B) from

C) with

D) for

13. Which of the following sentences contains a colon that introduces a list?

A) The walls of the art museum's stairwell are so beautiful: they are tiled in many shades of blue.

B) My favorite colors are different shades of blue and green: turquoise, lime green, periwinkle, bottle green, and royal blue.

C) Here is what I love: colors that remind me of the ocean.

D) My favorite colors are different shades of blue and green; I love turquoise, lime green, periwinkle, bottle green, and royal blue.

14. Which two words are used incorrectly in the following sentence?

We are not aloud to speak allowed in the public library.

A) We are

B) not, speak

C) aloud, allowed

D) public library

15. Which of the following sentences contains one independent clause and one dependent one?

A) I'm going home to change, and then I'm going to David's party.

B) I can't wear my work clothes to a party.

C) I'll take a shower, and then I'll put on my new dress.

D) If you need a ride to the party, I can pick you up on my way over there.

16. Which of the following sentences contains a prepositional phrase?

A) My cat is sitting in front of the computer screen.

B) She is blocking my view.

C) I'm going to shoo her away.

D) She will not be pleased.

17. Which of the following sentences uses capitalization correctly?

A) There are many Oceans on our planet; the Pacific and the Atlantic are the two largest.

B) There are many oceans on our Planet; the pacific and the Atlantic are the two largest.

C) There are many oceans on our planet; the Pacific and the Atlantic are the two largest.

D) There are many Oceans on our Planet; the Pacific and the Atlantic are the two Largest.

18. Select the best word for the blank in the following sentence.

If you will _____ me that book, I will show you which stories are the best ones.

A) bring

B) take

C) brink

D) tuck

19. Which of the following sentences contains a verb in the past-perfect tense?

A) We always give each other gifts on our shared birthday.

B) I gave Paria a scarf, and she gave me a coin purse.

C) We had already exchanged gifts by the time you arrived.

D) Your birthday is in August, isn't it?

20. Which punctuation mark is used incorrectly in the following sentence?

"That is a good plan;" Addie replied.

A) " (opening quotation mark)

B) " (closing quotation mark)

C) ; (semicolon)

D) . (period)

21. Which of the following sentences uses punctuation correctly?

A) When one of the cats approached her food bowl; Hollie showed her teeth and said "grrrr."

B) When one of the cats' approached her food bowl, Hollie showed her teeth and said "grrrr."

C) When one of the cats, approached her food bowl, Hollie showed her teeth and said "grrrr."

D) When one of the cats approached her food bowl, Hollie showed her teeth and said "grrrr."

22. Select the best word for the blank in the following sentence.

I'm so sorry, but I can't _____ your kind invitation—I'll be out of town on Friday night.

A) expect

B) accept

C) except

D) accede

23. Which word is used incorrectly in the following sentence?

Dr. Boynton has so many patience today that she will have no time for lunch.

A) Dr.

B) many

C) patience

D) lunch

24. Select the best word for the blank in the following sentence.

Wearing proper life jackets helps to _____ that sailors will not drown if their boat capsizes.

A) impure

B) enter

C) ensure

D) insure

25. Which of the following sentences is grammatically correct?

A) While I was baking cookies, I eat too much of the dough.

B) While I was baking cookies, I might eat too much of the dough.

C) While I was baking cookies, I ate too much of the dough.

D) While I was baking cookies, I will eat too much of the dough.

26. Which word is used incorrectly in the following sentence?

Are you going to die your hair green or purple?

A) Are

B) going

C) die

D) purple

27. Select the best words for the blank in the following sentence.

When I was in second grade, my _____ moved away to New Mexico.

A) best friend Jill

B) Best Friend Jill

C) best Friend Jill

D) best friend jill

28. Which word or phrase is used incorrectly in the following sentence?

Of my two sisters, Julie is the most responsible.

A) my two

B) two sisters

C) the most

D) responsible

29. Select the best word for the blank in the following sentence.

I sliced some _____ of bread for toast.

A) peas

B) peace

C) pieces

D) appeases

30. Which of the choices is a homophone for a word in the sentence below?

Priests perform religious rites such as christenings, weddings, and funerals.

A) princes

B) reform

C) rights

D) end

31. Which word is incorrectly capitalized or lowercased in the following sentence?

On Saturday, June 16th, we're traveling from Seattle to Victoria via Ferryboat.

A) Saturday

B) June

C) Victoria

D) Ferryboat

32. Which of the following sentences contains an interjection?

A) The dog has gray fur on its face, and it walks very slowly and stiffly.

B) Wow, how old is that dog, do you think?

C) I knew a German shepherd that lived to the age of fifteen.

D) If they are healthy, small dogs usually live longer than big ones.

33. Which of the following sentences is grammatically correct?

A) The clothes that I left at the drycleaner's shop was beautifully clean when I picked them up.

B) The clothes that I left at the drycleaner's shop were beautifully clean when I picked it up.

C) The clothes that I left at the drycleaner's shop were beautifully clean when I picked them up.

D) The coat that I left at the drycleaner's shop were beautifully clean when I picked them up.

34. Select the best word for the blank in the following sentence.

Dad thought it was important to _____ our home in case of a fire.

A) ensure
B) insure
C) assure
D) assay

35. Which two words are used incorrectly in the following sentences?

Do you know Janet and Brian Carter? There standing right over they're with their older sister.

A) Do, know
B) Janet, Brian
C) There, they're
D) their, sister

36. Which of the following sentences is grammatically correct?

A) You and Ana shouldn't take things that aren't yours.

B) You shouldn't take things that aren't theirs.

C) We shouldn't take things that aren't hers.

D) My sister and I shouldn't take things that aren't yours.

37. Select the best word for the blank in the following sentence.

At Andre's new job, he can only take _____ breaks during the workday.

A) to
B) too
C) two
D) tow

38. Which word is used incorrectly in the following sentence?

We always go to an evening picnic on Independence Day, but on Christmas Night we eat at home.

A) Independence
B) but
C) Christmas
D) Night

39. Which of the following sentences is grammatically correct?

A) Jenny enjoys swimming in pools but she hates swimming in lakes.

B) Jenny enjoys swimming in pools; but she hates swimming in lakes.

C) Jenny enjoys swimming in pools, but she hates swimming in lakes.

D) Jenny enjoys swimming in pools, but, she hates swimming in lakes.

40. Which of the following is a complex sentence?

A) Ferryboats provide a quick and easy way to cross San Francisco Bay.

B) You just jump on a boat in Oakland, and presto, you're in San Francisco within minutes.

C) Because San Francisco is so close to Oakland, the ferry ride is very short.

D) If you have heavy items, you can take the Bay Bridge, and the carpool lane can shorten the trip.

41. Which word or phrase from the following sentence is a continuous past-tense verb?

When Dad was going to college, he was in his early twenties.

A) Dad

B) was going

C) was

D) his early twenties

42. Select the best word for the blank in the following sentence.

Last night, after dropping easy flyballs all evening, left-fielder Danny Pine finally _____ one in the last play of the game.

A) catched

B) caught

C) catches

D) catch

43. Which of the following sentences is grammatically correct?

A) Let's take a coffee break in about fifteen minutes.

B) Let's take a coffee brake in about fifteen minutes.

C) Let's take a coffee bray in about fifteen minutes.

D) Let's take a coffee braid in about fifteen minutes.

44. Which of the following sentences contains a first-person plural verb?

A) My sister and I love shopping together.

B) You and your sister love shopping together, too.

C) Mom shops when she must, but she doesn't always love it.

D) She loves shopping only at hardware stores and antique shops.

45. Select the best words for the blank in the following sentence.

By the time Taylor arrived at the meeting, I was ready to leave. I _____ for her all evening.

A) had waited

B) have waited

C) had been waited

D) will wait

46. Which word is used incorrectly in the following sentence?

Use the rains to guide your horse, but don't yank on them so hard—that can hurt your horse's mouth.

A) Use

B) rains

C) yank

D) horse's

47. Select the best word for the blank in the following sentence.

By the time it began to _____, we were safely indoors.

A) rein

B) reign

C) rend

D) rain

48. Which of the following sentences is correctly punctuated?

A) Mom is afraid of flying; so she listens to a relaxation CD before she flies.

B) Mom is afraid of flying, so she listens to a relaxation CD before she flies.

C) Mom is afraid of flying: so she listens to a relaxation CD before she flies.

D) Mom is afraid of flying, so she listens to a relaxation CD before she flies?

49. Which of the following sentences uses capitalization correctly?

A) We celebrate Valentine's day in February, and we celebrate Independence Day in summer.

B) We celebrate Valentine's Day in February, and we celebrate Independence Day in summer.

C) We celebrate Valentine's day in February, and we celebrate Independence Day in Summer.

D) We celebrate valentine's day in February, and we celebrate Independence Day in Summer.

50. Which word is used incorrectly in the following sentence?

I need to do some errands: I need to shop for food, because I need to pick up my dry cleaning.

A) errands

B) food

C) because

D) cleaning

51. Which of the following sentences contains a semicolon?

A) Have you ever read anything by Edith Wharton?

B) She wrote the following novels: *The Age of Innocence, The House of Mirth, Ethan Frome,* and many more.

C) Wharton wrote mainly about wealthy people living in New York and Europe in the late 1800s; she also wrote about much humbler country folks, such as poor Ethan Frome and his family.

D) Many of Wharton's works have been adapted to create modern-day movies and television shows—my favorites are *The Age of Innocence* and *The Buccaneers.*

52. Which of the following sentences uses punctuation correctly?

A) I never eat cantaloupe; because I dislike the way it tastes.

B) I never eat cantaloupe: because I dislike the way it tastes.

C) I never eat cantaloupe because I dislike the way it tastes.

D) I never eat cantaloupe—because I dislike the way it tastes.

53. Which of the following sentences is grammatically correct?

A) On a mourning many months after my cat died, I awoke and realized I was still in deep morning.

B) On a mooring many months after my cat died, I awoke and realized I was still in deep morning.

C) On a morning many months after my cat died, I awoke and realized I was still in deep mourning.

D) On a marring many months after my cat died, I awoke and realized I was still in deep morning.

54. Which word is used incorrectly in the following sentence?

We invited everyone to our wedding accept people whom neither of us knew very well.

A) invited

B) everyone

C) accept

D) neither

55. Which of the following sentences contains a prepositional phrase?

A) My new coat is in the closet.

B) Where is my new coat?

C) Get your coat, and let's go.

D) I love my new coat!

Biology

Read the question carefully, and then choose the most correct answer.

1. What type of bond is formed between water molecules?

    A) covalent

    B) ionic

    C) hydrogen

    D) metallic

2. Which of the following is a polysaccharide?

    A) NADH

    B) cellulose

    C) cytosine

    D) histones

3. Seeds store proteins for use by the young growing plant. Which organelle would you expect to store these proteins?

    A) rough endoplasmic reticulum

    B) Golgi apparatus

    C) vacuole

    D) chloroplast

4. Which ATP-producing pathway occurs in the cytoplasm?

    A) Krebs cycle

    B) glycolysis

    D) photosynthesis

    C) Calvin cycle

5. A mouse that is heterozygous for the dominant trait of smooth fur is crossed with a mouse that is homozygous recessive for curly fur. What percentage of the F1 generation will have curly fur?

    A) 0 percent

    B) 25 percent

    C) 50 percent

    D) 100 percent

6. Why do telomeres get shorter each time a cell replicates?

    A) DNA polymerase does not read to the end of a DNA strand.

    B) Helicase cannot unwind the ends of chromosomes.

    C) DNA ligase cannot recover the Okazaki fragments from the end of a chromosome.

    D) Chromosome inversions occur as the cell ages.

7. In which phase of mitosis do homologous chromosomes separate?

    A) interphase

    B) prophase

    C) anaphase

    D) metaphase

8. Which of the following is necessary to initiate the transcription of a gene?

    A) DNA polymerase

    B) promoter

    C) centromere

    D) tRNA

9. Which of the following is a silent mutation?

    A) A mutation that does not change the DNA sequence.

    B) A mutation that occurs in the telomere of a chromosome.

    C) A mutation that causes a deletion of a single nucleotide, causing codons further down the strand to be read incorrectly.

    D) A mutation that changes the DNA code from GAA to GAG, both of which are codons for the amino acid glutamic acid.

10. Why does it take a large amount of energy to boil water?

   A) Water contains covalent bonds.

   B) Water repels energy.

   C) Water molecules remove energy.

   D) Water has a high specific heat.

11. Why do phospholipids form a bilayer when placed in water?

   A) They contain large macromolecules.

   B) They have a polar head and a nonpolar tail.

   C) They are lighter than water.

   D) They interact with proteins.

12. After proteins are synthesized, they are packaged for transport at:

   A) vacuoles.

   B) the Golgi apparatus.

   C) mitochondria.

   D) the cell membrane.

13. How many molecules of ATP are produced during the Krebs cycle?

   A) 0

   B) 8

   C) 16

   D) 32

14. Genes controlled by the lac operon are only expressed when lactose is attached to the operon. The lac operon uses:

   A) negative regulation.

   B) positive regulation.

   C) chromatin modification.

   D) promoter binding.

15. Where does transcription occur?

   A) nucleus

   B) cytoplasm

   C) ribosomes

   D) plasma membrane

16. During meiosis, crossing over occurs when:

   A) homologous chromosomes exchange genetic information.

   B) chromosomes are randomly sorted.

   C) a fragment of a chromosome is inverted.

   D) homologous chromosomes fail to separate.

17. The height of a certain plant is determined by a gene with two alleles—tall and short. Tallness is a recessive trait. If a homozygous tall plant is crossed with a homozygous short plant, what percentage of the F2 generation will be tall?

   A) 0 percent

   B) 25 percent

   C) 50 percent

   D) 100 percent

18. The head of a lipid is composed of which molecule?

   A) glycerol

   B) glucose

   C) phospholipid

   D) cellulose

19. Cell membranes are composed primarily of:

   A) nucleic acids.

   B) phospholipids.

   C) proteins.

   D) carbohydrates.

20. Which ATP-producing pathway occurs on membranes in mitochondria?

A) glycolysis

B) fermentation

C) electron transport chain

D) Krebs cycle

21. What is the mRNA sequence that would be transcribed from a strand of DNA with the nucleotide sequence TACAGCCC?

A) TACAGCCC

B) ATGTCGGG

C) UACAGCCC

D) AUGUCGGG

22. Mitosis produces:

A) two haploid cells.

B) two diploid cells.

C) four haploid cells.

D) four diploid cells.

23. Which of the following contains all the information necessary to produce a protein?

A) DNA

B) tRNA

C) a promoter

D) a codon

24. A woman who is homozygous for the dominant trait of curly hair has a child with a man who is homozygous for straight hair. All of their children have wavy hair. Curly hair is:

A) dominant over straight hair.

B) codominant with straight hair.

C) incomplete dominant with straight hair.

D) recessive to straight hair.

25. When a molecule is transported across a membrane by a protein that does not use energy, it is called:

A) osmosis.

B) active transport.

C) facilitated diffusion.

D) diffusion.

26. Which biochemical pathway releases $6CO_2$ and $6H_2O$?

A) photosynthesis

B) cellular respiration

C) Krebs cycle

D) electron transport chain

27. Which of the following is the enzyme that joins strands of DNA?

A) DNA polymerase

B) DNA telomerase

C) DNA ligase

D) DNA helicase

28. Which process produces four haploid daughter cells?

A) mitosis

B) meiosis I

C) meiosis II

D) interphase

29. A scientist who studies fruit flies notices that red-eyed flies have short antennae 95 percent of the time. Which of the following best explains why this happens?

A) Red-eyed flies only mate with other red-eyed flies.

B) Eye color and antenna length are linked genes.

C) Red eyes and short antennae are dominant traits.

D) Short antennae are a sex-linked trait.

30. Chromosomal inversions occur when:

A) a chromosome is flipped so the gene sequences are reversed.

B) a piece of one chromosome is flipped and reattached to another chromosome.

C) a chromosome is replicated, inverted, and then ligated together.

D) a fragment of DNA breaks from a single chromosome, flips, and is reattached.

Chemistry

Read the question carefully, and then choose the most correct answer.

1. An atom's chemical reactivity is determined by:

    A) the ratio of protons to neutrons.

    B) the number of full electron shells.

    C) the number of electrons in its valence shell.

    D) the atom's radius.

2. Which of the following groups of elements has the same number of valence electrons? Refer to the periodic table.

    A) F, C, Br

    B) Si, Al, S

    C) Al, Ga, B

    D) N, C, B

3. What type of bond can form single, double, or triple bonds?

    A) ionic

    B) covalent

    C) metallic

    D) hydrogen

4. Which of the following is a physical property?

    A) toxicity

    B) flammability

    C) heat of combustion

    D) density

5. Solutions that taste bitter and have a slippery texture are:

    A) acidic.

    B) basic.

    C) neutral.

    D) salts.

6. Which of the following mixtures is heterogeneous?

    A) coffee with sugar

    B) orange juice with pulp

    C) hot tea

    D) purified water

7. What type of reaction is shown below?
   $HCl + NaOH \rightarrow H_2O + NaCl$

    A) synthesis reaction

    B) decomposition reaction

    C) single displacement reaction

    D) double displacement reaction

8. Arrange the following elements in order of decreasing atomic radius: argon (Ar), antimony (Sb), bromine (Br), lead (Pb).

    A) Ar > Br > Sb > Pb

    B) Sb > Pb > Br > Ar

    C) Pb > Sb > Br > Ar

    D) Ar > Pb > Sb > Br

9. How many moles of $KClO_3$ are produced when 2 moles of KCl react with oxygen (O)?
   $2KCl + 3O_2 \rightarrow 2KClO_3$

    A) 0 moles of $KClO_3$

    B) 1 mole of $KClO_3$

    C) 2 moles of $KClO_3$

    D) 3 moles of $KClO_3$

10. Which element has the greatest number of protons? Refer to the periodic table.

    A) sulfur (S)

    B) oxygen (O)

    C) nitrogen (N)

    D) neon (Ne)

11. Which of the following elements are found in the same period on the periodic table?

   A) K, Br, Pt
   B) Na, Al, P
   C) C, N, Br
   D) Rb, Ga, Ge

12. What type of bond is formed when sodium (Na) bonds with chlorine (Cl) to form table salt?

   A) ionic
   B) covalent
   C) metallic
   D) hydrogen

13. The molecular weight of a substance is found by adding the atomic mass of each atom in the molecule. What is the molecular weight of methane (CH_4) in atomic mass units?

   A) 7
   B) 10
   C) 13
   D) 16

14. Orange juice is primarily composed of citric acid and malic acid. It likely has a pH of:

   A) 4.
   B) 7.
   C) 9.
   D) 13.

15. What are the coefficients needed to balance the equation below?

   $$\_CaCl_2 + \_Na_3PO_4 \rightarrow \_Ca_3(PO_4)_2 + \_NaCl$$

   A) 1, 1, 2, 2
   B) 2, 3, 2, 2
   C) 3, 2, 1, 6
   D) 1, 2, 3, 4

16. Which of the following elements has the largest atomic radius?

   A) barium (Ba)
   B) calcium (Ca)
   C) magnesium (Mg)
   D) strontium (Sr)

17. How many moles of water (H_2O) are produced when 2 moles of H_2 react with 1 mole of O_2?

   $$2H_2 + O_2 \rightarrow 2H_2O$$

   A) 0 moles of H_2O
   B) 1 mole of H_2O
   C) 2 moles of H_2O
   D) 4 moles of H_2O

18. What determines an atom's charge?

   A) the number of protons
   B) the number of electrons and protons
   C) the number of protons and neutrons
   D) the number of neutrons and electrons

19. List the elements arsenic (As), oxygen (O), phosphorus (P), and sulfur (S) in order of decreasing electronegativity.

   A) O > P > S > As
   B) O > S > P > As
   C) As > P > S > O
   D) As > S > P > O

20. What type of bond is formed when carbon (C) bonds with oxygen (O) to form carbon dioxide (CO_2)?

   A) ionic
   B) covalent
   C) metallic
   D) hydrogen

21. The molecular weight of a substance is found by adding the atomic mass of each atom in the molecule. What is the molecular weight of water (H_2O) in atomic mass units?

A) 8

B) 16

C) 18

D) 33

22. Which of the following mixtures is homogeneous?

A) salt water

B) vegetable soup

C) buttermilk

D) tomato juice

23. What are the coefficients needed to balance the equation below?

_AgI + _Na_2S → _Ag_2S + _NaI

A) 1, 1, 1, 2

B) 1, 2, 1, 2

C) 2, 1, 2, 1

D) 2, 1, 1, 2

24. What is the half-life of element Z if it takes 12 days to decay from 20 g to 5 g?

A) 6 days

B) 4 days

C) 3 days

D) 2 days

25. Which of the following elements has the smallest atomic radius?

A) oxygen (O)

B) boron (B)

C) nitrogen (N)

D) carbon (C)

26. The reaction shown below is endothermic.
$2NH_3(g) → 3H_2(g) + N_2(g)$
Heat should be added to:

A) the reactant side.

B) the product side.

C) both the reactant and the product side.

D) neither the product nor the reactant side.

27. List the elements barium (Ba), calcium (Ca), germanium (Ge), and nitrogen (N) in order of increasing electronegativity.

A) N < Ca < Ge < Ba

B) N < Ge < Ca < Ba

C) Ba < Ca < Ge < N

D) Ba < Ge <Ca < N

28. Which of the following phase changes releases energy?

A) condensation

B) melting

C) sublimation

D) evaporation

29. What is the oxidation state of the chlorine atom in HCl?

A) −1

B) 0

C) +1

D) +2

30. Technetium-99 exists in an excited state but decays to a lower energy state. During this process it releases high energy electromagnetic radiation. What type of radioactive decay does technetium-99 undergo?

A) alpha decay

B) beta decay

C) gamma decay

D) positron emission

Anatomy and Physiology

Read the question carefully, and then choose the most correct answer.

1. Which of the following organs is held and protected by the meninges?

    A) brain
    B) heart
    C) stomach
    D) uterus

2. Which of the following describes the function of osteoclasts?

    A) They transmit signals.
    B) They break down bone tissue.
    C) They repair bone fractures.
    D) They secrete collagen.

3. Which of the following valves prevents blood from going back to the left atrium?

    A) aortic
    B) mitral
    C) pulmonary
    D) tricuspid

4. Which type of muscle can be voluntarily relaxed and contracted?

    A) visceral
    B) smooth
    C) cardiac
    D) skeletal

5. How many bones comprise the thoracic vertebrae?

    A) 5
    B) 7
    C) 12
    D) 33

6. Which of the following surrounds neurons and provides protection?

    A) dendrite
    B) axon
    C) neuron
    D) neuroglia

7. Which of the following types of muscle is used for posture and stamina?

    A) type I
    B) type IIa
    C) type IIb
    D) visceral

8. Which of the following hormones is released by the kidneys and helps regulate blood pressure?

    A) renin
    B) calcitrol
    C) cortisol
    D) oxytocin

9. Which of the following is regulated by the parathyroid gland?

    A) phosphate level
    B) blood sugar level
    C) creatinine level
    D) sodium level

10. Which of the following kills pathogens in the body by disrupting the functioning of their DNA or membranes?

    A) antimicrobial peptides
    B) interferon
    C) histamines
    D) antigens

11. Which of the following describes the path followed by sperm as it exits the body?

A) vas deferens → epididymis → ejaculatory duct

B) epididymis → seminiferous tubes → urethra

C) seminiferous tubes → vas deferens → ejaculatory duct

D) ejaculatory duct → vas deferens → penis

12. Which type of neuron controls the movement of voluntary muscles?

A) sensory neurons

B) visceral afferent neurons

C) interneurons

D) efferent neurons

13. What carries oxygenated blood to the heart?

A) superior vena cava

B) inferior vena cava

C) pulmonary artery

D) pulmonary veins

14. Which of the following correctly describes the development of the blastocyst in humans?

A) The blastocyst is shed along with the uterine lining during menstruation.

B) Genetic material from only one parent is found in the blastocyst.

C) The placenta forms from the outer layer of the blastocyst.

D) The blastocyst contains only two cells.

15. Which of the following actions is controlled by the medulla oblongata?

A) sneezing

B) balancing

C) sleeping

D) smelling

16. Which of the following structures ensures that air enters the trachea and food enters the esophagus?

A) Eustachian tube

B) nasopharynx

C) epiglottis

D) voice box

17. Which of the following occurs when blood vessels close to the skin surface dilate?

A) Blood flow is reduced.

B) The blood absorbs more water.

C) The skin becomes cool.

D) Nerve cells in the skin become less responsive.

18. The digestive enzymes produced by the pancreas pass into which organ?

A) stomach

B) gall bladder

C) large intestine

D) small intestine

19. Which of the following is an important function of the pleural cavity?

A) It allows the lungs to expand.

B) It protects the lungs from the ribcage.

C) It produces fluid to protect the lungs.

D) It supports the diaphragm.

20. Which of the following is the network of capillaries in the kidneys where filtration begins?

A) renal pelvis

B) collecting ducts

C) ureters

D) glomerulus

21. Which of the following is a function of cerebrospinal fluid?

A) It prevents the layers of the meninges from sticking together.

B) It mixes with blood to nourish the brain.

C) It removes waste products from the brain.

D) It transmits signals to and from the brain.

22. Which of the following is the production of red and white blood cells from the stem cells of the red bone marrow?

A) ossification

B) hematopoiesis

C) osteosis

D) hemapheresis

23. In which part of the brain is language processed?

A) medulla oblongata

B) cerebral cortex

C) occipital lobe

D) temporal lobe

24. Sphincters close and open to prevent entry or escape of a substance. Which of the following does not have a sphincter?

A) bladder

B) esophagus

C) nares

D) capillaries

25. Which of the following bones is part of the vertebral column?

A) coccyx

B) hyoid

C) sternum

D) clavicle

26. Which of the following correctly describes true ribs?

A) They are the first four ribs.

B) They are attached directly to the sternum.

C) They are the eighth and ninth pairs of ribs.

D) Their main function is to protect the kidneys.

27. The coccygeal nerves belong to which group of peripheral nerves?

A) spinal nerves

B) cranial nerves

C) motor neurons

D) sensory neurons

28. Which of the following is the area of the small intestine where nutrients are absorbed?

A) duodenum

B) jejunum

C) rectum

D) cecum

29. What is the role of monocytes in wounds?

A) They increase blood clotting.

B) They release histamines.

C) They digest pathogens.

D) They prevent inflammation.

30. Which of the following is NOT a function of the placenta?

A) production of hormones

B) nourishment of the fetus

C) waste removal

D) production of red blood cells

Physics

Read the question carefully, and then choose the most correct answer.

1. A ball is thrown straight down off the top of a tall building with an initial speed of 5 meters per second. What is the speed of the ball when it has fallen 10 meters?

   A) 9.8 m/s
   B) 10.0 m/s
   C) 14.9 m/s
   D) 221.0 m/s

2. A quarterback throws a football at 18 meters per second at an angle of 45 degrees above the horizontal direction. What is the football's horizontal position after 4 seconds?

   A) 4.5 m
   B) 18 m
   C) 50.9 m
   D) 101.8 m

3. A fire station 800 meters away from a house sounds its alarm. If the speed of sound in air is 340 meters per second, how long does it take for the sound of the alarm to reach the house?

   A) 0.425 s
   B) 2.35 s
   C) 2.72 s
   D) 4.25 s

4. A 50 kilogram child jumps to the ground off a 2 meter wall. How much work does gravity do on the child?

   A) 98 J
   B) 100 J
   C) 490 J
   D) 980 J

5. Which of the following is NOT a scalar?

   A) The distance to the moon
   B) A person's height
   C) The number of degrees in a circle
   D) The acceleration due to gravity on the surface of the earth

6. A 40 kilogram object is pulled along a horizontal frictionless surface and accelerates at 2 meters per second squared. What is the magnitude and direction of the normal force on this object?

   A) 80 N vertically up
   B) 80 N vertically down
   C) 392 N vertically up
   D) 392 N vertically down

7. A billiard cue ball with a speed of 1.5 meters per second hits another at rest. If the cue ball moves directly backward at 0.5 meters per second after the collision, how fast is the one originally at rest now moving? Both billiard balls have a mass of 0.20 kilograms.

   A) 0 m/s
   B) 0.5 m/s
   C) 1.5 m/s
   D) 2 m/s

8. A small tabletop centrifuge with a radius of 18 centimeters applies a constant 18 meters per second squared of centripetal acceleration to its contents. What is the tangential velocity of its contents as the centrifuge spins?

   A) 0.18 m/s
   B) 1.8 m/s
   C) 3.24 m/s
   D) 18 m/s

9. Letting go of a compressed spring transmits what type of visual wave?

A) mechanical

B) electromagnetic

C) longitudinal

D) transverse

10. An ammeter reads a 0.5 ampere current through a series circuit with a total resistance of 60 ohms. What voltage is supplied by the battery?

A) 30 V

B) 60 V

C) 90 V

D) 120 V

11. A voltage across a plasma accelerates electrons from rest to 1000 kilometers per second in 1 microsecond. What is the acceleration of the electrons?

A) 1×10^{-12} m/s^2

B) 1×10^{-6} m/s^2

C) 1×10^{6} m/s^2

D) 1×10^{12} m/s^2

12. A pickup truck applies a constant 500 newton meters of torque to an axle with a radius of 10 centimeters. What perpendicular force acts on the axle?

A) 50 N

B) 500 N

C) 5000 N

D) 50,000 N

13. A 1 kilogram object is at rest on the surface of the earth. How hard does Earth push back on the object?

A) 0 N

B) 0.98 N

C) 4.9 N

D) 9.8 N

14. When dry, the human body has a resistance of about 100 kiloohms. If a person touches the leads of a car battery at 12 volts, how much current flows through the person?

A) 0.12 mA

B) 1.2 mA

C) 1,200 mA

D) 12,000 mA

15. A 2.5 gram penny is dropped from rest from the top of a building that is 400 meters tall. With what speed does it hit the ground?

A) 4.4 m/s

B) 88.5 m/s

C) 177.1 m/s

D) 1770.8 m/s

16. What is the total resistance of a 2 ohm, 5 ohm, and 10 ohm parallel combination of resistors?

A) 0.4 Ω

B) 0.5 Ω

C) 1.25 Ω

D) 17 Ω

17. A material has an index of refraction of 1.33. What is the speed of light in this material?

A) 2.26×10^{8} m/s

B) 2.86×10^{8} m/s

C) 2.99×10^{8} m/s

D) 3.99×10^{8} m/s

18. A 7 nanocoulomb charge is placed 8 centimeters from a 15 nanocoulomb charge. In what direction will the charges move?

A) They will move together.

B) They will move farther apart.

C) They will not move.

D) They will move together in the same direction.

19. The distance between a satellite and the center of a planet is increased by a factor of three. By what factor is the force due to gravity changed?

A) $\frac{1}{9}$

B) $\frac{1}{3}$

C) 3

D) 9

20. For a radio wave with a wavelength of 10 meters moving at the speed of light (c = 3 × 10⁸ meters per second), what is the time period of a single oscillation?

A) 3.33×10^{-8} s

B) 3.33×10^{-7} s

C) 3.33×10^{-6} s

D) 3.33×10^{-5} s

21. How much work is done by a 500 watt engine over 30 minutes?

A) 1.5×10^{4} J

B) 9×10^{4} J

C) 1.5×10^{5} J

D) 9×10^{5} J

22. What is the speed of light in a diamond with an index of refraction of 2.4?

A) 1.25×10^{8} m/s

B) 2.25×10^{8} m/s

C) 1.25×10^{12} m/s

D) 2.25×10^{12} m/s

23. A 6 kilogram plant hangs from a massless string on a porch. What is the magnitude of the tension in the string?

A) 0 N

B) 6 N

C) 9.8 N

D) 58.8 N

24. Two waves destructively interfere to produce a wave with a wavelength of 7×10^{-3} meters and a period of oscillation of 5 microseconds. What is the velocity of this resulting wave?

A) 3.5×10^{-8} m/s

B) 7.1×10^{-4} m/s

C) 350 m/s

D) 1400 m/s

25. A person weighing 70 kilograms is driving a car. With what speed must they take a 10 meter-radius turn so that the centripetal acceleration is equal to their weight?

A) 4.8 m/s

B) 4.9 m/s

C) 9.8 m/s

D) 9.9 m/s

26. On a certain planet, a mass dropped from an 8 meter height hits the ground with a speed of 15 meters per second. What is the acceleration due to gravity on this planet?

A) 0.9 m/s²

B) 8.0 m/s²

C) 14.1 m/s²

D) 15.0 m/s²

27. What is the speed of light in glass with an index of refraction 1.50?

A) 2×10^{8} m/s

B) 2.33×10^{8} m/s

C) 2.66×10^{8} m/s

D) 3×10^{8} m/s

28. A compass points toward its north direction. Which of Earth's magnetic poles is this?

A) north

B) south

C) west

D) none (Magnetic field is a scalar.)

29. A company is designing a parallel plate capacitor. How far apart must the plates be to generate an electric field of 100 volts per meter with 5 volts of potential difference?

A) 0.05 cm

B) 0.5 cm

C) 5 cm

D) 500 cm

30. Seventeen 12 ohm resistors are connected in parallel. What is the total resistance of this circuit?

A) 0.71 Ω

B) 1.42 Ω

C) 194 Ω

D) 204 Ω

ANSWER KEY

MATHEMATICS

1. **D)**

$$\frac{15\text{ ft}}{\text{sec}} \times \frac{3600\text{ sec}}{1\text{ hr}} \times \frac{1\text{ mi}}{5280\text{ ft}} \approx \textbf{10.2 mph}$$

2. **A)**

$2(-1)(5) - (-1 + 5)^2$

$-10 - 4^2$

$-10 - 16 = \textbf{--26}$

3. **D)**

$\frac{4}{5} - \frac{1}{3} = \frac{12}{15} - \frac{5}{15} = \mathbf{\frac{7}{15}}$

4. **A)**

$66{,}653.2 - 66{,}284.8 = \textbf{368.4}$

5. **C)**

$9^2 + 2(7^2 - 1)$

$= 81 + 2(49 - 1)$

$= 81 + 2(48)$

$= 81 + 96$

$= \textbf{177}$

6. **C)**

Times greater than 1200 are p.m. on the 12-hour clock. $1315 - 1200 = 115$, which means it is **1:15 p.m.**

7. **B)**

$(5 + 1)^2 \div 4 + 1$

$= 6^2 \div 4 + 1$

$= 36 \div 4 + 1$

$= 9 + 1 = \textbf{10}$

8. **B)**

$8.7 - 4.243 = \textbf{4.457}$

9. **A)**

$8\frac{1}{4} - 5\frac{4}{5} = \frac{33}{4} - \frac{29}{5} = \frac{165}{20} - \frac{116}{20}$

$= \frac{49}{20} = \mathbf{2\frac{9}{20}}$

10. **D)**

$6.25(25{,}000) - 19{,}000 = 156{,}250 - 19{,}000$

$= \textbf{137,250}$

11. **C)**

$\frac{4}{50} = \frac{x}{175}$

$50x = 700$

$\textbf{x = 14}$

12. **C)**

part = whole × percent

$124 \times 0.40 = \textbf{49.6}$

13. **B)**

$\frac{2}{5} = 0.4$

$\frac{1}{3} = 0.\overline{3}$

$0.45 > 0.4 > 0.\overline{3}$

Zack has the most walnuts.

14. **A)**

$4.368 \div 2.8 = \textbf{1.56}$

15. **A)**

$10 + 5 = 15$ units per day

$15 \times 30 = \textbf{450}$

16. **C)**

$1250 + 675 = \textbf{1925}$

17. **D)**

$2.7 \times 9.6 = \textbf{25.92}$

18. **B)**

$\frac{375 \div 125}{1000 \div 125} = \mathbf{\frac{3}{8}}$

19. **B)**

$\frac{7}{10} = 0.7$

$\frac{3}{5} = 0.6$

0.6 < 0.613 < 0.65 < 0.7

20. D)

Military time is given in four digits; a.m. times do not add 1200.

6 a.m. = **0600**

21. B)

$\frac{0.5}{18} = \frac{2}{x}$

$0.5x = 36$

$x = 72$

22. C)

whole = $\frac{part}{percent}$

$\frac{33}{0.15} = 220$

23. A)

$C = \frac{5}{9}(F - 32)$

$C = \frac{5}{9}(98.6 - 32)$

$C = \frac{5}{9}(66.6) = 37°$

24. A)

$2(3x + 1) - 3 = 4x + 3$

$6x + 2 - 3 = 4x + 3$

$6x - 1 = 4x + 3$

$6x = 4x + 4$

$2x = 4$

$x = 2$

25. D)

$5\frac{2}{3} \times 2\frac{8}{17} = \frac{17}{3} \times \frac{42}{17} = \frac{42}{3} = 14$

26. A)

$5\frac{2}{3} \div 1\frac{1}{2} = \frac{17}{3} \div \frac{3}{2} = \frac{17}{3} \times \frac{2}{3} = \frac{34}{9} = 3\frac{7}{9}$

27. D)

$10 \text{ km} \times \frac{1 \text{ mi}}{1.61 \text{ km}} \approx 6.2 \text{ mi}$

28. C)

$7x - 2(3x + 7) = 2x + 1$

$7x - 6x - 14 = 2x + 1$

$x - 14 = 2x + 1$

$-x - 14 = 1$

$-x = 15$

$x = -15$

29. C)

whole = $\frac{part}{percent}$

$\frac{85}{0.17} = 500$

30. A)

$4 \div 5 = 0.8$

31. D)

whole = $\frac{part}{percent}$

$\frac{550}{0.25} = 2200$

32. B)

Multiply by the least common denominator to clear the fractions.

$(12)\frac{x}{4} - (12)\frac{1}{3} = (12)\frac{7x}{12} + (12)\frac{5}{6}$

$3x - 4 = 7x + 10$

$-4x - 4 = 10$

$-4x = 14$

$x = -\frac{7}{2}$

33. D)

$712 \text{ ml} \times \frac{1 \text{ L}}{1000 \text{ ml}} = 0.712 \text{ L}$

34. B)

$4x - 3y + 12z + 2x - 7y - 10z$

$= 4x + 2x - 3y - 7y + 12z - 10z$

$= 6x - 10y + 2z$

35. A)

$2\frac{1}{2} \times \frac{2}{5} = \frac{5}{2} \times \frac{2}{5} = 1$

36. D)

$3\frac{3}{8} \div 9 = \frac{27}{8} \div \frac{9}{1} = \frac{27}{8} \times \frac{1}{9} = \frac{3}{8}$

37. C)

Distribute by multiplying coefficients and adding exponents.

$2x^2(4x^2 + 2xy - 3y^2)$

$= \mathbf{8x^4 + 4x^3y - 6x^2y^2}$

38. **D)**

$927 \times 0.187 = 173.349 \approx \mathbf{\$173.35}$

39. **C)**

$6.3 \div 18 = \mathbf{0.35}$

40. **A)**

$0.52 \text{ g} \times \dfrac{1000 \text{ mg}}{1 \text{ g}} = \mathbf{520 \text{ mg}}$

41. **D)**

$4x - 3(y - 2x)$

$= 4x - 3y + 6x$

$= 4x + 6x - 3y$

$= \mathbf{10x - 3y}$

42. **C)**

$11.50 - 9.75 = 1.75$

$\text{percent} = \dfrac{\text{part}}{\text{whole}}$

$\dfrac{1.75}{9.75} \approx 0.179 = \mathbf{17.9\%}$

43. **C)**

Reduce coefficients, subtract exponents.

$\dfrac{9a^7b^3}{18a^2b^5} = \mathbf{\dfrac{a^5}{2b^2}}$

44. **B)**

$\dfrac{2}{600} = \dfrac{0.5}{x}$

$2x = 300$

$\mathbf{x = 150}$

45. **A)**

$\text{part} = \text{whole} \times \text{percent}$

$62 \times 0.90 = \mathbf{55.8}$

46. **B)**

$\dfrac{2}{5} - \dfrac{1}{3} = \dfrac{6}{15} - \dfrac{5}{15} = \mathbf{\dfrac{1}{15}}$

47. **C)**

$65 - 14.46 + 5.8 = \mathbf{56.34}$

48. **B)**

negative ÷ negative = positive

$-48 \div (-6) = \mathbf{8}$

49. **A)**

$\$13.50 \times 7.5 = \mathbf{\$101.25}$

50. **D)**

$5 - 3\dfrac{1}{3} = \dfrac{15}{3} - \dfrac{10}{3} = \dfrac{5}{3} = \mathbf{1\dfrac{2}{3}}$

51. **D)**

$\dfrac{1}{22} = \dfrac{4.5}{x}$

$\mathbf{x = 99}$

52. **D)**

Five and a half hours after 1:00 p.m. is 6:30 p.m., which is **1830**.

53. **B)**

$\text{whole} = \dfrac{\text{part}}{\text{percent}}$

$\dfrac{140}{0.35} = \mathbf{400}$

54. **A)**

$-2 - 10 = -2 + (-10) = \mathbf{-12}$

55. **B)**

Multiply by the least common denominator to clear the fractions.

$(4)\dfrac{x}{4} = (4)\dfrac{(x + 2)}{2}$

$x = 2(x + 2)$

$x = 2x + 4$

$-x = 4$

$\mathbf{x = -4}$

1.   B)

In the last sentence, the author states that "good hand-washing hygiene, not cozier sweaters, is our best defense from the common cold." The reader can infer from this information that frequent hand washing gives us a better chance of avoiding a cold; however, this will not absolutely guarantee that we remain cold-free. We might touch an infected person or surface between hand washings, or we might eat food off an infected person's plate.

2.   B)

In the first paragraph, the author states, "There is a cultural myth that pervades discussions surrounding the common cold. According to this myth, exposure to cold temperatures causes people to catch a cold. This, however, is simply not true."

3.   B)

The author writes, "Cases of the cold definitely tend to skyrocket when it is coldest and wettest outside—namely, winter. But the cause is not the snow and ice outside; it's the pathogens and crowded spaces inside." There are no sentences supporting the other claims.

4.   C)

In the last sentence of the first paragraph, the author writes, "The common cold is caused by viruses, not cold weather; low temperatures alone will not leave us sneezing."

5.   C)

In the second paragraph, the author states that "good hand-washing hygiene, not cozier sweaters, is our best defense from the common cold."

6.   B)

In the second paragraph, the author states that "consistently high or low blood pressure can be a sign of illness." The passage deals with the heart and the circulatory system, so readers can infer that "illness" refers to one or both of these. There is no support for any of the other claims.

7.   D)

The primary purpose of the essay is to inform; its general focus is on blood pressure. It is not primarily persuasive or advisory. The author provides details about hypertension, but not about low blood pressure.

8.   A)

As the first sentence indicates, the passage explains what blood pressure is. In the second paragraph the author goes into more detail about hypertension (high blood pressure).

9.   B)

In the last sentence, the author writes, "It is important to visit your doctor regularly to monitor your blood pressure and take steps to keep it under control." Readers can infer from context that the phrase "to monitor your blood pressure" means to regularly check it and make sure it is normal; if it is high or low, a doctor can "take steps" to treat the condition and bring it "under control."

10.   A)

The author writes that low blood pressure can be a sign of illness, but he or she does not explain what causes this condition.

11.   C)

A chronic medical condition persists—it occurs consistently. While *regularly* can be a synonym for *chronically*, the author does not use *regularly* to describe a recurring medical condition.

12.   C)

In the third paragraph, the author writes, "The amount of water an individual needs varies based on such factors as metabolism or diet, but conventional wisdom is that humans should take in anywhere between 2.7 and 3.7 liters of water each day." Readers can infer that by "conventional wisdom," the author means the standard advice that medical professionals give their patients.

13.   A)

In the first paragraph, the author writes, "Dehydration ... can be caused by illness, exercise, heat, stress, or lack of self-care."

14.   B)

In the second paragraph, the author writes, "If you are waiting until you are thirsty to drink something, then you are already dehydrated; our thirst mechanism fails to 'notify' our body of dehydration in time." There is no support for any of the other claims.

15. **C)**

In the first sentence, the author writes, "Water accounts for roughly 60 percent of an adult human's body weight and is essential for most bodily functions." Readers can infer from context that the phrase "essential for most bodily functions" means that without water, the body could not function—so water is crucial for "most bodily functions."

16. **C)**

The primary purpose of the essay is to explain; its general focus is on dehydration. It is not primarily cautionary or advisory. The author does not tell a story about a specific patient.

17. **D)**

The passage defines dehydration and details its causes, possible effects, and prevention. The other sentences give details from the passage.

18. **C)**

In the first paragraph, the author writes, "E-cigarettes ... contain a liquid that is heated to produce an aerosol that is then inhaled. The liquid usually contains nicotine, the primary addictive substance in tobacco." Readers can infer that, since e-cigarettes usually contain an addictive substance (nicotine), they are usually addictive.

19. **C)**

In the first sentence, the author writes, "E-cigarettes have only been around for about fifteen years, but they are a booming business." In the last sentence, the author refers to "the growth of the e-cigarette industry." The context shows that by "booming business" the author means that the e-cigarette business is very successful: many consumers have bought this product.

20. **B)**

In the second paragraph, the author states, "Other medical professionals believe e-cigarettes may, in fact, help [the war on smoking tobacco] by providing smokers with an alternative to smoking tobacco, which, in addition to nicotine, contains many harmful substances and is unequivocally linked with multiple types of cancer." The reader can infer from this information that the author thinks it is good to quit smoking tobacco, since scientists know for sure that tobacco is harmful and causes cancer.

21. **C)**

The passage does not contain this detail. According to the passage, smoking e-cigarettes may cause "popcorn lung," but the author does not identify this disorder as lung cancer.

22. **B)**

The text is informative, not persuasive or reassuring. Probably the author wants readers to be aware that the harmful effects of e-cigarettes are still not clear.

23. **D)**

The passage is mainly about an ongoing debate over the pros and cons of e-cigarettes. The author points out that research has raised more questions rather than provide answers. The other answer choices provide details from the passage.

24. **B)**

The second paragraph ends with this statement: "Larger-scale clinical studies have not provided conclusive evidence for these benefits." By "these benefits," the author means claims that turmeric can heal inflammation. The last paragraph begins with "Regardless of its true health benefits ...." The author goes on to summarize how popular turmeric has become. The reader can infer that the author does not think there is proof for turmeric's effectiveness as an anti-inflammatory health aid.

25. **B)**

In paragraph 1, the author writes, "Once the root is boiled, dried, and ground, it creates a bitter yellow powdered spice that gives Indian curry its distinctive color." The word *distinctive* is related to the words *distinct* and *distinguish*. Indian curry's deep yellow color distinguishes it—sets it apart—from other dishes: this color is one of Indian curry's identifying characteristics.

26. **D)**

The passage is mainly about turmeric's current popularity among people who believe in the spice's health benefits. The other sentences provide details that support the main idea.

27. **C)**

The primary purpose of the essay is to explain; its focus is on the history of turmeric, its uses, and current popularity. The essay is not persuasive or cautionary. The author's tone is mildly critical or ironic, but he or she does not seem worried that consumers will be duped by all the "buzz" about turmeric.

28. A)

In paragraph 1, the author writes, "Turmeric has been used medicinally—as well as in cooking, as a dye, and in religious rituals—in India and Southeast Asia for millennia." A millennium is one hundred years, and the plural *millennia* refers to as least two hundred years.

29. B)

In the second paragraph, the author writes, "Small-scale studies have shown that curcumin, a key compound found in turmeric, can help with both skin inflammation and joint inflammation."

30. B)

The author writes that, due to new studies that show it can take up to six months to fully heal from a concussion, school districts and doctors may now advise that an injured student athlete wait much longer than just two weeks—perhaps a full six months—before returning to play.

31. B)

In the second paragraph, the author writes, "The brain is commonly known for its fragility; ironically, it may be its resiliency that is hiding the long-term effects of concussions. A concussion is a mild traumatic brain injury. The brain is tremendously resilient in how it deals with the damage: it can 'rewire' around the area of trauma and make new neurological connections." The context shows that the author uses the words *resiliency* and *resilient* to refer to the brain's ability to heal itself quickly.

32. B)

The passage does not contain this detail. The passage does not mention school coaches' role in deciding when injured athletes must or should start playing again.

33. B)

The author points out that new studies have shown that, following a concussion, the brain may take up to six months to heal completely. The passage deals primarily with implications for school athletes.

34. A)

In the first paragraph, the author writes, "New studies indicate that the impact of a single concussion, even if it is a person's first, can cause longer-lasting neurological damage than we previously knew—possibly even permanent."

35. C)

In the first sentence, the author writes, "New studies indicate that the impact of a single concussion, even if it is a person's first, can cause longer-lasting neurological damage than we previously knew." In the second paragraph, the author writes, "A concussion is a mild traumatic brain injury." Readers can infer that neurology is the study of the human brain and nervous system.

36. B)

The passage is primarily informative. However, the author uses jokes like the one in the last paragraph to entertain readers.

37. C)

To entertain readers, the author is referring to the following rhyme: "I scream, you scream, we all scream for ice cream."

38. D)

In paragraph 2, the author writes, "When a cold substance ... presses against the roof of your mouth, it causes blood vessels there to begin to constrict." *Constrict* is a synonym for *narrow* or *shrink*.

39. B)

As the first two sentences show, the passage is mainly about the causes of "brain freeze." The other sentences provide details that support the main idea.

40. B)

Readers can infer that when the tongue grows cold due to contact with cold substances such as ice cream, snow cones, or iced drinks, it does not trigger "brain freeze."

41. A)

In the last sentence, the author writes, "The duration of the pain varies from a few seconds up to about a minute." Readers can infer that "duration of the pain" means "how long the pain lasts." An ice cream headache is short, luckily.

42. B)

The passage is mainly about the composition of snake venom. The other sentences give details from the passage.

43. C)

In the last paragraph, the author writes, "Researchers have been studying the chemical compositions of these venoms and have been making strides in using the science behind the toxins to combat major diseases such as cancer, heart disease, and Alzheimer's." Readers can infer that the author is using the phrase "making strides in using the science" to refer to making discoveries that greatly improve medical science's ability to cure diseases.

44. A)

In the first paragraph, the author writes, "The two key ingredients in all snake venoms are enzymes and polypeptides. Some enzymes help the snake disable its prey, and others help the snake digest its prey." Later in the passage the author goes into more detail about these processes.

45. C)

The primary purpose of the essay is to inform; its general focus is on the composition of snake venoms. It is not primarily cautionary or advisory. The author does not tell a story about a specific research scientist.

46. B)

In the first sentence, the author writes, "Many snakes produce a toxic fluid in their salivary glands called venom." Readers can infer from this that some snakes do *not* produce venom. There is no support for any of the other claims.

47. D)

In the last sentence in the second paragraph, the author writes, "Some cytotoxins target specific types of cells—myotoxins affect muscles, cardiotoxins attack the heart, and nephrotoxins damage the kidneys." Readers can infer that *myo* refers to muscles, *cardio* refers to the heart, and *nephro* refers to the kidneys, as in *nephritis* (inflammation of the kidneys).

48. B)

The first paragraph tells how, in 1796, surgeon Edward Jenner invented a precursor to the modern smallpox vaccine.

49. D)

Injecting patients with vaccines (vaccinating them) immunizes them—makes patients immune to—diseases. Here, the nouns *vaccination* and *immunization* are synonyms.

50. B)

In the second paragraph, the author writes, "Vaccines work by stimulating the immune system to produce antibodies against a particular disease .... Your immune system hangs on to the antibodies it creates; if you are exposed to the pathogen in the future, your body is ready to fight it off."

51. D)

In the last sentence, the author writes, "Today, every state requires some immunizations for children entering public schools, though all allow medical exemptions and most allow exemptions on religious or philosophical grounds." There are no sentences supporting the other claims.

52. A)

In the last paragraph, the author writes, "Vaccines ... have helped eradicate or almost eradicate previously widespread diseases such as whooping cough, polio, rubella, tetanus, tuberculosis, smallpox, diphtheria, and measles." Readers can infer from this and from their own experiences that, despite flu shots, many people in the United States still get sick with the flu.

53. D)

The primary purpose of the essay is to inform; its focus is the history of vaccines. It is not persuasive or cautionary, and it does not give advice.

54. D)

The primary purpose of the passage is to inform; its focus is on types and functions of sweat glands. It is not persuasive. It does define the word *sweat*, but it covers more information than a simple definition.

55. C)

In the last paragraph the author writes, "Mammary glands are specialized examples of apocrine glands."

1. **A)**

    Triage is "the act of sorting patients according to the urgency of their needs."

2. **D)**

    Patience should be spelled "patient's."

3. **C)**

    Severe means "to a great degree."

4. **D)**

    Transient means "lasting for only a short period of time."

5. **A)**

    Enteral means "having passed through the intestine."

6. **B)**

    When something *recurs* it "returns" or "appears again." *Recurrence* is the noun form of the verb recur.

7. **C)**

    Neuro comes from the Greek meaning "nerve," and *vascular* comes from the Latin meaning "small vessel." The combination of the two—*neurovascular*—pertains to the nervous system and blood vessels.

8. **A)**

    Symmetric means "having similar proportion in size or shape"; a change in symmetry affects size or shape.

9. **A)**

    Sufficient means "that which is needed, desired, or necessary."

10. **C)**

    An *analgesic* is a "drug that relieves pain."

11. **B)**

    Status means "relative standing; position; condition."

12. **B)**

    Initiate means to "begin; originate."

13. **B)**

    Transdermal means "passing through the skin."

14. **C)**

    Incompatible means "unable to work together," so the co-workers are mismatched.

15. **D)**

    Diabeetes should be spelled "diabetes."

16. **B)**

    Diminish means "become less in amount or intensity."

17. **A)**

    Dilate means "expand; make larger."

18. **A)**

    A *shunt* is "a tube that diverts the path of fluid in the body."

19. **D)**

    Musculoskeletal disorders affect both the muscles and the skeleton.

20. **D)**

    In this sentence, *jerk* means "a quick, sudden movement."

21. **D)**

    Hypovolemic means "low volume." Hypovolemic shock is caused by severe loss of fluid or blood.

22. **B)**

    Aseptic means "free from bacteria or other pathogens."

23. **C)**

    Malaise means "a general feeling of illness and discomfort."

24. **C)**

    Hygiene refers to "habits and conditions, like cleanliness, that promote health."

25. B)

Apnea is "a temporary pause in breathing."

26. A)

Fatigue means "weariness from physical or mental exertion."

27. B)

Incompatible means "unable to associate in harmony."

28. D)

Empathy means "understanding of another's feelings."

29. A)

Cease means "to stop doing an action; discontinue."

30. A)

Endogenous means "something produced within the body."

31. C)

Vital means "necessary to the maintenance of life."

32. C)

A *contingent* activity is one that is "conditional; depending on something not certain."

33. B)

Gaping means "to be open; to have a break in continuity."

34. D)

Consistency means "conforming to regular patterns, habits, principles, etc."

35. D)

Languid means "tired and slow."

36. B)

Copious means "abundant and plentiful."

37. B)

Deleterious means "harmful or deadly to living things."

38. A)

Bilateral is from the Latin *bi–*, meaning "two," and *lateralis*, meaning "belonging to the side." *Bilateral* means "having two sides."

39. A)

Something that is *systemic* or occurs systemically "affects the whole body or organization."

40. C)

Benign means "not harmful; not malignant."

41. C)

Resilience means "the ability to bounce back or recover quickly."

42. A)

Adhere means "to follow devotedly; to hold closely to an idea or course."

43. B)

Recur means "to return."

44. C)

Something that is *deleterious* is "harmful or deadly to living things."

45. B)

Collaborate means to "work together on a common project."

46. B)

Deter means "to prevent or discourage" from happening.

47. C)

Cohort means "a group of people with something in common."

48. A)

Access means "to enter or gain admission."

49. C)

Pragmatic means "dealing with things sensibly and realistically based on practical considerations."

50. C)

Abstain means "to refrain; choose to avoid or not participate."

51. A)

Flushed means "colored red, especially in the face."

52. D)

Abbreviate means "to shorten or abridge."

53. A)

Resect means "to remove" or "cut out."

54. B)

Absorb means "incorporate or take in information."

55. B)

Excess means "an overabundance or a surplus."

1. C)

Choice C contains the correctly paired conjunctions *either . . . or*. In choice A, *either* is incorrectly paired with *nor*. Choice B includes a double negative (*can't . . . neither*), and choice D contains a verb error (*can taking*).

2. B)

Choice B is correct. *Good* is an adjective, but because it is modifying the verb *played*, it should be replaced with the adverb *well*.

3. C)

Choice C is correct because the quotation is a statement with a speaker tag attached. Commas are used to attach a speaker tag to a quotation that is a declarative statement. In choice A, the question mark is incorrect because the speaker is not asking a question. Choice B is incorrect because a period incorrectly separates the quotation from the speaker tag (*Adelaide said*). Choice D is incorrect because a semicolon is only used to join two complete independent clauses or items in a list.

4. D)

Choice D correctly uses the contractions *you're* (*you are*) and *you'll* (*you will*). Choice A incorrectly uses the pronoun *your* instead of the contraction *you're*. Choice B misspells the contraction *you'll* by leaving out the apostrophe. Choice C incorrectly uses *rightly* instead of *right*; the phrase *rightly now* is not idiomatic in English.

5. C)

Choice C is correct. The conjunction *because* correctly connects the opening independent clause "I can't go with you to the meeting tonight" to the dependent clause "because I have too much work to complete for class." It provides a cause-and-effect relationship between the two clauses. Choices A and B, *yet* and *nor*, must both be preceded by a comma. They also describe a contrasting relationship rather than a cause-and-effect relationship. Choice D, *although*, is nonsensical here because it too implies a contrasting relationship between the clauses rather than a cause-and-effect relationship.

6. A)

Choice A is correct. To agree with the plural noun *cats*, the singular verb *sleeps* should be replaced with the plural verb *sleep*.

7. A)

In choice A, the adverb *amazingly* modifies the adjective *hot*, and the adverb so modifies the adverb *amazingly*. Each of the other choices contains only one adverb (*amazingly*, *too*, and *quite*).

8. A)

Choice A is correct. The word *let's* should be capitalized—it begins the sentence.

9. D)

The correct answer is choice D: *had been* and *said*. The correctly completed sentence uses the continuous past-perfect verb *had been taking* to show that one past event ("my coach said") happened after a second past event ("I had been taking ice-skating lessons"). The other answer choices use incorrect tenses to show the order of events.

10. A)

Choice A correctly uses the verb *meet* ("to go to see someone") and the noun *meat* ("food made from animal tissues"). Choice B incorrectly reverses the two words *meet* and *meat*. In choice C, the verb *mate* means "to marry or join with," and the noun *mead* means "an alcoholic drink." In choice D, a *moot* point is one that does not matter, having already been settled; the noun *might* means "great strength." While choices C and D use words that fit the part of speech needed, the meanings of these words do not make sense in the context of this sentence.

11. C)

Choice C is correct. The conjunction *for* does not make sense in the sentence and should be replaced with the conjunction *but* or *yet*. This change would make it clear that <u>even though</u> Max left home early that morning, he was still late for work, <u>despite his good intentions</u>.

12. D)

Choice D is correct. The preposition *for* correctly completes the phrase "love for espresso drinks." The phrases "love about espresso drinks," "love from espresso drinks," and "love with espresso drinks" do not express the correct relationship and are all idiomatically incorrect in English.

13. B)

In choice B, the colon follows the phrase "shades of blue and green," after which the writer lists specific shades that he or she likes. Choices A and C each open with an introductory phrase that ends with a colon; however, neither sentence includes a list. Choice D's second clause does contain a list; however, it does not contain a colon.

14. C)

Choice C is correct. The homophones *aloud* and *allowed* should be transposed: *We are not allowed to speak aloud in the public library.* The verb *allowed* means "given permission to," and the adverb *aloud* means "out loud."

15. D)

Choice D is correct. "If you need a ride to the party" is a dependent clause, and "I can pick you up on my way over there" is an independent clause. Choices A and C each contain two independent clauses joined by a conjunction (*and*). Choice B contains only an independent clause.

16. A)

In choice A, the prepositional phrase "in front of the computer screen" tells where the cat is sitting. Choices B, C, and D do not contain prepositions or prepositional phrases.

17. C)

Choice C correctly capitalizes the proper nouns *Pacific* and *Atlantic*. In choice A, the common noun *oceans* is incorrectly capitalized. Choice B incorrectly capitalizes the common noun *planet* and incorrectly lowercases the proper noun *Pacific*. Choice D incorrectly capitalizes the common nouns *oceans* and *planet* and the adjective *largest*.

18. A)

The correct choice is A; the verb *bring* means "to come to a place with [something]." Choice B, *take*, means "to remove from a place." Choice C, *brink*, means "the edge of something." Choice D, *tuck*,

means "to put something away so that it is hidden or safe."

19. C)

Choice C is correct; it contains the past-perfect verb *had exchanged*. Choices A and D contain present-tense verbs (*give* and *is*). Choice B contains the past-tense verb *gave* twice.

20. C)

Choice C is correct. A comma, not a semicolon, should be used after *plan*. The period and both of the quotation marks are used correctly.

21. D)

Choice D uses the following punctuation marks correctly: a comma, an opening quotation mark, a period, and a closing quotation mark. In choice A, the semicolon after *bowl* should be changed to a comma. In choice B, there should not be an apostrophe at the end of *cats*—this plural noun is not possessive. In choice C, there should not be a comma separating the subject (*cats*) from the verb (*approached*).

22. B)

The correct choice is B. The verb *accept* means "to consent to receive [something that someone offers to you]." None of the other choices makes sense in the sentence. Choice A, *expect*, means "to assume that something will occur." Choice C, *except*, means "not including." Choice D, *accede*, means "to agree to a demand" and is usually followed by a prepositional phrase beginning with *to*.

23. C)

Choice C is correct. *Patience* should be replaced with its homophone, *patients*: *Dr. Boynton has so many patients today that she will have no time for lunch.* *Patience* is a noun, synonymous to *tolerance*, *serenity*, and *persistence*. *Patients* is a plural noun that means "sick or injured people who a medical professional examines and treats."

24. C)

The correct choice is C. The sentence correctly uses the verb *ensure*, which means "to make sure." *Impure* is an adjective that means "not pure," *enter* is a verb that means "to come in," and *insure* is a verb that

means "to give [someone] insurance coverage."
None of these choices make sense in the sentence.

25. C)

Choice C correctly pairs two past-tense verbs, *was baking* and *ate*. Choice A incorrectly pairs a past-tense verb, *was baking*, with a present-tense verb, *eat*. Choice B incorrectly pairs a past-tense verb, *was baking*, with a conditional-tense verb, *might eat*. Choice D incorrectly pairs a past-tense verb, *was baking*, with a future-tense verb, *will eat*.

26. C)

Choice C is correct. The verb *die* should be replaced with its homophone, *dye: Are you going to dye your hair green or purple? Die* means "to perish," and *dye* means "to color [something] using dye."

27. A)

Choice A is correct. Here, *best* is a common adjective, *friend* is a common noun, and *Jill* is a proper noun. The other choices are incorrectly capitalized and/or lowercased.

28. C)

Choice C is correct. The speaker is comparing only two people: his or her two sisters. *The most* should be replaced with the word *more*.

29. C)

The correct choice is C. The sentence correctly uses the plural noun *pieces* to complete the phrase "pieces of bread." In choice A, *peas* are "a small green legume." In choice B, *peace* means "quiet and tranquility." In choice D, the verb *appeases* means "soothes, mollifies, or placates." None of these other words make sense in the sentence.

30. C)

Choice C is correct. *Rites* and *rights* sound alike but have different spellings and meanings, which makes them a homophone pair. Choices A (*priests/prince*), B (*perform/reform*), and D (*and/end*) are not homophone pairs because they do not sound enough alike.

31. D)

Choice D is correct. The word *ferryboat* should be lowercased—it is a common noun.

32. B)

Choice B is correct. The interjection *wow* expresses emotion. In this sentence, the speaker might be expressing surprise or pity. None of the other choices contains an interjection.

33. C)

Choice C correctly matches the plural noun *clothes* with the plural verb *were* and the plural pronoun *them*. Choice A incorrectly pairs the plural noun *clothes* with the singular verb *was*. Choice B incorrectly matches the plural noun *clothes* with the singular pronoun *it*. Choice D incorrectly matches the singular noun *coat* with the plural verb *were* and the plural pronoun *them*.

34. B)

Choice B is correct. The verb *insure* means "to cover with an insurance policy." None of the other choices make sense in the sentence. Choice A, *ensure*, means "to guarantee." Choice C, *assure*, means "to dispel any doubts." Choice D, *assay*, means "to determine content or quality."

35. C)

Choice C is correct. The homophones *there* and *they're* should be transposed: *They're standing right over there . . .* The contraction *they're* means "they are," and the adverb *there* (which modifies the verb *standing*) means "in or at that place."

36. A)

Choice A correctly pairs the plural second-person subject "you and Ana" with the plural second-person possessive pronoun *yours*. Choice B incorrectly pairs the singular second-person subject *you* with the plural third-person possessive pronoun *theirs*. Choice C incorrectly pairs the plural first-person subject *we* with the singular feminine third-person possessive pronoun *hers*. Choice D incorrectly pairs the plural first-person subject "my sister and I" with the plural second-person possessive pronoun *yours*.

37. C)

Choice C, the adjective *two* is correct. This choice refers to the number; Andre can take more than one break but less than three. The blank requires an adjective, and the number makes sense in context. *To* is a preposition that indicates direction, position, or purpose. *Too* is an adverb meaning "in addition" or "also." The verb *tow* means "to drag or pull behind";

a car might tow a trailer, for instance. None of the other three choices make sense in the context of the sentence.

38. D)

Choice D is correct. The common noun *night* should not be capitalized, even though it follows a proper noun (the holiday name *Christmas*). The word *Day* in *Independence Day* is part of the name of the holiday, so it is capitalized.

39. C)

Choice C correctly connects two independent clauses ("Jenny enjoys swimming in pools" and "she hates swimming in lakes") with a comma and the coordinating conjunction *but*. Choice A is a run-on sentence lacking punctuation (a comma after *pools*). Choice B incorrectly uses a semicolon instead of a comma. Choice D incorrectly includes a comma after *but*.

40. C)

Choice C has one dependent clause and one independent one, joined by the subordinating conjunction *because*, so it is a complex sentence. Choice A is a simple sentence with one subject (*ferryboats*) and one verb (*provide*). Choice B is a compound sentence (two independent clauses joined by the coordinating conjunction *and*). Choice D is a compound-complex sentence: it has one dependent clause ("If you . . . items") and two independent clauses ("you can . . . Bay Bridge" and "the carpool . . . trip").

41. B)

Choice B is correct. The past-tense verb *was going* suggests that Dad was in college continuously for several years. Choice A, *Dad*, is a proper noun. In choice C, the verb *was* in the second clause is past-tense, but not continuous. Choice D, "his early twenties," is a noun modified by a possessive pronoun and adjective.

42. B)

Choice B is correct: the verb *to catch* is irregular, and its past-tense form is *caught*. Choice A is incorrect: there is no such word as *catched*. Choice C incorrectly uses a present-tense verb, *catches*, in a sentence in which the action takes place "last night." Choice D incorrectly matches a singular noun, *Danny Pine*, with a plural verb, *catch*. Also, *catch* is

a present-tense verb, and this sentence's action takes place "last night."

43. A)

Choice A correctly uses the noun *break*, which means "rest" or "respite." Choice B incorrectly uses *brake*, a noun meaning "braking mechanism in a vehicle," in place of its homophone *break*. Choice C incorrectly uses the verb *bray* (meaning "to make a braying noise like a donkey") in place of *break*. Choice D incorrectly uses the noun *braid* (meaning "plaited hair") in place of *break*.

44. A)

Choice A is correct; this choice contains a first-person plural subject ("my sister and I") and a first-person plural verb (*love*). Choice B contains a second-person plural subject ("you and your sister") and a second-person plural verb (*love*). Choices C and D both contain third-person singular subjects (*Mom* and *she*) and third-person singular verbs (*shops*, *does [not] love*, *loves*).

45. A)

The sentence uses the past-perfect verb *had waited* to show that one past event ("I had waited for her all evening") happened before a second past event ("Taylor arrived").

46. B)

Choice B is correct. *Rains* should be replaced with its homophone, *reins*: *Use the reins to guide your horse . . . Rains* is a plural noun in this sentence, synonymous to *showers*, *floods*, and *deluges*. In this corrected sentence, *reins* is a plural noun that means "straps that are attached to a horse's bridle; a rider uses them to control and guide the horse."

47. D)

Choice D, the verb *rain*, is correct. It is a synonym for *pour* or *sprinkle*. A *rein* is a strap attached to a horse's bridle. The verb *reign* means "to rule [a kingdom]." The verb *rend* means "to rip or tear [something]." None of these answer choices make sense in the context of the sentence.

48. B)

Choice B correctly uses a comma at the end of the independent clause "Mom . . . flying" and before the subordinating conjunction so; it also correctly ends the sentence with a period. Choice A incorrectly uses a semicolon at the end of the independent clause "Mom . . . flying" and before the subordinating conjunction so. Choice C incorrectly uses a colon at the end of the independent clause "Mom . . . flying" and before the subordinating conjunction so. Choice D incorrectly ends the sentence, which is not a question, with a question mark instead of a period.

49. B)

Choice B correctly capitalizes the holiday names and lowercases the common noun *summer*. In choice A, the proper noun *Day* (in *Valentine's Day*) is incorrectly lowercased. Choice C incorrectly lowercases *Day* (in *Valentine's Day*) and incorrectly capitalizes the common noun *summer*. Choice D incorrectly lowercases the holiday name *Valentine's Day* and incorrectly capitalizes the common noun *summer*.

50. C)

Choice C is correct. The subordinating conjunction *because* should be replaced with the coordinating conjunction *and*. The writer does not need to shop for food *as a result* of needing to pick up dry cleaning. He or she needs to do both, and the two errands do not have a cause-effect relationship.

51. C)

The semicolon in choice C joins two related independent clauses. Choice A ends with a question mark. Choice B has a colon, three commas, and a period. Choice D has an apostrophe (in *Wharton's*), a hyphen (in *modern-day*), an em dash (between *television shows* and *my favorites*), and ends with a period.

52. C)

No punctuation is required between independent and dependent clauses, so choice C is correct. The semicolon in choice A, the colon in choice B, and the em dash in choice D are all incorrect.

53. C)

Choice C correctly uses *morning* and *mourning*. *Morning* is the early part of a day, and *mourning* is a grieving process someone goes through after a loved one has died. Choice A reverses *morning* and *mourning*. In choice B, a *mooring* is a place to secure a boat in a harbor. In choice D, *marring* is a verb that means "spoiling [something]," and *morning* is used incorrectly in place of *mourning*.

54. C)

Choice C is correct. *Accept* (a verb meaning "to agree to take [something]") should be replaced with its homophone, *except: We invited everyone to our wedding except people whom neither of us knew very well. Except* is a preposition that means "other than."

55. A)

Choice A is correct. The prepositional phrase "in the closet" tells where the speaker's new coat is. None of the other choices contain a preposition.

1.   C)

Hydrogen bonds form between the slight negative charge on the oxygen atom in one water molecule and the slight positive charge on the hydrogen atoms in another water molecule.

2.   B)

Cellulose is a polysaccharide, a sugar molecule made from repeating monosaccharides. NADH is a complex molecule that carries electrons. Cytosine is a nucleic acid, and histones are proteins found in chromosomes.

3.   C)

Vacuoles are large organelles found in plant cells and some animals cells. They store water, waste, and compounds that are needed for specialized tasks, including proteins.

4.   B)

Glycolysis is the energy-producing pathway that occurs in the cell's cytoplasm.

5.   C)

Half of the offspring will inherit two recessive alleles for curly fur.

	S	s
s	Ss	ss
s	Ss	ss

6.   A)

DNA polymerase cannot replicate the ends of chromosomes (telomeres).

7.   C)

Chromosomes are separated to opposite ends of the cell during anaphase.

8.   B)

A promoter is necessary to initiate gene transcription. If a promoter is not present, the gene cannot be expressed.

9.   D)

Each amino acid is encoded by multiple codons. In a silent mutation, a change in the DNA sequence results in a new codon that codes for the same amino acid.

10.   D)

When a substance is heated, atoms gain energy and move faster. Eventually, the atoms move fast enough that they begin to move away from each other. Since water is polar, hydrogen bonds form. Hydrogen bonds make it difficult to separate molecules of water.

11.   B)

Lipids form layers because they have a polar head and a nonpolar tail. The polar heads interact with water, and the nonpolar tails are repelled by water. Thus, they arrange themselves into a bilayer with two layers of polar heads facing outward toward water with the nonpolar tails between them.

12.   B)

The Golgi apparatus packages proteins so they can be transported to the appropriate location either inside or outside the cell.

13.   A)

ATP is not produced during the Krebs cycle. The Krebs cycle generates electrons used in the electron transport chain.

14.   B)

Positive regulation of gene expression happens when an activator is present. The lac operon is repressed unless lactose is present to activate gene transcription.

15.   A)

During transcription, a strand of mRNA is produced using the template provided by DNA. This process occurs in the nucleus.

16.   A)

Crossing over happens during meiosis I when homologous chromosomes are aligned at the equator of the cell during metaphase. During this process, genetic information is exchanged between paternal and maternal chromosomes, increasing the variability between parents and offspring.

17.   A)

All the offspring will have one copy of each allele, so they will be short because that is the dominant trait.

	T	**T**
t	Tt	Tt
t	Tt	Tt

18.   A)

Most lipids have a polar head made of phosphate or glycerol.

19.   B)

Cell membranes are composed of two layers of phospholipids. Other molecules, such as proteins and carbohydrates, may be embedded in the cell membrane but do not compose the membrane's primary structure.

20.   C)

In the electron transport chain, electrons are passed between proteins embedded in the mitochondrial membranes. This process creates a proton gradient that is then used to produce ATP.

21.   C)

RNA does not contain thymidine, which eliminates A and B as correct responses. D is not complementary to the sequence, so it can be eliminated as well.

22.   B)

During mitosis, the two sets of identical DNA are separated into two daughter cells, creating two cells with a full set (2n) of chromosomes.

23.   A)

DNA contains the instructions for making proteins. mRNA is made using the code in DNA, and then ribosomes construct proteins using the information in mRNA.

24.   C)

Since the heterozygous offspring have neither curly nor straight hair, but something in between, the dominant trait, curly hair, does not completely dominate the recessive trait, straight hair.

25.   C)

Both active transport and facilitated diffusion use membrane proteins to cross the membrane, but active transport also requires energy in the form of ATP.

26.   C)

During the Krebs cycle, pyruvate is broken down to CO_2 and water.

27.   C)

DNA ligase joins broken strands of DNA. Enzymes are often named for their function: *ligate* means "to join or tie together."

28.   C)

Meiosis II results in four haploid daughter cells.

29.   B)

Genes that are close to each other on a chromosome (linked genes) are likely to be inherited together.

30.   D)

Chromosomal inversion happens when a fragment of a single chromosome inverts and is reattached to the chromosome. This changes the DNA sequence in the area where the inversion occurs, leading to mutations.

CHEMISTRY

1. **C)**

    The number of atoms in an electron's valence shell determines its chemical reactivity. Elements with shells that are close to full are the most reactive; elements with full shells (noble gases) are the least reactive.

2. **C)**

    Al, Ga, and B are in group 13 and have three valence electrons.

3. **B)**

    Covalent bonds can share one pair of electrons (single bond), two pairs of electrons (double bond), or three pairs of electrons (triple bond).

4. **D)**

    Density is a physical property: when measuring the density of a material, the chemical identity of that material will not change.

5. **B)**

    Solutions that taste bitter and have a slippery texture are basic.

6. **B)**

    Orange juice contains bits of solid pulp that are not uniformly spread out, making it a heterogeneous mixture.

7. **D)**

    The reactants swap ions, so this is a double replacement reaction. The H^+ joins the OH^- to form H_2O, and the Na^+ bonds to the Cl^- ion to form NaCl.

8. **C)**

    Atomic radius decreases from bottom to top across a group and from left to right across a period. Lead (Pb) is the farthest down and left, so it has the largest radius.

9. **C)**

    Two moles of $KClO_3$ are produced from 2 moles of KCl.

10. **A)**

    Sulfur (S) is element 16, which means it has sixteen protons.

11. **B)**

    Na, Al, and P are all found in the third period on the periodic table.

12. **A)**

    Sodium (Na) donates one electron to chlorine (Cl), resulting in the ions Na^+ and Cl^-. The two ions then form an ionic bond to produce NaCl.

13. **D)**

    The atomic mass of carbon (C) is 12, and the atomic mass of hydrogen (H) is 1: $12 + 1(4) = 16$ amu.

14. **A)**

    Acids have a pH between 0 and 7.

15. **C)**

    The balanced equation is $3CaCl_2 + 2Na_3PO_4 \rightarrow Ca_3(PO_4)_2 + 6NaCl$, showing 3 Ca, 6 Cl, 6 Na and 2 (PO_4) on both sides of the arrow. The answer choice is 3, 2, 1, 6.

16. **A)**

    All elements are in group 2. Atomic radius increases from top to bottom within a specific group; since barium (Ba) is the element farthest down the group, it will have the largest atomic radius.

17. **C)**

    Two moles of hydrogen gas and 1 mole of oxygen gas will produce 2 moles of water.

18. **B)**

    The number of electrons (which have a negative charge) and protons (which have a positive charge) determine the atom's total charge.

19. **B)**

    On the periodic table, the electronegativity of an element increases from left to right across a row or period. The electronegativity also increases from bottom to top within a column or group. Therefore, oxygen (O) will be more electronegative than sulfur (S) since it is one row above. phosphorus (P) will be less electronegative than sulfur since it is one column to the left. Arsenic (As) will be the least electronegative since it is one row beneath phosphorous.

20. B)

Carbon (C) and oxygen (O) share electrons when forming CO_2, resulting in a covalent bond.

21. C)

The atomic mass of oxygen (O) is 16, and the atomic mass of hydrogen (H) is 1: 1(2) + 16 = 18 amu.

22. A)

The salt in salt water is uniformly distributed, making it a homogeneous mixture.

23. D)

The balanced equation is $2AgI + Na_2S \rightarrow Ag_2S + 2NaI$, showing 2Ag, 2I, 2Na and 1S on both sides of the arrow. The answer choice is 2, 1, 1, 2.

24. A)

20 g will decay to 10 g after the first half-life. 10 g will decay to five g after the second half-life. If 2 half-lives take 12 days, each half-life is 12 ÷ 2 = 6 days.

25. A)

All of these elements are in the same period. Atomic radius decreases from left to right across the periodic table; since oxygen (O) is the element farthest to the right in the period, it will have the smallest atomic radius.

26. A)

In an endothermic reaction, heat is absorbed by the reaction, so it is included on the reactant side of the equation.

27. C)

On the periodic table, the electronegativity of an element increases from left to right and bottom to top. Therefore, barium (Ba) will be less electronegative than calcium (Ca) since it is farther down within group 2 or IIA. Calcium is to the left of germanium (Ge), and thus is less electronegative in comparison. Nitrogen (N) is more electronegative than germanium since it is in group 15 or VA (one column to the right of Ge) and within period 2 (two rows up).

28. A)

The process of condensation releases energy: substances transition from a high-energy state (gas) to a lower energy state (water).

29. A)

Hydrogen (H) always has an oxidation number of +1. To create a neutral molecule, the chlorine (Cl) must then have an oxidation number of −1.

30. C)

During gamma decay, atoms maintain the same number of protons and neutrons but release high energy electromagnetic radiation known as gamma radiation (written as $_0^0\gamma$).

1. **A)**

Meninges are present only in the dorsal cavity, which holds the spinal cord and brain.

2. **B)**

Osteoclasts are the bone cells that break down or degrade bone tissue.

3. **B)**

The mitral valve prevents backflow of blood to the left atrium.

4. **D)**

Skeletal muscle can be controlled voluntarily.

5. **C)**

There are twelve bones in the thoracic, or chest, vertebrae.

6. **D)**

The neuroglia protect the neuron by surrounding it.

7. **A)**

Type I muscle fibers contract slowly but are useful for posture and stamina.

8. **A)**

Renin is released by the kidneys and plays a role in regulating blood pressure.

9. **A)**

Phosphate and calcium levels are regulated by parathyroid hormone, which is released by the parathyroid gland.

10. **A)**

Antimicrobial peptides kill pathogens by altering their DNA or membrane functions.

11. **C)**

Sperm travels from the seminiferous tubes through the vas deferens to the ejaculatory duct.

12. **D)**

Efferent neurons control the movement of voluntary muscles.

13. **D)**

Pulmonary veins carry oxygenated blood from the lungs to the right atrium of the heart.

14. **C)**

The outer layer of the blastocyst (the trophoblast) gives rise to the placenta.

15. **A)**

The medulla oblongata is gray matter that regulates involuntary bodily functions like sneezing, blood pressure, and oxygen level in the blood.

16. **C)**

The epiglottis prevents food from entering the lungs through the trachea.

17. **C)**

Heat is released when blood vessels close to the skin's surface dilate.

18. **D)**

The digestive enzymes produced by the pancreas pass into the small intestine.

19. **A)**

The pleural cavity provides a space for the lungs to expand.

20. **D)**

The glomerulus is a network of capillaries that begins the filtration process by filtering blood plasma, the result of which is then excreted as urine.

21. **C)**

Cerebrospinal fluid absorbs waste products from the brain, allowing them to be transferred into the bloodstream.

22.   B)

Hematopoiesis is the process whereby stem cells in the red bone marrow produce red and white blood cells.

23.   B)

Language is processed in the cerebral cortex.

24.   C)

The nares (nostrils) do not have sphincters and are always open.

25.   A)

The coccyx is located at the tip of the vertebral column.

26.   B)

The true ribs are the first seven pairs of ribs, which are attached directly to the sternum.

27.   A)

The coccygeal nerves belong to the group of spinal nerves.

28.   B)

Most nutrients are absorbed in the jejunum.

29.   C)

Monocytes use phagocytosis to "swallow" and break down pathogens.

30.   D)

The placenta does not produce red blood cells for the fetus.

PHYSICS

1. C)

Plug the variables into the appropriate formula and solve.

$v_f^2 = v_i^2 + 2ad$

$v_f^2 = 5^2 + 2 \times 9.8 \times 10$

$v_f = \sqrt{5^2 + 2 \times 9.8 \times 10} = \textbf{14.9 m/s}$

2. D)

Plug the variables into the appropriate formula and solve.

$d = \frac{1}{2}at^2 + v_i t$

$x = \frac{1}{2} \times 0 \times 4^2 + 18\cos45° \times 4 = \textbf{101.8 m}$

3. B)

Plug the variables into the appropriate formula and solve.

$v = \frac{d}{t}$

$t = \frac{d}{v}$

$t = \frac{800\text{ m}}{340\text{ m/s}} = \textbf{2.35 s}$

4. D)

Plug the variables into the appropriate formula and solve.

$W = Fd$

$W = mgd$

$W = (50\text{ N})(9.8\text{ m/s}^2)(2\text{ m}) = \textbf{980 J}$

5. D)

The acceleration due to gravity is a vector with a magnitude and a direction.

6. C)

Plug the variables into the appropriate formula and solve.

$N = mg$

$N = (40\text{ kg})(9.8\text{ m/s}^2) = \textbf{392 N vertically up}$

7. D)

Plug the variables into the appropriate formula and solve.

$mv_{1i} + mv_{2i} = mv_{1f} + mv_{2f}$

The mass of each ball is the same, so m cancels out of the equation.

$v_{1i} + 0 = v_{1f} + v_{2f}$

$v_{2f} = v_{1i} - v_{1f} = 1.5\text{ m/s} - (-0.5\text{ m/s}) = \textbf{2 m/s}$

8. B)

Plug the variables into the appropriate formula and solve.

$a_{rad} = \frac{v^2}{r}$

$v = \sqrt{(18\text{ m/s}^2)(0.18\text{ m})} = \textbf{1.8 m/s}$

9. C)

A relaxing spring visually transmits longitudinal waves.

10. A)

Plug the variables into the appropriate formula and solve.

$V = IR$

$V = (0.5\text{ A})(60\ \Omega) = \textbf{30 V}$

11. D)

Plug the variables into the appropriate formula and solve.

$v_f = v_i + at$

$a = \frac{v_f - v_i}{t}$

$a = \frac{1 \times 10^6\text{ m/s} - 0\text{ m/s}}{1 \times 10^{-6}\text{ s}} = \textbf{1} \times \textbf{10}^{\textbf{12}}\textbf{ m/s}^2$

12. C)

Plug the variables into the appropriate formula and solve.

$\tau = rF\sin\theta$

$F = \frac{\tau}{r\sin\theta}$

$F = \frac{500\text{ N m}}{(0.10\text{ m})\sin90°} = \textbf{5000 N}$

13. D)

Gravity is pulling down on the object with a force of $F = ma = (1\text{ kg})(9.8\text{ m/s}^2) = 9.8$ N. According to Newton's Third Law, Earth exerts an equal force back on the object.

14. A)

Plug the variables into the appropriate formula and solve.

$V = IR$

$I = \dfrac{V}{R}$

$I = \dfrac{12\ V}{1 \times 10^5\ \Omega} = 1.2 \times 10^{-4}\ A = \mathbf{0.12\ mA}$

15. B)

Plug the variables into the appropriate formula and solve.

$PE_g = mgh$

$\dfrac{1}{2}mv^2 = mgh$

$v = \sqrt{2gh}$

$v = \sqrt{2(9.8\ m/s^2)(400\ m)} = \mathbf{88.5\ m/s}$

16. C)

Plug the variables into the appropriate formula and solve.

$\dfrac{1}{R_t} = \dfrac{1}{2} + \dfrac{1}{5} + \dfrac{1}{10}$

$= \dfrac{5}{10} + \dfrac{2}{10} + \dfrac{1}{10}$

$= \dfrac{8}{10} = \dfrac{4}{5}$

$R_t = \dfrac{5}{4}\Omega = \mathbf{1.25\ \Omega}$

17. A)

Plug the variables into the appropriate formula and solve.

$n = \dfrac{c}{v_s}$

$v_s = \dfrac{c}{n}$

$v_s = \dfrac{3 \times 10^8\ m/s}{1.33} = \mathbf{2.26 \times 10^8\ m/s}$

18. B)

Like charges repel.

19. A)

Plug the variables into the appropriate formula and solve.

$F_g = \dfrac{GmM}{r^2}$

$F_g = \dfrac{GmM}{(3r)^2} = \dfrac{1}{9}\left(\dfrac{GmM}{r^2}\right)$

20. A)

Plug the variables into the appropriate formula and solve.

$T = \dfrac{\lambda}{v} = \dfrac{10\ m}{3 \times 10^8\ m/s} = \mathbf{3.33 \times 10^{-8}\ s}$

21. D)

Plug the variables into the appropriate formula and solve.

$P = \dfrac{W}{t}$

$W = Pt = (500\ W)(1800\ s) = \mathbf{9 \times 10^5\ J}$

22. A)

Plug the variables into the appropriate formula and solve.

$n = \dfrac{c}{v_s}$

$v_s = \dfrac{c}{n}$

$v_s = \dfrac{3 \times 10^8\ m/s}{2.4} = \mathbf{1.25 \times 10^8\ m/s}$

23. D)

Plug the variables into the appropriate formula and solve.

$T = mg$

$T = 6\ kg(9.8\ m/s^2) = \mathbf{58.8\ N}$

24. D)

Plug the variables into the appropriate formula and solve.

$v = \lambda f$

$v = \dfrac{7 \times 10^{-3}\ m}{5 \times 10^{-6}\ s} = \mathbf{1400\ m/s}$

25. D)

Plug the variables into the appropriate formula and solve.

$F_c = m\dfrac{v^2}{r}$

$g = \dfrac{v^2}{r}$

$v = \sqrt{gr} = \sqrt{(9.8\ m/s^2)(10\ m)} = \mathbf{9.9\ m/s}$

26. C)

Plug the variables into the appropriate formula and solve.

$PE_g = mgh$

$\frac{1}{2}mv^2 = mgh$

$g = \frac{v^2}{2h}$

$g = \frac{(15 \text{ m/s})^2}{2(8 \text{ m})} = \textbf{14.1 m/s}^2$

27. A)

Plug the variables into the appropriate formula and solve.

$n = \frac{c}{v_s}$

$v_s = \frac{3 \times 10^8 \text{ m-s}}{1.50} = \textbf{2} \times \textbf{10}^8 \textbf{ m/s}$

28. B)

A compass pointing to its north direction points toward Earth's south magnetic pole. Opposite poles attract.

29. C)

Plug the variables into the appropriate formula and solve.

$\Delta V = Ed$

$d = \frac{\Delta V}{E}$

$d = \frac{5V}{100 \text{ V/m}} = 0.05 \text{ m} = \textbf{5 cm}$

30. A)

Plug the variables into the appropriate formula and solve.

$\frac{1}{R_t} = \frac{1}{R_1} + \frac{1}{R_2} + \frac{1}{R_3} + \ldots$

$\frac{1}{R_t} = 17\left(\frac{1}{12}\right)$

$R_t = \frac{12\,\Omega}{17} = \textbf{0.71 }\boldsymbol{\Omega}$

THREE: PRACTICE TEST THREE

Mathematics

Directions: Work the problem carefully, and choose the best answer.

1. The dosage for a certain medication is 2 milligrams per kilogram. What dosage should be given to a patient weighing 165 pounds?

   A) 150 mg
   B) 250 mg
   C) 132 mg
   D) 50 mg

2. Rita's new boss tells her to arrive at 0500 hours. What time should she report to work?

   A) 7:00 a.m.
   B) 5:00 p.m.
   C) 5:00 a.m.
   D) 7:00 p.m.

3. A doctor advises her prediabetic patient to decrease his sugar consumption by 25%. If he currently consumes 40 grams of sugar per day on average, how many grams of sugar per day should he have now?

   A) 10 g
   B) 16 g
   C) 24 g
   D) 30 g

4. If Tim is driving 75 miles per hour, how far will he travel in 24 minutes?

   A) 187.5 mi
   B) 30 mi
   C) 24 mi
   D) 40 mi

5. Sandra has $1400 in savings. If she saves $125 a month, which expression represents her balance after x months?

   A) 1525x
   B) 125(x + 1400)
   C) 125x + 1400
   D) 1400x + 125

6. Find the sum of $\frac{2}{5}$, $\frac{3}{4}$, and $\frac{7}{10}$.

   A) $1\frac{9}{20}$
   B) $\frac{37}{60}$
   C) $1\frac{17}{20}$
   D) $\frac{12}{19}$

7. Andre welded together three pieces of metal pipe, measuring 26.5 inches, 18.9 inches, and 35.1 inches. How long was the welded pipe?

A) 10.3 in

B) 80.5 in

C) 27.5 in

D) 42.7 in

8. A patient has a condition that requires her to limit her fluid intake to 1800 milliliters per day. A family member brings her a bottle of water that contains 591 milliliters, and she drinks the whole bottle. How many milliliters of water can the patient ingest the rest of the day?

A) 1391 ml

B) 1209 ml

C) 2391 ml

D) 1309 ml

9. A doctor has prescribed Norco 10-325, which contains 10 milligrams of hydrocodone and 325 milligrams of acetaminophen, to help control a patient's post-op pain. The warning on the prescription label cautions patients to limit their intake of acetaminophen to less than 3500 milligrams per day. How many tablets can the patient take while staying under the daily limit?

A) 9

B) 10

C) 11

D) 12

10. A bank account is $20 overdrawn. The bank charges the customer a $25 overdraft fee. What is the bank account balance now?

A) −$5

B) $15

C) $5

D) −$45

11. One day in January, the low temperature was −7°F. During the day the temperature rose 15 degrees. What was the high temperature?

A) −23°F

B) 23°F

C) −8°F

D) 8°F

12. Simplify the following expression:
$(9 + 6) \times (2 - 5)$

A) −45

B) 45

C) 25

D) 16

13. Simplify the following expression:
$-10 + 15 \div (-5) \times 3^2 - 10^2$

A) −48

B) −137

C) −91

D) −73

14. Ruby has $\frac{1}{3}$ box of laundry detergent, and her roommate has $\frac{3}{5}$ box. How much detergent do they have together?

A) $\frac{14}{15}$ box

B) $\frac{1}{2}$ box

C) $\frac{3}{4}$ box

D) $\frac{7}{15}$ box

15. $23 + 19.09 + 4.7 =$

A) 19.79

B) 24.02

C) 26.09

D) 46.79

16. 26 is 40% of what number?

    A) 65

    B) 10.4

    C) 66

    D) 650

17. Maria's salary is $1975 per month. Taxes and insurance taken out of her check total 35%. What is Maria's take-home pay?

    A) $1283.75

    B) $1940

    C) $1175

    D) $691.25

18. The recommended ratio of nurses to patients in a critical care unit is 1 to 4. How many nurses should be on duty if there are 20 patients in the unit?

    A) 10 nurses

    B) 8 nurses

    C) 7 nurses

    D) 5 nurses

19. Which of the following numbers is the greatest?

    A) 0.29

    B) $\frac{2}{9}$

    C) $\frac{1}{4}$

    D) 0.26

20. The ratio of men to women in a nursing program is 2 to 7. If there are 72 men in the program, how many women are there?

    A) 504 women

    B) 21 women

    C) 252 women

    D) 210 women

21. Asha has saved $96 toward the purchase of a new laptop, 20% of its price. What is the price of the laptop?

    A) $864

    B) $960

    C) $380

    D) $480

22. Bob's hospital bill is $1896. If Bob pays $158 per month, which expression represents his balance after x months?

    A) 158(1896 – x)

    B) 158x + 1896

    C) 1738x

    D) 1896 – 158x

23. A pencil is 19 centimeters long. What is its approximate length in inches?

    A) 48.26 in

    B) 7.5 in

    C) 15 in

    D) 3.75 in

24. Simplify the following expression: $(3x^2y^5)(4x^4y)$

    A) $12x^6y^6$

    B) $7x^6y^6$

    C) $7x^8y^5$

    D) $12x^8y^5$

25. Kenna lost an average of 1.1 pounds per week for an entire year. How much weight did she lose? (Round to the nearest whole number.)

    A) 47 lb

    B) 53 lb

    C) 46 lb

    D) 57 lb

26. Convert 10:30 p.m. to military time.
    A) 1030
    B) 2230
    C) 2030
    D) 1230

27. Felicia has earned 57.5 hours of sick leave. Assuming she works 8-hour shifts, how many days of sick leave has she earned? (Round to the nearest tenth.)
    A) 460 days
    B) 49.5 days
    C) 72 days
    D) 7.2 days

28. Convert 0.46 to a fraction in lowest terms.
    A) $\frac{23}{500}$
    B) $\frac{23}{10}$
    C) $\frac{23}{50}$
    D) $\frac{2}{3}$

29. Simplify the following expression:
    $4(a^2 + 2a) - 3(a + 7)$
    A) $4a^2 + 5a - 21$
    B) $4a^2 + 11a - 21$
    C) $9a^2 + 21$
    D) $4a^2 + 5a + 21$

30. Convert 6.5 feet to meters. Round the answer to the nearest hundredth.
    A) 1.98 m
    B) 198 m
    C) 78 m
    D) 7.8 m

31. Solve for x: $2x - 3y = -7$
    A) 2
    B) $\frac{3y - 7}{2}$
    C) -2
    D) $\frac{2y - 7}{3}$

32. Rosie has $145. She needs to buy a new dishwasher that costs $520. How much will she need to save each week to be able to buy the dishwasher in five weeks?
    A) $75
    B) $80
    C) $104
    D) $133

33. Alyssa weighs 65 kilograms. What is her weight in pounds?
    A) 30 lb
    B) 32.5 lb
    C) 143 lb
    D) 130 lb

34. The orthopedic post-surgery unit at Smith Hospital is 75% full. There are 36 patients in the unit. What is the capacity of the unit?
    A) 27 patients
    B) 48 patients
    C) 12 patients
    D) 45 patients

35. Over the course of a year, Jamie saved $1530. On average, how much did she save per month?
    A) $153.00
    B) $183.60
    C) $127.50
    D) $140.00

36. Solve: $7x + 3 = 38$

A) -5

B) 5

C) $5\frac{6}{7}$

D) 245

37. An employee is given $100 petty cash to purchase 6 binders and 6 sets of dividers at the office supply store. Divider sets are $3.49 each, and the binders come in packages of two for $10.49 per package. How much money will the employee return to petty cash?

A) $52.41

B) $16.12

C) $83.88

D) $47.59

38. If three lengths of copper wire, $6\frac{2}{5}$ feet each, are cut off a 100-foot roll of copper wire, how much wire is left on the roll?

A) $19\frac{1}{5}$ ft

B) $93\frac{3}{5}$ ft

C) $80\frac{4}{5}$ ft

D) $81\frac{1}{5}$ ft

39. Find the product of $\frac{10}{21}$ and $\frac{14}{25}$.

A) $\frac{125}{147}$

B) $\frac{12}{23}$

C) 1

D) $\frac{4}{15}$

40. Simplify the expression: $6a^3b^2(5a^2b^5c)$.

A) $11a5b^7c$

B) $30ab^2c$

C) $30a^6b^{10}c$

D) $30a^5b^7c$

41. 88 is what percent of 160?

A) 72%

B) 55%

C) 2.2%

D) 22%

42. How many $1\frac{1}{3}$-pound loaves of bread can be made from 8 pounds of dough?

A) $3\frac{2}{3}$ loaves

B) 12 loaves

C) 6 loaves

D) $6\frac{2}{3}$ loaves

43. What is the price of 2.7 pounds of steak at $5.40 per pound?

A) $16.20

B) $8.10

C) $13.50

D) $14.58

44. Find the product of 6.2 and 8.5.

A) 527

B) 14.7

C) 52.7

D) 2.3

45. Eduardo has made $24\frac{1}{2}$ ounces of homemade tomato sauce. How many $3\frac{1}{2}$-ounce jars can he fill?

A) 7 jars

B) 8 jars

C) 12 jars

D) 6 jars

46. Solve: $\frac{x}{3} + \frac{7}{6} = \frac{5}{2}$

A) 11

B) 4

C) 0

D) -11

47. Two units of a certain gas weigh 175 grams. What is the weight of 5 units of this gas?

A) 70 g

B) 875 g

C) 1750 g

D) 437.5 g

48. Convert $\frac{2}{3}$ to a decimal number. Round the answer to the nearest hundredth.

A) 0.6

B) 0.67

C) 0.66

D) 0.7

49. If property taxes are figured at $1.50 for every $100 in evaluation, what taxes will be paid on a home valued at $85,000?

A) $567

B) $12,750

C) $1275

D) $5670

50. John lost 10% of his body weight. If he now weighs 171 pounds, how much did he weigh originally?

A) 154 lb

B) 210 lb

C) 190 lb

D) 181 lb

51. Juan is packing a shipment of three books weighing 0.8 pounds, 0.49 pounds, and 0.89 pounds. The maximum weight for the shipping box is 2.5 pounds. How much more weight will the box hold?

A) 2.18 lb

B) 0.32 lb

C) 0.48 lb

D) 4.68 lb

52. A telemarketer determined that during a single shift, he pushed 2,112 buttons making long-distance phone calls. If each call requires the telemarketer to push 11 buttons, how many calls did he make during his shift?

A) 302 calls

B) 192 calls

C) 250 calls

D) 210 calls

53. Yvonne ran 4.6 miles, 4.8 miles, 5.3 miles, 5.2 miles, and 6 miles on five consecutive days. What was her average distance over the five days?

A) 4.1 mi

B) 25.9 mi

C) 5.18 mi

D) 4.975 mi

54. Given the numbers 5.63, 5.6, and 5.627, find the sum of the two with larger decimals decreased by the one with the smallest decimal.

A) 5.657

B) 5.297

C) 5.603

D) 16.857

55. Which decimal number is equivalent to $\frac{3}{16}$?

A) 5.3

B) 0.2125

C) 0.2

D) 0.1875

Reading

Directions: Read the passage carefully, and then read the questions that follow and choose the most correct answer.

In 1733, Stephen Hales, an English clergyman with a great interest in a variety of sciences, experimented with inserting tubes into the arteries of animals such as horses to measure "the force of the blood," thereby becoming the first person to measure blood pressure. He described his findings in a study titled *Haemastaticks*, noting how high the blood would rise in the tube's column as he entered it into the animals' arteries.

Fortunately, we no longer have to use such invasive methods to study blood pressure. In 1896, Italian physician Scipione Riva-Rocci, building on earlier noninvasive methods of measuring blood pressure, created what we still recognize as a sphygmomanometer, the conventional blood pressure meter that we use today.

Shortly after Riva-Rocci's invention was made available to the medical world, Nikolai Korotkov, a Russian surgeon, combined the use of a sphygmomanometer with a stethoscope to create a new way to monitor blood pressure, the auscultatory (listening) technique. The cuff of the sphygmomanometer is placed around the patient's upper arm and tightened enough to stop the blood flow. It is then released gradually while a health care provider listens with the stethoscope and monitors a column of liquid mercury on the sphygmomanometer. Even though we now also have digital methods that do not use mercury, blood pressure is still described in millimeters of mercury (mm Hg). Discoveries and inventions from more than one hundred years ago still form the basis of the way we measure blood pressure today.

1. Which of the following statements can be considered a statement of FACT according to the content offered in the paragraphs above?

   A) Doctor Hales was a veterinarian who measured farm animals' blood pressure in the 1700s.

   B) Doctor Korotkov invented the stethoscope, a new way to "listen" to patients' blood pressure.

   C) Doctor Riva-Rocci invented the earliest version of the sphygmomanometer, a blood pressure meter.

   D) Today, a health care provider listens with a stethoscope and monitors a column of liquid mercury on the sphygmomanometer.

2. Like a shirt cuff, a blood-pressure cuff _____.

   A) buttons at the wrist

   B) encircles part of the arm

   C) is made of heavy cloth

   D) cuts off the blood flow

3. Which sentence best summarizes the passage?

   A) "In 1733, Stephen Hales, an English clergyman with a great interest in a variety of sciences, experimented with inserting tubes into the arteries of animals such as horses to measure 'the force of the blood,' thereby becoming the first person to measure blood pressure."

   B) "In 1896, Italian physician Scipione Riva-Rocci, building on earlier noninvasive methods of measuring blood pressure, created what we still recognize as a sphygmomanometer, the conventional blood pressure meter that we use today."

   C) "The cuff of the sphygmomanometer is placed around the patient's upper arm and tightened enough to stop the blood flow."

   D) "Discoveries and inventions from more than one hundred years ago still form the basis of the way we measure blood pressure today."

4. According to the passage, what is true of mercury?

A) Using a sphygmomanometer, we still use mercury to measure blood pressure.

B) We still describe blood pressure in millimeters of mercury (mm Hg).

C) Using a stethoscope, we still use mercury to "listen" to blood pressure.

D) In invasive treatments, we still insert tubes of mercury into horses' arteries.

5. The author begins paragraph 2 with the word *fortunately* because he or she thinks we are lucky to have _____.

A) excellent health care that is not very expensive

B) ways to treat hypertension and low blood pressure

C) noninvasive methods of measuring blood pressure

D) animals that doctors can use in invasive experiments

6. What is the author's primary purpose in writing this essay?

A) to provide biographies of Hales, Riva-Rocci, and Korotkov

B) to provide a history of inventions that measure blood pressure

C) to explain how medical professionals measure blood pressure today

D) to warn readers to avoid contact with mercury, which is poisonous

Biotechnology has been revolutionizing the medical profession for decades. Pills that can transmit medical data and smartphones that can monitor asthma symptoms are among the advances being made. Now biotechnologists are taking aim at one of the most fear-inducing medical instruments in history: the hypodermic syringe needle.

The hypodermic syringe needle has been sticking patients since the 1850s, but the creation of a new, transdermal vaccine delivery system may make the needle obsolete. This new device is a pain-free vaccination tool that does not need refrigeration like some vaccines delivered via syringe. The tiny patch, which is smaller than a postage stamp, latches on to human skin via a spring-loading mechanism. The patch injects medications into the body's cells without injuring patients like hypodermic needles do. It has thousands of tiny needles—just microns in diameter—coated in the vaccine that pierce only the top layer of the skin. This causes no pain, does not require special training to deliver, and should alleviate the fear felt by the needle-phobic. Scientists believe transdermal vaccines may be able to supplant hypodermic needles for medical practitioners carrying out vaccination efforts in developing nations. While diseases like polio have been eradicated in the United States, they still affect populations in developing nations. This new technology could change the lives of millions of people around the globe.

7. Which of the following statements can the reader infer from the passage?

A) The tiny patch is a cheaper vaccine delivery system than the hypodermic syringe needle.

B) The hypodermic syringe needle is a cheaper vaccine delivery system than the tiny patch.

C) The tiny patch is a more convenient vaccine delivery system than the hypodermic syringe needle.

D) The hypodermic syringe needle is a more convenient vaccine delivery system than the tiny patch.

8. What is the author's primary purpose in writing this passage?

   A) to advise readers on ways to vaccinate patients around the globe

   B) to warn readers that hypodermic syringe needles can scare patients

   C) to tell readers some exciting news about a pain-free vaccination tool

   D) to tell a story about a doctor who travels the world vaccinating people

9. Which sentence best summarizes the passage's main idea?

   A) "Biotechnology has been revolutionizing the medical profession for decades."

   B) "Pills that can transmit medical data and smartphones that can monitor asthma symptoms are among the advances being made."

   C) "The hypodermic syringe needle has been sticking patients since the 1850s, but the creation of a new, transdermal vaccine delivery system may make the needle obsolete."

   D) "It has thousands of tiny needles—just microns in diameter—coated in the vaccine that pierce only the top layer of the skin."

10. According to the passage, how might the invention of transdermal vaccines affect people around the globe?

    A) by eradicating diseases more quickly and efficiently

    B) by making the vaccination process pleasurable rather than painful

    C) by doubling the cost of vaccines used by world health professionals

    D) by encouraging young people to enter the biotechnology field

11. In the second paragraph, what does the word part *dermal* in the word *transdermal* most likely mean?

    A) data

    B) fear

    C) needle

    D) skin

12. In the second paragraph, what does the word *supplant* mean?

    A) improve

    B) replace

    C) outlaw

    D) buy

We all know how vital blood is for the human body—it transports oxygen from our lungs, removes waste from our organs, and protects our bodies from infections. It plays an integral part in the processes of all other systems in the human body. Blood feeds and stimulates the neurological processes of the nervous system; it pumps waste products through the liver and kidneys of the excretory system; it even releases antibodies so the immune system can help destroy potentially harmful microorganisms in the body. Blood is one of the most versatile components of human life. But what exactly is blood made of?

The composition of blood can be broken down into two categories: plasma and cells. Plasma, a pale, yellowish fluid, makes up about 55 percent of the volume of our blood. It contains proteins, salts, hormones, glucose, and other elements. Plasma is the liquid that transports the cells of the blood. Cells make up the other 45 percent of our blood. The three major types of cells in the blood are red blood cells, white blood cells, and platelets. Red blood cells are shaped like doughnuts but with a depression in the center instead of a hole. They are the cells that carry oxygen around the body. There are different types of white blood cells, but they are all involved in immunity. They engulf and ingest microorganisms. And platelets are cells that are essential for blood clotting. Without platelets, we would not be able to stop bleeding once injured. Together, these major components of the blood add up to an average of about five liters of fluid in an adult human, making blood not only a vital component of the human body but a plentiful one as well.

13. What does the first paragraph mainly concern?

A) reasons why the human body needs blood

B) the composition of human blood

C) the functions of red and white blood cells

D) the amount of blood that an adult human's body contains

14. What is the author's primary purpose in writing this essay?

A) to explain how to take good care of the blood in our bodies

B) to persuade readers that blood is more important than other fluids

C) to advise readers about different treatments for blood diseases

D) to inform readers about the importance and composition of blood

15. Readers can infer that without plasma, blood could not _____.

A) clot

B) be red

C) move around

D) remain in the body

16. Which of the following statements can be considered a statement of FACT according to the content offered in the paragraphs above?

A) Blood is a fascinating topic that interests most people.

B) Blood is the most important fluid our bodies excrete.

C) Red blood cells are more important than white blood cells.

D) An adult human's body contains about five liters of blood.

17. According to the passage, what is true about platelets?

A) They make up 55 percent of the volume of our blood.

B) They carry oxygen around the body.

C) They engulf and ingest microorganisms.

D) They are essential for blood clotting.

18. What is the meaning of the word *plentiful* in the last sentence?

A) overflowing

B) abundant

C) liquid

D) reddish

The word *bacteria* typically conjures images of disease-inducing invaders that attack our immune systems. However, recent research is changing that perception; plenty of scholarly articles point to the benefits of healthy bacteria that actually reinforce the immune system. New research indicates that the "microbiome"—that is, the resident bacteria in your digestive system—may impact your health in multiple ways. Scientists who have been studying microbial DNA now believe that internal bacteria can influence metabolism, mental health, and mood. Some even suggest that imbalances in your digestive microbiome correlate with such disorders as obesity and autoimmune diseases.

It appears that a healthy, diverse microbiome is optimal, and one of the easiest ways to promote that is to eat an array of healthy foods. High-fiber foods, such as fruits and vegetables, can help your gut bacteria thrive. Some foods, for example, yogurt or kimchi, contain healthy bacteria that may confer health benefits when we consume them.

There is also increasing evidence that our national obsession with antibacterial products is detrimental to our microbiomes and thus our health. Children who live with pets and play outdoors seem to have lower rates of allergies, attention deficit disorder, and obesity. This line of research suggests that we can and should live in harmony with many of our bacterial neighbors (and residents) rather than fighting them.

19. Readers can infer from the passage that the author believes bacteria is _____.

    A) primarily harmful
    B) always good for us
    C) sometimes healthy
    D) one cause of obesity

20. What does the word *conjures* mean in the first sentence?

    A) charms
    B) mesmerizes
    C) disappears
    D) brings up

21. Which sentence best summarizes the passage's main idea?

    A) Most people think that bacteria causes diseases and attacks the human immune system.
    B) Scientists are learning that some kinds of bacteria—especially kinds that live in our digestive systems—provide health benefits.
    C) Foods such as yogurt and kimchi contain healthy bacteria, so people should eat these foods every day.
    D) In the United States, people are obsessed with antibacterial products that harm our microbiomes, thereby harming our health.

22. According to the passage, what is true of children who live with pets and play outdoors?

    A) They have good metabolisms, strong mental health, and sunny moods.
    B) They have imbalances in their digestive microbiomes, disorders such as obesity, and autoimmune diseases.
    C) They tend to eat healthy foods such as fruits, vegetables, yogurt, and kimchi.
    D) They are less likely to have allergies, attention-deficit disorders, and obesity.

23. On which two systems of the human body does the author focus in this passage?

    A) the nervous system and the excretory system
    B) the immune system and the digestive system
    C) the endocrine system and the circulatory system
    D) the hormone feedback system and the cardiovascular system

24. In the first paragraph, the phrase "resident bacteria in your digestive system" means bacteria that lives in _____.

    A) your kitchen
    B) your bathroom
    C) your stomach and intestines
    D) rotting food and garden clippings

Most people are familiar with influenza viruses, or the flu. Every winter, US citizens are bombarded with stories about flu outbreaks; stories about the flu have become as common as headlines about holiday discounts. Many people seem to think that the flu is just the far end of a continuum with the common cold at the "mild" end, and it's true that many people recover quickly having suffered relatively mild symptoms.

But influenza viruses can pose a great danger. They are constantly mutating and producing new strains that challenge our immune systems. Influenza outbreaks already lead to up to a half million deaths across the globe each year. Now imagine what would happen if an outbreak of a dangerous new strain of influenza spread across the global community. It would not be the first time the flu has caused widespread death across the world. The "Spanish flu" pandemic of 1918 killed between 50 million and 100 million people. Doctors and scientists around the world are constantly preparing for the next potential flu pandemic by analyzing strains of swine flu and avian flu that may be passed to human populations.

Strains of swine flu and avian flu have wreaked havoc on farms all over the world in the recent past. Some of these strains have the potential to be passed from domesticated animals to human beings. A form of avian flu, the H5N1 strain, is devastating to bird populations, and although it is difficult to pass to humans (and among humans), it can be deadly when it happens. Consequently, scientists are scrambling to develop a universal antivirus for all influenza strains. They are hoping that a universal vaccine can save millions of human lives.

25. What is the meaning of the word *bombarded* in the second sentence?

  A) bombed

  B) showered

  C) flooded

  D) overwhelmed

26. Which of the following is NOT listed as a detail in the passage?

  A) Many flu sufferers have fairly mild symptoms and recover quickly.

  B) Worldwide, about half a million people die of the flu each year.

  C) The 1918 "Spanish flu" killed between 50 million and 100 million people.

  D) The deadly H5N1 strain of avian flu easily passes from birds to humans.

27. Which sentence best summarizes the passage's main idea?

  A) Some people believe that the flu is just a severe version of the common cold.

  B) Flu viruses can be very dangerous because they constantly mutate and make new strains.

  C) In 1918, the worldwide "Spanish flu" epidemic killed between 50 million and 100 million people.

  D) Scientists are desperate to develop a universal antivirus for all strains of the flu.

28. What is the author's primary purpose in writing this essay?

  A) to reassure readers that probably there will be no more flu pandemics

  B) to inform readers that the flu is a serious threat to public health worldwide

  C) to persuade readers to get an influenza vaccination every year

  D) to tell a story about a human farmer who contracted swine flu

29. In the last paragraph, what does the phrase "wreaked havoc" mean?

  A) interrupted daily routines

  B) quickly mutated and spread

  C) caused devastation

  D) made a mess

30. Readers can infer from reading this passage that scientists have not yet _____.

  A) learned what causes flu epidemics and pandemics

  B) developed a universal antivirus for all influenza strains

  C) developed different vaccines for specific influenza viruses

  D) studied the causes and effects of the 1918 "Spanish flu" pandemic

Across the globe, women are, on average, outliving their male counterparts. Although this gender gap has shrunk over the last decade thanks to medical improvements and lifestyle changes, women are still expected to live four and a half years longer than men. What is the reason for this trend? The answer may lie in our sex hormones.

Men are more likely to exhibit riskier behaviors than women, especially between the ages of fifteen and twenty-four, when testosterone production is at its peak. Testosterone is correlated with aggressive and reckless behaviors that contribute to high mortality rates—think road rage, alcohol consumption, drug use, and smoking.

Estrogen, on the other hand, seems to be correlated with cholesterol levels: an increase in estrogen is accompanied by a decrease in "bad" cholesterol, which may confer advantages by reducing the risk of heart attack and stroke.

Of course, lifestyle and diet are also components of this difference in life expectancy. Men are more likely to be involved in more physically dangerous jobs, such as manufacturing or construction. They may be less likely to eat as many fruits and vegetables as their female counterparts. And they may be more likely to consume more red meat, including processed meat. These types of meats have been linked to high cholesterol, hypertension, and cancer. Better health decisions and better nutrition may eventually even the score in men's and women's life expectancy.

31. What does the second paragraph mainly concern?

A) testosterone production

B) young men's behavior

C) reasons why some men die young

D) reasons why women outlive men

32. What is the author's primary purpose in writing this essay?

A) to warn men to stop behaving riskily and eating unhealthy foods

B) to explain why, on average, women today outlive men

C) to advise readers about ways to extend life expectancy

D) to express the hope that men's life expectancy will go up

33. According to the passage, what is true about women and men?

A) In general, women care more about life expectancy than men do.

B) In general, men care more about having fun than women do.

C) In general, women take better care of themselves than men do.

D) In general, men's bodies contain more sex hormones than women's do.

34. What is the meaning of the word *correlated* in the second paragraph?

A) associated

B) incompatible

C) isolated

D) mismatched

35. Which of the following statements can be considered a statement of FACT according to the content offered in the paragraphs above?

A) Sex hormones are the sole cause of the gender gap in life expectancy.

B) Women's diets are better than men's, so women are slimmer and live longer.

C) Because of risky behavior, most men die before they reach middle age.

D) Worldwide, the average woman lives four and a half years longer than the average man.

36. Readers can infer that in the past decade, men have been _____.

A) engaging in riskier behavior

B) eating more red meat

C) making positive lifestyle changes

D) visiting their primary care doctors more often

Autism is a psychiatric condition that exists along a spectrum that ranges from mild to severe. It affects communication, social interaction, and behavior. People with severe cases of autism are likely to be unable to communicate verbally or nonverbally. They do not initiate social interactions and may be unable to respond appropriately when spoken to. They often engage in repetitive behaviors. People at this end of the spectrum need lifelong support.

On the other hand, people at the mild end of the spectrum may appear to have good social skills, making their condition less likely to be detected. However, they may struggle with social situations. They may have to be taught to make eye contact and how to engage in back-and-forth conversation with friends, peers, teachers, employers, and others. They may have extremely focused interests and require routines to stay on an even keel.

There is not a one-size-fits-all way to interact with people with autism spectrum disorder, so it is best for teachers, employers, coworkers, and friends to collaborate with these unique learners on a case-by-case basis.

37. Which sentence provides the best summary of the passage?

   A) "Autism is a psychiatric condition that exists along a spectrum that ranges from mild to severe."

   B) "People with severe cases of autism are likely to be unable to communicate verbally or nonverbally."

   C) "They may have extremely focused interests and require routines to stay on an even keel."

   D) "There is not a one-size-fits-all way to interact with people with autism spectrum disorder, so it is best for teachers, employers, coworkers, and friends to collaborate with these unique learners on a case-by-case basis."

38. According to the passage, what do people living with severe autism need?

   A) lifelong support

   B) speech therapy

   C) regimented routines

   D) quiet, dimly lighted environments

39. What is the author's primary purpose in writing this essay?

   A) to warn readers not to treat people with autism in a one-size-fits-all manner

   B) to persuade parents who suspect their child is autistic to have him or her tested

   C) to inform readers about ways people with autism behave and interact with others

   D) to advise medical practitioners about detecting autism and treating autistic patients

40. What is the meaning of the phrase "collaborate with" in the last sentence?

   A) start a business with

   B) complete a project with

   C) work with

   D) provide treatment for

41. Which of the following statements can be considered a statement of FACT according to the content offered in the paragraphs above?

   A) Most people with autism have poor communication skills and abnormal behavior.

   B) If someone engages in repetitive behaviors, he or she is almost certainly autistic.

   C) Mildly autistic people may have extremely focused interests and require routines.

   D) Treating people with autism in a one-size-fits-all way is a sure sign of ignorance.

42. According to the passage, how should we treat people who have autism?

   A) We should not expect them to communicate well with others.

   B) We should support their interest in narrowly focused topics.

   C) We should make sure they have access to speech therapy from a young age.

   D) We should not treat them as a group, but as unique individuals.

Empathy is different from mimicry or sympathy—it is neither imitating someone else's emotions nor feeling concern for their suffering. Empathy is much more complex; it is the ability to actually share and comprehend the emotions of others.

Empathy takes on two major forms: cognitive empathy and affective, or emotional, empathy. Cognitive empathy is the ability to identify and understand the emotions, mental state, or perspective of others. Affective empathy is the ability to experience an emotional response to the emotions of others—either to feel what they are feeling or to have an appropriate emotional reaction, such as feeling sad when hearing about someone's bad news. Related to affective empathy is compassionate empathy, the ability to control your own emotions while helping others deal with theirs.

Empathy is crucial for being able to respond properly in social settings. People who suffer from some psychiatric conditions, such as autism spectrum disorder, may struggle with being empathetic. Conversely, some people with very strong cognitive empathy may abuse their social understanding as a means to take advantage of others. Most people, however, choose moments and contexts in which they are likely to relate to the emotions of others.

43. The reader can infer from the passage that the author believes empathy is _____.

A) a primarily positive quality

B) similar to autism spectrum disorder

C) similar to mimicry or sympathy

D) a good quality is some cases and a bad quality in others

44. According to the passage, what is one negative use of empathy?

A) People who actually possess little or no empathy may fake this quality.

B) People who are empathetic may feel too much concern for others' suffering.

C) People with affective empathy may experience an emotional response to others' emotions.

D) People who are able to identify and understand others' emotions, mental state, or perspective may abuse this knowledge by taking advantage of others.

45. What is the author's primary purpose in writing these paragraphs?

A) to define empathy

B) to persuade readers to show more empathy

C) to advise readers about ways to appear empathetic

D) to show that empathy is a better quality than sympathy

46. Readers can infer that _____ might be most useful to a medical professional who responds to emergencies.

A) sympathy and mimicry

B) cognitive empathy

C) affective empathy

D) compassionate empathy

Ancient people saw epilepsy as a supernatural phenomenon—a divine punishment or possession by gods or demons—and feared and sometimes cast out people who exhibited frequent seizures. Even into modern times, epilepsy has been stigmatized; until recently, those who have it were thought to be affected by mental health issues. In fact, epilepsy is a neurological disorder, which means it originates in the nervous system. It is one of the most common neurological disorders, affecting millions of people across the globe, though it does disproportionately occur in adolescents.

The cause of its telltale seizures is an electrical abnormality in the brain. In about half the people diagnosed with epilepsy, there is no apparent cause for these abnormalities. Among the other half, epilepsy is associated with genetics, brain tumors, head trauma, infections, strokes, and other diverse causes. In most cases, seizures can be controlled with medication. In drug-resistant or more severe cases, surgery or brain implants can eliminate seizures or at least reduce their frequency.

Modern, sophisticated medical practices, such as different types of brain imaging, can help neurologists understand the mechanism of epilepsy. They can consequently provide the necessary medical advice and care to assist patients in their journey to maintenance and recovery. Most people with epilepsy function normally in society without much support.

47. Which of the following statements can the reader infer from the passage?

   A) Epilepsy is a supernatural phenomenon.

   B) People with epilepsy are mentally ill.

   C) Epilepsy is more common than many people think.

   D) Most people with epilepsy cannot behave normally.

48. What is the author's primary purpose in writing this essay?

   A) to advise readers on ways to treat patients who have seizures

   B) to warn readers with epilepsy to take prescribed medications regularly

   C) to explain how common epilepsy is and list its causes, symptoms, and treatment

   D) to relate a medical mystery: scientists are still searching for the causes of epilepsy

49. Which sentence best summarizes the passage's main idea?

   A) Surgery or brain implants can eliminate or reduce the frequency of epileptic seizures.

   B) Even today, ignorant people believe that epilepsy is a mental illness.

   C) Ancient people believed that epilepsy was either a divine punishment or possession by demons.

   D) Epilepsy is one of the most common neurological disorders, affecting millions of patients.

50. In the last sentence, what does the word *function* mean?

   A) job

   B) party

   C) act

   D) purpose

51. In the first sentence, what does the word *supernatural* mean?

   A) unnatural

   B) psychic

   C) having to do with superheroes in comic books

   D) having to do with supernatural beings such as gods

52. According to the passage, what causes epilepsy?

   A) an electrical abnormality in the brain

   B) a divine punishment or possession by gods or demons

   C) mental health issues

   D) different types of brain imaging

From the outside, your ears may look like floppy satellite dishes that are perpetually begging you to insert the latest wireless earphones. But did you know that your ears are more than just auditory conduits for the latest tunes? When you move past these whirlpools of flesh and cartilage and into the narrow catacombs of your inner ear, you enter an entirely different physiological realm. The ear has a secret secondary job: balance.

The labyrinth of your inner ear—literally called the bony labyrinth—is composed of a series of waxy canals and fluid-filled ducts. In addition to the cochlea, which is responsible for hearing, you have five balance receptors. Two receptors detect linear motion: one for up-and-down movement and the other for forward-and-backward or side-to-side movements. The other three receptors—the semicircular canals—work together to detect head rotation. The semicircular canals are at right angles to each other, replicating the three dimensions of the world around us. They contain a special fluid called endolymph, which "sloshes" with the movement of your head, stimulating tiny hairlike structures that then send signals to your brain about the direction you are moving—or whether you are still. So think twice before you inundate your dual-purpose ears with the deafening reverberations of the top forty—you might be throwing your whole world off balance.

53. Readers can infer from the passage that the author is trying to _____ us.

A) inform and persuade

B) inform and entertain

C) warn and persuade

D) amuse and entertain

54. Why does the author use the hyphenated word *dual-purpose* in the last sentence?

A) to show that our ears have two jobs: hearing and helping us keep our balance

B) to show that we have two ears and two eyes, but only one nose

C) to jokingly refer to a play on words: "you might be throwing your whole world off balance"

D) to rhyme with the phrase "cruel chirp hiss"

55. According to the passage, two out of five "receptors" in the ear "detect linear motion." What do the other three receptors do?

A) They allow us to hear sounds.

B) They form a bony labyrinth.

C) They detect head rotation.

D) They tell us when music is too noisy.

Vocabulary

Directions: Read the question and then choose the most correct answer.

1. Select the meaning of the underlined word in the sentence.

After her terminal diagnosis, the patient chose <u>palliative</u> care.

A) experimental

B) conventional

C) leading to a cure

D) easing symptoms

2. Which word is not spelled correctly in the context of this sentence?

During delevery, many women experience vaginal tearing.

A) delevery

B) women

C) experience

D) tearing

3. Select the word that means "increase in extent, bulk, or amount."

The search committee expanded its recruitment efforts by interviewing nurses with a range of licenses.

A) expanded

B) efforts

C) range

D) licenses

4. Select the meaning of the underlined word in the sentence.

In end-stage illnesses, palliative care is a <u>standard</u> protocol.

A) normal

B) atypical

C) legal

D) unlikely

5. Most people mistakenly believe that most nutrients are <u>absorbed</u> in the stomach.

A) broken down

B) processed

C) taken in

D) dissolved

6. Select the word that best completes the sentence.

By law, employers cannot demonstrate racial or gender _____ in the hiring of potential candidates.

A) bias

B) knowledge

C) pretense

D) selection

7. Select the meaning of the underlined word in the sentence.

Applying pressure to a wound <u>occludes</u> blood flow.

A) obstructs

B) promotes

C) damages

D) sustains

8. Select the meaning of the underlined word in the sentence.

The <u>latent</u> effects of childhood violence are only just now being studied.

A) obvious

B) lasting

C) hidden

D) misunderstood

9. Which word means "the cause of a disease or condition"?

   A) hematological

   B) etiology

   C) aegis

   D) predisposition

10. Select the meaning of the underlined word in the sentence.

    In an emergency situation, nurses will have to rely on <u>oral</u> instructions from the physician.

    A) written

    B) spoken

    C) confusing

    D) unclear

11. What best describes the term *gastric*?

    A) pertaining to the stomach

    B) pertaining to the liver

    C) an excess of liquids

    D) an episode of flatulence

12. Select the meaning of the underlined word in the sentence.

    When the dermis surrounding a splinter becomes <u>inflamed</u>, precaution must be taken to prevent infection.

    A) covered in blisters

    B) red and swollen

    C) cold and clammy

    D) blackened and numb

13. Select the meaning of the underlined word in the sentence.

    The policy of certain companies is to deny benefits for <u>preexisting</u> conditions.

    A) highly contagious

    B) life-threatening

    C) undiagnosed

    D) already occurring

14. Select the word that best completes the sentence.

    An inner ear infection can affect _____, causing patients to fall.

    A) equilibrium

    B) temperature

    C) hearing

    D) acuity

15. Select the meaning of the underlined word in the sentence.

    The expression "first, do no harm" is the <u>primary</u> rule of those who practice medicine.

    A) unspoken

    B) principal

    C) forgotten

    D) minor

16. Which word means "relating to the liver"?

    A) renal

    B) cephalic

    C) hematologic

    D) hepatic

17. Select the meaning of the underlined word in the sentence.

    The onset of diabetes can lead to high blood pressure and <u>renal</u> failure.

    A) heart

    B) kidney

    C) circulation

    D) pulmonary

18. Which best describes the term *palliative*?

    A) to feel extreme discomfort

    B) to apply pressure to a wound

    C) to experience palpitations

    D) care administered at an end-stage illness

19. Select the word that means "the growth of microorganisms in an artificial environment."

Henrietta Lacks never knew that her cancer cell cultures would be immortalized as a vaccine.

A) cancer

B) cultures

C) immortalized

D) vaccine

20. Select the meaning of the underlined word in the sentence.

While overexposure to the sun may seem innocuous, repeated sunburns can prove detrimental over time.

A) glamorous

B) healthy

C) harmless

D) worrisome

21. Select the word that means "weaken or lower."

Chemotherapy infusions depress the immune system and may necessitate additional therapy.

A) infusions

B) depress

C) necessitate

D) therapy

22. Select the meaning of the underlined word in the sentence.

Left arm pain can be an indication that a cardiac event is imminent.

A) delayed

B) avoidable

C) fatal

D) impending

23. Select the word that best completes the sentence.

The patient's _____ infection was being treated with long-term antibiotics.

A) primary

B) chronic

C) potential

D) recent

24. Select the meaning of the underlined word in the sentence.

The neurological problems, including stuttering and shaking, were the first indications of his medical disorder.

A) muscular system

B) nervous system

C) skeletal system

D) endocrine system

25. Which word means "lasting only for a short period of time"?

A) ephemeral

B) eternal

C) terminal

D) potential

26. Select the meaning of the underlined word in the sentence.

Increased longevity due to improved medical procedures has placed a strain on the Social Security program.

A) prosperity

B) health

C) nutrition

D) survival

27. Select the meaning of the underlined word in the sentence.

Therapeutic massage provides relief for sore muscles.

A) healing

B) prescribed

C) systemic

D) targeted

28. What best describes the term *primary*?

A) the final stage

B) an unlikely symptom

C) the first occurrence

D) a close race

29. Select the meaning of the underlined word in the sentence.

The internal audit revealed accounting anomalies in the medical practice's finances.

A) crimes

B) mistakes

C) irregularities

D) improvements

30. A renal stent is placed in the

A) intestine.

B) liver.

C) lungs.

D) kidney.

31. Consistent physical therapy can enhance the effects of pain relievers.

A) complicate

B) prevent

C) cancel

D) improve

32. Select the word that best completes the sentence.

The board of directors and the nurses' association negotiated an agreeable _____ on a pay increase.

A) controversy

B) complication

C) argument

D) compromise

33. Select the meaning of the underlined word in the sentence.

The long, boring lecture left the audience lethargic.

A) energized

B) curious

C) tired

D) confused

34. What best describes the term *prognosis*?

A) to forecast an outcome

B) to diagnose an illness

C) to prescribe a particular medication

D) to suggest physical therapy

35. Select the meaning of the underlined word in the sentence.

Exogenously administered hormones can be used to treat many medical conditions.

A) in high doses

B) from outside the body

C) given intravenously

D) into the digestive system

36. If a patient presents with a unilateral tendon rupture, she

A) has suffered a fall.

B) has ruptured one tendon.

C) has ruptured multiple tendons.

D) will require amputation.

37. Select the meaning of the underlined word in the sentence.

The patient's discomfort was caused by his inability to <u>void</u> his bowels.

A) ease

B) strengthen

C) empty

D) feel

38. Select the meaning of the underlined word in the sentence.

Exercise is <u>vital</u> to health.

A) contrary

B) necessary

C) unrelated

D) secondary

39. Which word means "becoming worse"?

A) lacerating

B) preexisting

C) deteriorating

D) impending

40. What best describes the term *subtle*?

A) barely perceptible

B) noticeable changes

C) frequent movement

D) observable actions

41. Select the meaning of the underlined word in the sentence.

Vaccinations prevent the acquisition and <u>transmission</u> of diseases.

A) treatment

B) study

C) passing

D) elimination

42. Vascular dementia is caused by

A) disrupted blood flow in the brain.

B) bacteria found in spinal fluid.

C) the inability to digest certain proteins.

D) the breakdown of cardiac tissue.

43. Analgesics are used for

A) going to sleep.

B) preventing infection.

C) the relief of pain.

D) inducing fever.

44. Which word is not spelled correctly in the context of this sentence?

The students failed to supress their laughter during the lecture on the causes of flatulence.

A) supress

B) laughter

C) lecture

D) flatulence

45. Select the meaning of the underlined word in the sentence.

Promotions go to those who demonstrate efficiency, <u>diligence</u>, and loyalty.

A) persistence

B) proficiency

C) resistance

D) discretion

46. Select the meaning of the underlined word in the sentence.

Wearing sunscreen for <u>dermal</u> protection is advisable.

A) facial

B) skin

C) muscular

D) eyes

47. Which word means "separate or discontinuous"?

  A) adjusted

  B) diluted

  C) uncertain

  D) discrete

48. Select the meaning of the underlined word in the sentence.

  Patients may <u>seek</u> a second opinion when they question a diagnosis.

  A) be angered by

  B) be confused

  C) fight against

  D) look for

49. Select the meaning of the underlined word in the sentence.

  Health professionals have to be <u>discreet</u> when discussing a patient's medical history.

  A) careful

  B) accurate

  C) loud

  D) exact

50. What best describes the term *precaution*?

  A) an alarm

  B) a safeguard

  C) an event

  D) a monitor

51. Select the meaning of the underlined word in the sentence.

  Advertising campaigns that show the debilitating effects of tobacco <u>deter</u> smoking.

  A) promote

  B) highlight

  C) discourage

  D) encourage

52. A label on a drug contraindicating consumption of grapefruit means eating it

  A) is discouraged.

  B) is encouraged.

  C) will benefit the patient.

  D) is mandatory.

53. Select the meaning of the underlined word in the sentence.

  The <u>volume</u> of urine generated daily by a healthy individual is 800 to 2,000 milliliters.

  A) color

  B) odor

  C) amount

  D) concentration

54. Someone who has succumbed to an illness has likely

  A) died.

  B) recovered.

  C) relapsed.

  D) responded to treatment.

55. Select the meaning of the underlined word in the sentence.

  Children often have difficulty <u>ingesting</u> tablets and require liquid medications instead.

  A) swallowing

  B) holding

  C) measuring

  D) processing

Grammar

Directions: Read the question and then choose the most correct answer.

1. Which of the following sentences is grammatically correct?

   A) If Pablo studies diligently, Pablo will probably do good on the test.

   B) If Pablo studies diligently, he will probably do well on the test.

   C) If Pablo studies diligently, he will probably do good on the test.

   D) If Pablo studies diligent, he will probably do well on the test.

2. Select the best words for the blanks in the following sentence.

   If _____ ready to leave now, please get _____ coat, and I'll pick you up at the front door.

   A) your, our

   B) you're, your

   C) you're, hour

   D) yore, you're

3. Which word is used incorrectly in the following sentence?

   The dresses that the customer wanted to return was torn and dirty, so Mr. Wu refused to accept them.

   A) customer

   B) return

   C) was

   D) them

4. Select the best words for the blanks in the following sentence.

   I felt nervous _____ happy, _____ I was about to start the next chapter of my life.

   A) nor, so

   B) or, and

   C) yet, for

   D) so, yet

5. Which of the following sentences is grammatically correct?

   A) There are too many stares; I'd rather take the elevator.

   B) There are too many steers; I'd rather take the elevator.

   C) There are too many stairs; I'd rather take the elevator.

   D) There are too many stars; I'd rather take the elevator.

6. Which word from the following sentence is an adjective?

   Do you truly believe that Heidi is prettier than Adelaide?

   A) truly

   B) believe

   C) Heidi

   D) prettier

7. Which word is used incorrectly in the following sentence?

   We are going to Los angeles on the third Wednesday in March.

   A) Los

   B) angeles

   C) third

   D) Wednesday

8. Select the best punctuation marks for the blanks in the following sentence.

   Older sister Hollie said she didn't like the way Katrina always answered _____No!" whenever Mom asked the little girl to do something_____

   A) an opening quotation mark and a period

   B) a colon and a question mark

   C) an opening quotation mark and an exclamation point

   D) a semicolon and a period

9. Which of the following sentences is grammatically correct?

A) On Monday, either my sisters or our parents picks me up at the bus station.

B) On Monday, either my sisters or our parents pick me up at the bus station.

C) On Monday, either my sisters nor our parents pick me up at the bus station.

D) On Monday, neither my sisters or our parents pick me up at the bus station.

10. Which word in the following sentence begins a dependent clause?

When I offered her a ride, Mazie accepted gratefully.

A) When

B) offered

C) Mazie

D) accepted

11. Select the best words for the blanks in the following sentence.

"Mom," I said, "no one has ever _____ from _____ his or her hair bright pink."

A) dyed, dying

B) dye, die

C) died, dyeing

D) die, dye

12. Which word from the following sentence is a conjunction?

I dislike hearing about real-life wars, yet I usually enjoy war movies.

A) dislike

B) wars

C) yet

D) I

13. Which <u>two</u> words are used incorrectly in the following sentence?

That bare in the circus is wearing a funny costume, but I'm sure the poor animal would rather go bear.

A) bare, bear

B) circus, costume

C) I'm sure

D) would rather

14. Which of the following sentences uses punctuation correctly?

A) "Please shut *up*, Matty?" I said to my cat, who had been yowling all morning.

B) "Please shut *up*, Matty," I said to my cat; who had been yowling all morning.

C) "Please shut *up*, Matty." I said to my cat: who had been yowling all morning.

D) "Please shut *up*, Matty!" I said to my cat, who had been yowling all morning.

15. Select the best word for the blank in the following sentence.

In the future, whenever I think about my mom, I _____ that she is my hero.

A) realize

B) will realize

C) will have realized

D) had realized

16. Which punctuation mark is used incorrectly in the following sentence?

"What a wonderful time we're going to have next weekend:" Ana said.

A) " (opening quotation mark)

B) ' (apostrophe)

C) : (colon)

D) . (period)

17. Select the best words for the blanks in the following sentences.

You should put _____ teaspoons of sugar in your coffee. Then you will feel _____ jittery by noon.

A) fewer, less

B) less, fewer

C) five, less

D) more, less

18. Which word is used incorrectly in the following sentence?

My most warmest jacket is made of synthetic fleece.

A) My

B) most

C) jacket

D) synthetic

19. Select the best words for the blanks in the following sentence.

Why aren't we _____ to speak _____ in the public library?

A) alloyed, aglow

B) aloud, allowed

C) allowed, aloud

D) aglow, alloyed

20. Which word is used incorrectly in the following sentence?

Oh wow, I hope we don't loose the game!

A) wow

B) hope

C) don't

D) loose

21. Which word from the following sentence <u>begins</u> the sentence's predicate?

A professor from the chemistry department is conducting a seminar on toxic chemicals.

A) A

B) from

C) is

D) on

22. Select the best word for the blank in the following sentence.

I cannot _____ this gift; it is far too expensive.

A) except

B) accede

C) expect

D) accept

23. Which word is used incorrectly in the following sentence?

Everybody in our class have applied to one or more colleges.

A) Everybody

B) our

C) have

D) colleges

24. Select the best word for the blank in the following sentence.

Who is a millennial? Researchers _____ that generation as those born between 1981 and 1996.

A) define

B) defend

C) defer

D) differ

25. Which word is used incorrectly in the following sentence?

Lots of people agrees with me when I say that cool weather is better than a heat wave.

A) Lots

B) agrees

C) weather

D) better

26. Which word from the following sentence is a comparative adjective?

Of the two dogs, Finley seems healthier than Hollie.

A) two

B) dogs

C) seems

D) healthier

27. Select the best word for the blank in the following sentence.

Juanita could _____ gone out with her friends last night, but she stayed home to study.

A) of

B) have

C) had

D) ave

28. Which word is incorrectly capitalized or lowercased in the following sentence?

On Valentine's Day my parents went out to dinner together, and on Easter Morning they seemed happy as they watched Ana and me as we examined the pretty candy and colored eggs in our baskets.

A) Day

B) Easter

C) Morning

D) Ana

29. Which of the following sentences is grammatically correct?

A) Danny leaves for work after he walked the dog.

B) Danny left for work after he will walk the dog.

C) Danny left for work after he would have walked the dog.

D) Danny left for work after he walked the dog.

30. Select the best words for the blanks in the following sentences.

The large family was too _____ to waste even a drop of milk. Each day the parents would carefully _____ a small portion of milk into each child's cereal bowl.

A) poor, pour

B) pour, poor

C) pure, purr

D) purr, pure

31. Which word from the following sentence is a contraction?

If you can't stand the heat, get out of the kitchen.

A) If

B) can't

C) heat

D) kitchen

32. Which of the following sentences uses capitalization correctly?

A) My aunt, my Mom's sister, lives in British Columbia, Canada, with her Husband.

B) My aunt, my mom's sister, lives in British Columbia, Canada, with her husband.

C) My Aunt, my mom's sister, lives in British columbia, Canada, with her husband.

D) My Aunt, my Mom's sister, lives in British Columbia, Canada, with her Husband.

33. Which of the choices is a homophone for a word in the sentence below?

The new member of the royal family has a sweet smile and a poised manner.

A) stew

B) mumble

C) hiss

D) manor

34. Which of the following sentences is grammatically correct?

A) Please take me a take-out dinner from the restaurant.

B) Please bring me a take-out dinner from the restaurant.

C) Please prepare me a take-out dinner from the restaurant.

D) Please eat me a take-out dinner from the restaurant.

35. Which word is used incorrectly in the following sentence?

During the 1960s, many college students marched in piece marches to protest the Vietnam War.

A) 1960s

B) college

C) piece

D) Vietnam

36. Which of the following sentences uses capitalization and lowercasing correctly?

A) We're going to new Mexico so we can take hikes in the desert.

B) We're going to New Mexico so we can take hikes in the Desert.

C) We're going to New mexico so we can take hikes in the desert.

D) We're going to New Mexico so we can take hikes in the desert.

37. Select the best words for the blanks in the following sentence.

Watching TV news usually angers _____ depresses me, _____ it occasionally interests me very much.

A) and, although

B) for, if

C) nor, because

D) yet, so

38. Which word from the following sentence is a subordinating conjunction?

Because San Francisco is such a beautiful city, tourists flock there all year long.

A) Because

B) San Francisco

C) tourists

D) flock

39. Select the best word for the blank in the following sentence.

The tests determined there were _____ drugs in the patient's blood.

A) unjust

B) injust

C) elicit

D) illicit

40. Which words from the following sentence form a noun phrase?

The janitor who works at our school has a very difficult job.

A) who works at our school

B) has a very difficult job

C) very difficult

D) has a . . . job

41. Which of the following sentences is grammatically correct?

   A) May I have another peace of cake?

   B) May I have another piece of cake?

   C) May I have another peas of cake?

   D) May I have another place of cake?

42. Which punctuation mark is used incorrectly in the following sentence?

   "At what time do you want to eat dinner," she asked.

   A) " (opening quotation mark)

   B) , (comma)

   C) " (closing quotation mark)

   D) . (period)

43. Which word or phrase from the following sentence is a future-tense verb?

   Promise to bring your famous brownies, and I will invite you to my birthday party.

   A) promise

   B) bring

   C) will invite

   D) birthday party

44. Which word is incorrectly capitalized or lowercased in the following sentence?

   I am leaving for the city of seattle on Saturday, June 16th.

   A) I

   B) seattle

   C) Saturday

   D) June

45. Select the best helping verbs for the blanks in the following sentence.

   Because I _____ always wanted to stay at the Grand Hotel, my great-aunt _____ generously offered to take me and my sister there for a "girls' weekend."

   A) have, has

   B) was, is

   C) have been, might

   D) will have, have

46. Which two words are used incorrectly in the following sentence?

   I accidentally through my baseball threw my neighbor's window, and it shattered.

   A) I accidentally

   B) through, threw

   C) baseball, window

   D) it shattered

47. Which of the following sentences is grammatically correct?

   A) Alexa is the smartest of the three sisters.

   B) Alexa is the smarter of the three sisters.

   C) Alexa is the most smart of the three sisters.

   D) Alexa is more smart than her two sisters.

48. Which two words are used incorrectly in the following sentence?

   Yes, you're write: we should always try hard to right sentences that are grammatically correct.

   A) Yes, you're

   B) write, right

   C) always, grammatically

   D) hard, correct

49. Which of the following sentences is grammatically correct?

A) When the club members arrives, they hang their coats on hooks.

B) When the club members arrive, they hang their coats on hooks.

C) When the club members arrived, they hang their coats on hooks.

D) When the club members had arrived, they hang their coats on hooks.

50. Which of the following sentences contains a proper noun?

A) My sister will be starting college in August.

B) I always buy bread from the bakery down the street.

C) Please close the door behind you when you leave.

D) We are thinking about buying a new car.

51. Select the best word for the blank in the following sentence.

The boy was so tired that he fell asleep as soon as his mother _____ him down on the bed.

A) laid

B) lied

C) ley

D) lei

52. Which of the choices is a homophone for a word in the sentence below?

At the ball following the royal wedding, the queen danced with her grandson, the groom.

A) bawl

B) flowing

C) winding

D) grim

53. Which of the following sentences is grammatically correct?

A) The presidential sweet includes two bedrooms, two bathrooms, a living room, and a kitchen.

B) The presidential Swede includes two bedrooms, two bathrooms, a living room, and a kitchen.

C) The presidential sweat includes two bedrooms, two bathrooms, a living room, and a kitchen.

D) The presidential suite includes two bedrooms, two bathrooms, a living room, and a kitchen.

54. Which of the following sentences is grammatically correct?

A) You can have either oatmeal nor pancakes.

B) You can't have neither oatmeal nor pancakes.

C) You can have either oatmeal or pancakes.

D) You can having either oatmeal or pancakes.

55. Which word is used incorrectly in the following sentence?

Are you aloud to stay out later on weekend nights than on school nights?

A) Are

B) aloud

C) weekend

D) school

Biology

Directions: Read the question carefully, and then choose the most correct answer.

1. As heat is added to water, why does the surface tension decrease?

   A) Hydrogen bonding decreases with heat.

   B) Ionic bonding decreases with heat.

   C) Adhesion increases with heat.

   D) Cohesion increases with heat.

2. Proteins are built from monomers called:

   A) carboxylic acids.

   B) nitrogenous bases.

   C) nucleic acids.

   D) amino acids.

3. A student places a cell with an internal concentration of 20 percent NaCl in a solution with a concentration of 10 percent NaCl. Which of the following will happen?

   A) Water will move into the cell.

   B) NaCl will move into the cell.

   C) Osmosis will cause the cell to shrink.

   D) Na^+ ions will move out of the cell.

4. In plants, what does the Calvin cycle do?

   A) convert CO_2 into a sugar

   B) produce ATP when light is not available

   C) use the energy in light to split water into hydrogen and oxygen

   D) generate ATP, NADPH, and oxygen

5. In some cells, the repeated sequences at the end of chromosomes can be extended by:

   A) DNA polymerase.

   B) DNA ligase.

   C) DNA telomerase.

   D) DNA helicase.

6. The exchange of genetic material between maternal and paternal chromosomes is:

   A) transcription.

   B) crossing over.

   C) replication.

   D) fertilization.

7. Which molecule carries the nucleotide code for a specific protein to a ribosome?

   A) DNA

   B) tRNA

   C) mRNA

   D) rRNA

8. Mitochondrial myopathy, a mitochondrial disease that leads to low energy, heart issues, and kidney problems, happens when a cytosine is replaced by a thymine. What type of mutation causes mitochondrial myopathy?

   A) frameshift mutation

   B) deletion

   C) point mutation

   D) chromosome inversion

9. The structure that holds two chromatids together is a:

   A) telomere.

   B) centromere.

   C) centrosome.

   D) nucleosome.

10. Which property of water prevents oil from being dissolved in water?

    A. adhesion

    B. polarity

    C. cohesion

    D. specific heat

11. A black mouse with the genotype BB is mated with a white mouse with the phenotype bb. All of the resulting offspring have black and white spotted fur. Which type of dominance do these genes show?

   A) Black is dominant over white.

   B) Black is codominant with white.

   C) Black is incompletely dominant over white.

   D) Black is recessive to white.

12. Which component of an amino acid is unique?

   A) the functional R group

   B) the amino group

   C) the carboxyl group

   D) the nitrogenous base

13. The hormone adrenaline attaches to receptors on the surface of the cell membrane but cannot pass through it. The molecule that activates the cellular response to adrenaline is:

   A) ATP.

   B) cyclic AMP.

   C) RNA.

   D) DNA polymerase.

14. How many molecules of CO_2 are needed to form a molecule of glucose during photosynthesis?

   A) 0

   B) 3

   C) 6

   D) 12

15. How many amino acids are synthesized by the human body?

   A) 4

   B) 20

   C) 16

   D) 64

16. During DNA replication, which enzyme adds complementary nucleotides to each of the parent strands to form the new strands of DNA?

   A) DNA polymerase

   B) DNA ligase

   C) DNA telomerase

   D) DNA helicase

17. An individual's phenotype is the:

   A) number of genes encoded by their DNA.

   B) physical traits encoded in their DNA.

   C) physical features determined by ribosomes.

   D) number of their traits repressed by modification.

18. DNA and RNA are built from monomers called:

   A) amino acids.

   B) sugars.

   C) nucleotides.

   D) polymerases.

19. The hormone that regulates the metabolism of carbohydrates is:

   A) insulin.

   B) glucose.

   C) epinephrine.

   D) cyclic AMP.

20. Which process do cells use to produce ATP when oxygen availability is low?

   A) Krebs cycle

   B) fermentation

   C) glycolysis

   D) electron transport chain

21. How many possible codons can be formed by the four nucleotides in DNA?

A) 3

B) 12

C) 20

D) 64

22. Which is the final phase of mitosis?

A) interphase

B) metaphase

C) anaphase

D) telophase

23. A student is looking at a tissue sample under a microscope and notes that very few cells are undergoing mitosis. What is the most likely explanation for his observation?

A) Cells that have recently divided through mitosis are smaller.

B) Cells in mitosis cannot be differentiated from cells in interphase.

C) Cells spend most of their lifetime in interphase.

D) Somatic cells only divide once in their lifetime.

24. Which of the following causes translation to end?

A) Anticodons bind to the ribosome.

B) Stop codons are reached by the ribosome.

C) Codons are misread by the ribosomes.

D) tRNA binds to release factor.

25. The hypothalamus produces hormones that affect cells in the pituitary gland. This is an example of:

A) a gap junction.

B) endocrine signaling.

C) intracellular transport.

D) neurotransmitters.

26. The primary purpose of fermentation is to:

A) move glucose into muscle tissues.

B) produce energy in the form of ATP.

C) store energy when oxygen is low.

D) create oxygen that can be used by muscles.

27. How can two people with a different genotype have the same phenotype?

A) One person is heterozygous for a dominant trait while the other is homozygous for the dominant trait.

B) The heterozygous individual resembles the homozygous recessive individual because the dominant trait is masked by the recessive allele.

C) One person has codominant alleles and resembles the other individual who is homozygous for the dominant trait.

D) The heterozygous individual is showing incomplete dominance, while the other is homozygous for the recessive trait.

28. What are Okazaki fragments?

A) Short fragments of DNA that result from replicating the 3' to 5' DNA strand.

B) Fragments of DNA at the end of a chromosome that are not replicated.

C) A fragment of DNA that has been unwound by DNA helicase.

D) Single-stranded DNA that has been bound by single-stranded binding protein.

29. In which phase of mitosis do the chromosomes align in the center of the cell?

A) telophase

B) anaphase

C) prophase

D) metaphase

30. An organism has a total of 36 chromosomes. How many chromosomes will be in each of the organism's gametes?

A) 9

B) 18

C) 36

D) 72

Chemistry

Directions: Read the question carefully, and then choose the most correct answer.

1. An atom is most chemically stable when:

    A) its nucleus contains no neutrons.

    B) it has more protons than electrons.

    C) its valence shell is full.

    D) the shell closest to the nucleus is full.

2. Arrange the following elements in order of increasing ionization energy: oxygen (O), silicon (Si), sulfur (S).

    A) S < Si < O

    B) Si < S < O

    C) O < S < Si

    D) S < O < Si

3. What type of intermolecular forces are exerted between two neon (Ne) atoms?

    A) London dispersion forces

    B) dipole-dipole forces

    C) hydrogen-bonding forces

    D) Van der Waals Forces

4. Which of the following processes is an example of a physical change?

    A) turning on a propane gas stove

    B) igniting a match

    C) roasting a green coffee bean

    D) sublimation of iodine

5. The air in the atmosphere is a solution composed of 78.09% nitrogen (N), 20.95% oxygen (O), 0.93% argon (Ar), and 0.04% carbon dioxide (CO_2) by volume. Which of these gases is the solvent?

    A) nitrogen (N_2)

    B) oxygen (O_2)

    C) argon (Ar)

    D) carbon dioxide (CO_2)

6. Bleach has a pH of:

    A) 7.

    B) 9.

    C) 11.

    D) 13.

7. What is the oxidation state of the sulfur atom in H_2S?

    A) −2

    B) −1

    C) +1

    D) +2

8. If 8 moles of hydrogen (H) react completely with oxygen (O), how many moles of water are produced?

    $2H_2 + O_2 \rightarrow 2H_2O$

    A) 2 moles of H_2O

    B) 4 moles of H_2O

    C) 6 moles of H_2O

    D) 8 moles of H_2O

9. What type of electrons participate in chemical reactions?

    A) innermost electrons

    B) core electrons

    C) valence electrons

    D) shielded electrons

10. Arrange the following elements in order of decreasing ionization energy: carbon (C), magnesium (Mg), silicon (Si).

    A) Si > Mg > C

    B) Mg > Si > C

    C) C > Si > Mg

    D) C > Mg > Si

11. Which of the following is acidic?

    A) soda

    B) bleach

    C) pure water

    D) baking soda solution

12. Which of the following particles is found in the nucleus of an atom?

    A) neutron

    B) valence electron

    C) core electron

    D) photon

13. Which of the following elements are considered semi-metallic or metalloids?

    A) B, Si, P, N

    B) B, Al, Ga, In

    C) B, Si, As, Te

    D) C, Si, Ge, Sn

14. Which phase change is shown by the arrow on the phase diagram below?

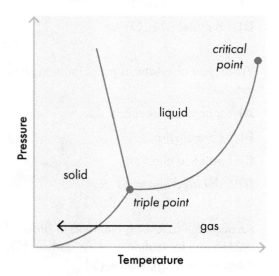

    A) sublimation

    B) freezing

    C) condensation

    D) deposition

15. What is the oxidization number of sodium (Na) in sodium oxide (Na_2O)?

    A) −1

    B) 0

    C) +1

    D) +2

16. Which of the following molecules experiences dipole-dipole intermolecular forces?

    A) N_2

    B) Cl_2

    C) HCl

    D) H_2

17. In the following acid-base reaction, which species acts as an Arrhenius acid?

$$HCl(aq) + KOH(aq) \rightarrow KCl(aq) + H_2O(l)$$

    A) HCl

    B) KOH

    C) KCl

    D) H_2O

18. One gram of pure sugar cane is added to 200 grams of coffee. In this solution, sugar is best described as:

    A) an acid.

    B) a base.

    C) the solute.

    D) the solvent.

19. If an oxygen atom acquires enough electrons to fill its valence shell, what will the charge be on the atom?

    A) O^{3-}

    B) O^{2-}

    C) O^{3+}

    D) O^{2+}

20. Which of the following molecules exhibits hydrogen bonding?

A) F_2

B) CH_3CH_2OH

C) CH_3CH_3

D) H_2

21. How many valence electrons does sulfur (S) need to obtain a full valence shell?

A) 4

B) 3

C) 2

D) 1

22. Which phase change is shown by the arrow on the phase diagram below?

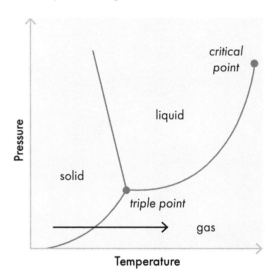

A) sublimation

B) freezing

C) condensation

D) deposition

23. How many valence electrons does nitrogen (N) have?

A) 7

B) 6

C) 5

D) 4

24. What is the oxidization number of oxygen in potassium peroxide (K_2O_2)?

A) −2

B) −1

C) 0

D) +1

25. What type of radioactive decay results in the formation of a helium nucleus?

A) Alpha decay

B) Beta decay

C) Gamma decay

D) positron emission

26. In the following chemical reaction, which species is the precipitate?

$2KI(aq) + Pb(NO_3)_2(aq) \rightarrow 2KNO_3(aq) + PbI_2(s)$

A) potassium iodide (KI)

B) lead (II) nitrate ($Pb(NO_3)_2$)

C) potassium nitrate (KNO_3)

D) lead (II) iodide (PbI_2)

27. According to the octet rule, how many bonds do elements in group 16 typically form?

A) 1

B) 2

C) 3

D) 4

28. What phase transition does water (H_2O) go through when the temperature raises from −5°C to 10°C?

A) sublimation

B) melting

C) condensation

D) deposition

29. If 6 moles of KNO_3 react completely with $PbCrO_4$, how many moles of $Pb(NO_3)_2$ are produced?

$$PbCrO_4 + 2KNO_3 \rightarrow Pb(NO_3)_2 + K_2CrO_4$$

A) 1 mole of $Pb(NO_3)_2$

B) 2 moles of $Pb(NO_3)_2$

C) 3 moles of $Pb(NO_3)_2$

D) 6 moles of $Pb(NO_3)_2$

30. Which species is oxidized in the following reaction?

$$Zn(s) + 2AgNO_3(aq) \rightarrow 2Ag(s) + Zn(NO_3)_2(aq)$$

A) zinc (Zn)

B) silver (Ag)

C) silver nitrate ($AgNO_3$)

D) zinc nitrate ($Zn(NO_3)_2$)

Anatomy and Physiology

Directions: Read the question carefully, and then choose the most correct answer.

1. Which body cavity holds the appendix?

   A) dorsal

   B) thoracic

   C) abdominal

   D) pelvic

2. What type of bones make up the wrist and the foot?

   A) irregular

   B) sesamoid

   C) short

   D) compact

3. Which of the following is the part of the larynx that produces a sound when air passes through it?

   A) olfactory membrane

   B) epiglottis

   C) elastic cartilage

   D) mucous membrane folds

4. Which vitamin is produced when the skin is exposed to sunlight?

   A) vitamin A

   B) vitamin E

   C) vitamin K

   D) vitamin D

5. Which of the following is a function of antibodies during an immune response?

   A) They store information for antibody production when the antigen reappears.

   B) They ingest the pathogen and destroy it.

   C) They produce an enzyme to coat and protect healthy cells.

   D) They bind to the antigen to neutralize pathogens.

6. Where are the adrenal glands located?

   A) in the brain

   B) on the back of the thyroid

   C) on the kidneys

   D) in the pelvic area

7. Which of the following tasks is performed by bones and joints?

   A) They store iron, calcium, and fat.

   B) They disintegrate old blood cells.

   C) They produce fluids for protection.

   D) They promote muscle growth.

8. Which layer of the stomach has cells that secrete hydrochloric acid and digestive enzymes?

   A) serosa

   B) submucosa

   C) muscularis

   D) mucosa

9. Which chamber of the heart pumps deoxygenated blood to the lungs?

   A) right atrium

   B) right ventricle

   C) left atrium

   D) left ventricle

10. Which of the following stores mature sperm?

    A) testes

    B) seminiferous tubules

    C) vas deferens

    D) epididymis

11. What is the role of nephrons in the genitourinary system?

A) filter metabolic waste from the blood

B) secrete enzymes that facilitate urine excretion

C) reabsorb protein molecules from the blood

D) collect dead cells and excrete them in urine

12. Which of the following describes the biceps when the elbow is flexed?

A) antagonist

B) agonist

C) fixator

D) synergist

13. What substance does a Schwann cell secrete that increases the speed of signals traveling to and from neurons?

A) myelin

B) cerebrospinal fluid

C) corpus callosum

D) collagen

14. Which of the following occurs when a neuron sends a single, short nerve impulse to a muscle?

A) muscle tone

B) twitch contraction

C) isometric contraction

D) temporal summation

15. Which of the following is found in the blood in high levels as a result of muscle fatigue?

A) ATP

B) platelets

C) lactic acid

D) glucose

16. In which part of the kidneys are the collecting ducts located?

A) renal cortex

B) renal medulla

C) renal pelvis

D) renal calculus

17. Which part of the brain coordinates the muscle actions required for complex movement?

A) cerebrum

B) hypothalamus

C) cerebellum

D) pineal gland

18. Which of the following is the largest bone in the human body?

A) femur

B) humerus

C) scapula

D) tibia

19. What is the role of the fallopian tubes in the female reproductive system?

A) They produce and release eggs.

B) They secrete hormones that regulate pregnancy.

C) They prevent foreign substances from entering the uterus.

D) They transport eggs from the ovaries to the uterus.

20. Which blood vessels are closest to the cells of the body, making the exchange of nutrients, gases, and cellular waste possible?

A) veins

B) arteries

C) capillaries

D) venules

21. Which lobe of the liver spirals around the inferior vena cava?

    A) left

    B) right

    C) caudate

    D) quadrate

22. Which of the following is the calcified tissue that forms the solid inner part of the teeth?

    A) enamel

    B) dentin

    C) pulp

    D) cementum

23. Which of the following are the hollow spaces in the brain that are filled with cerebrospinal fluid?

    A) canals

    B) sacs

    C) ventricles

    D) pouches

24. Which of the following hormones is produced by the ovaries?

    A) progesterone

    B) growth hormone

    C) follicle-stimulating hormone

    D) dopamine

25. What does the diaphragm do during inspiration?

    A) It relaxes.

    B) It contracts.

    C) It vibrates.

    D) It expands.

26. A physician makes a diagnosis of a right tibia fracture. Which part of the body is affected?

    A) upper arm

    B) lower arm

    C) upper leg

    D) lower leg

27. Which chamber of the heart pumps oxygenated blood throughout the body?

    A) right atrium

    B) right ventricle

    C) left atrium

    D) left ventricle

28. Which of the following regulates the fight-or-flight response to stimuli?

    A) central nervous system

    B) somatic nervous system

    C) parasympathetic nervous system

    D) sympathetic nervous system

29. Which of the following is a function of the pancreas?

    A) It absorbs the nutrients that pass through the small intestine.

    B) It stores and releases glycogen to help digest food.

    C) It secretes insulin to control blood sugar level.

    D) It filters waste from the blood and produces plasma components.

30. Which of the following muscles is found in the lower leg?

    A) gluteus maximus

    B) pectoralis major

    C) gastrocnemius

    D) latissimus dorsi

Physics

Directions: Read the question carefully, and then choose the most correct answer.

1. X-rays are what type of wave?

    A) mechanical

    B) electromagnetic

    C) longitudinal

    D) transverse

2. What is the magnitude of the force of friction on a box of books with a mass of 100 kilograms pulled across a wooden floor with a coefficient of kinetic friction of 0.30?

    A) 30 N

    B) 294 N

    C) 882 N

    D) 980 N

3. Which of the following are NOT electromagnetic waves?

    A) infrared light

    B) sonar

    C) microwaves

    D) gamma rays

4. What constant force is required to act on a 1 kilogram mass to do 850 joules of work over a distance of 100 meters?

    A) 0.85 N

    B) 8.5 N

    C) 85 N

    D) 850 N

5. What is the kinetic energy of an electron with velocity of 1000 kilometers per second and a mass of 9.1×10^{-31} kilograms?

    A) 4.55×10^{-25} J

    B) 4.55×10^{-19} J

    C) 4.55×10^{19} J

    D) 4.55×10^{25} J

6. A ball is thrown straight down off the top of a tall building with an initial speed of 5 meters per second. How long does it take the ball to fall the 10 meter distance?

    A) 0.501 s

    B) 0.755 s

    C) 0.899 s

    D) 1.01 s

7. A wrench is dropped from rest on the surface of Mars from a height of 2 meters. If the acceleration due to gravity on Mars is 3.8 meters per second squared, with what speed does the wrench hit the ground?

    A) 3.8 m/s

    B) 3.9 m/s

    C) 7.6 m/s

    D) 15.2 m/s

8. How much kinetic energy does a 0.145-kilogram baseball have if it is pitched at 100 miles per hour?

    A) 3.24 J

    B) 145 J

    C) 324 J

    D) 14,486 J

9. A rock is thrown at 30 meters per second on Earth. The same rock is then thrown at 30 meters per second on the moon, where $g_M = \frac{g_E}{6}$. How does the kinetic energy of the rock change?

    A) It does not change.

    B) It halves.

    C) It doubles.

    D) It quadruples.

10. Three 5 ohm resistors are connected in series with a 15 volt power supply. What current will an ammeter read flowing through this circuit?

A) 0.07 A

B) 1 A

C) 3 A

D) 15 A

11. What is the total resistance of a 2 ohm, 5 ohm, and 10 ohm parallel combination of resistors?

A) 0.4 Ω

B) 0.5 Ω

C) 1.25 Ω

D) 17 Ω

12. In free space, a 10 kilogram bowling ball is pushed with a constant force of 15 newtons. What is its acceleration?

A) 0.67 m/s^2

B) 1.5 m/s^2

C) 15 m/s^2

D) 150 m/s^2

13. What is the momentum of a 3 gram bullet moving with a velocity of 300 meters per second?

A) 0.9 kg m/s

B) 1 kg m/s

C) 9 kg m/s

D) 90 kg m/s

14. A 1 ampere current flowing through the human body can be fatal. For a body with 100 kiloohms of resistance, what potential difference is required to reach the fatal current?

A) 0.100 V

B) 100 V

C) 100,000 V

D) 100,000,000 V

15. An amusement park Gravitron ride presses riders against the wall with three times their weight. What is the centripetal acceleration of the ride?

A) 3 m/s^2

B) 3.4 m/s^2

C) 9.8 m/s^2

D) 29.4 m/s^2

16. What is the change in kinetic energy of a car with a mass of 1200 kilograms as it speeds up from 11.2 meters per second on a residential street to 29.1 meters per second on a highway?

A) 75,264 J

B) 432,822 J

C) 508,086 J

D) 583,350 J

17. A 5 kilogram rifle fires a 3 gram bullet at 300 meters per second. What is the recoil velocity of the rifle?

A) 18 cm/s, in the opposite direction of the bullet

B) 18 cm/s, in the same direction as the bullet

C) 50 cm/s, in the opposite direction of the bullet

D) 50 cm/s, in the same direction as the bullet

18. A 5 kilogram bowling ball falls from an open window 10 meters above the ground. Which of the following correctly describes the work done by gravity?

A) The work is done in the down direction.

B) The work is done in the up direction.

C) The work is done perpendicular to motion.

D) The work is a scalar that has no direction.

19. A merry-go-round accelerates at a constant 1.5 radians per second squared starting from rest. What is its angular velocity after 5 seconds?

A) 5 rad/s

B) 7.5 rad/s

C) 10 rad/s

D) 12.5 rad/s

20. A siren changes its frequency from 10,000 hertz to 1000 hertz. What happens to the pitch of the sound heard by a person nearby?

A) It stays the same.

B) It increases.

C) It decreases.

D) It becomes inaudible.

21. What is the wavelength of a wave traveling with a speed of 343 meters per second and oscillating 600 times per second?

A) 0.57×10^{-5} m

B) 2.06×10^{-5} m

C) 5.7×10^{-1} m

D) 2.06×10^{5} m

22. How close to one another do two electrons need to be placed to generate a repulsive force of 1 newton?

A) 1.51×10^{-11} m

B) 1.51×10^{-12} m

C) 1.51×10^{-13} m

D) 1.51×10^{-14} m

23. The earth ($M_{Earth} = 6 \times 10^{24}$ kg) and Moon ($M_{Moon} = 7.4 \times 10^{22}$ kg) are separated by 384,000 kilometers. What is the force of gravity between the earth and moon?

A) 7.7×10^{8} N

B) 2×10^{20} N

C) 2×10^{22} N

D) 7.7×10^{28} N

24. Two waves, one with an amplitude of 2.5 meters and the other with an amplitude of 0.3 meters, destructively interfere. What is the minimum possible amplitude that can be achieved?

A) 0 m

B) 0.3 m

C) 2.2 m

D) 2.5 m

25. Electromagnetic waves propagate at the speed of light. Gamma rays are electromagnetic waves with the shortest wavelength; radio waves have the longest. What happens to the period of oscillations going from gamma rays to radio waves?

A) The period increases.

B) The period decreases.

C) The period remains the same.

D) Electromagnetic waves do not have a period of oscillation.

26. A 15-newton force is applied at an angle of 180 radians to the radial direction of a 20 centimeter wrench. What is the applied torque?

A) 0 N m

B) 3 N m

C) 10 N m

D) 30 N m

27. If a light ray passes from air into a material with an index of refraction of 1.25, what is true about the transmitted light ray?

A) It will be deflected toward the normal.

B) It will be deflected away from the normal.

C) It will not be deflected.

D) It will not be transmitted into the material.

28. An electric field of 3×10^4 newtons per coulomb is produced in a laboratory. What is the magnitude of the force exerted on a 7 millicoulomb charge placed in this field?

A) 2.1 N

B) 21 N

C) 210 N

D) 4.3×10^6 N

29. Two 9 volt batteries are wired in series. If they are connected to a 200 ohm resistor, what current will flow in the circuit?

A) 0.09 A

B) 0.9 A

C) 0.018 A

D) 0.18 A

30. The same object is dropped from rest from the same height, first on Earth, then later on the moon. Which two variables remain constant in the equation $v_f^2 = v_i^2 + 2ad$?

A) v_f, v_i

B) v_f, a

C) v_i, a

D) v_i, d

ANSWER KEY

MATHEMATICS

1. **A)**

$$\frac{2\ mg}{kg} \times \frac{1\ kg}{2.2\ lb} \times 165\ lb = \textbf{150 mg}$$

2. **C)**

Military times less than 1200 correspond directly to a.m. on the 12-hour clock.

0500 = **5:00 a.m.**

3. **D)**

part = whole × percent

40 × 0.25 = 10

40 − 10 = **30**

4. **B)**

$$\frac{75\ mi}{hr} \times \frac{1\ hr}{60\ min} \times 24\ min = \textbf{30 mi}$$

5. **C)**

If Sandra saves $125, that amount would be multiplied by the number of months, x, which would be added to the $1400 she began with.

6. **C)**

$$\frac{2}{5} + \frac{3}{4} + \frac{7}{10} = \frac{8}{20} + \frac{15}{20} + \frac{14}{20} = \frac{37}{20} = 1\frac{17}{20}$$

7. **B)**

26.5 + 18.9 + 35.1 = **80.5**

8. **B)**

1800 − 591 = **1209**

9. **B)**

3500 ÷ 325 ≈ 10.8, so **10 tablets** will stay under the limit.

10. **D)**

−20 + (−25) = **−45**

11. **D)**

−7 + 15 = **8**

12. **A)**

= (9 + 6) × (2 − 5)

= 15 × (−3)

= **−45**

13. **B)**

$-10 + 15 \div (-5) \times 3^2 - 10^2$

= −10 + 15 ÷ (−5) × 9 − 100

= −10 + (−3) × 9 − 100

= −10 + (−27) − 100

= **−137**

14. **A)**

$$\frac{1}{3} + \frac{3}{5} = \frac{5}{15} + \frac{9}{15} = \frac{14}{15}$$

15. **D)**

23 + 19.09 + 4.7 = **46.79**

16. **A)**

$$whole = \frac{part}{percent}$$

$$\frac{26}{0.40} = \textbf{65}$$

17. **A)**

part = whole × percent

1975 × 0.35 = 691.25

1975 − 691.25 = **1283.75**

18. **D)**

$$\frac{1}{4} = \frac{x}{20}$$

4x = 20

x = 5

19. **A)**

$$\frac{2}{9} = 0.\overline{2}$$

$$\frac{1}{4} = 0.25$$

0.29 > 0.26 > 0.25 > 0.22

20. **C)**

$$\frac{2}{7} = \frac{72}{x}$$

$$2x = 504$$

x = 252

21. **D)**

$$\text{whole} = \frac{\text{part}}{\text{percent}}$$

$$\frac{96}{0.20} = \textbf{480}$$

22. **D)**

If Bob pays $158 per month, the amount he has paid on his bill would be 158 times the number of months, x. Bob's balance will be decreased by the amount he has paid.

23. **B)**

$$19 \text{ cm} \times \frac{1 \text{ in}}{2.54 \text{ cm}} \approx \textbf{7.5 in}$$

24. **A)**

Multiply coefficients and add exponents.

$$(3x^2y^5)(4x^4y)$$

$$= \textbf{12}x^\textbf{6}y^\textbf{6}$$

25. **D)**

1 year = 52 weeks

$$1.1 \times 52 = 57.2 \approx \textbf{57}$$

26. **B)**

To convert p.m. times to military time, add 1200.

$$1030 + 1200 = \textbf{2230}$$

27. **D)**

$$57.5 \div 8 = 7.1875 \approx \textbf{7.2}$$

28. **C)**

$$\frac{46 \div 2}{100 \div 2} = \frac{\textbf{23}}{\textbf{50}}$$

29. **A)**

$$4(a^2 + 2a) - 3(a + 7)$$

$$= 4a^2 + 8a - 3a - 21$$

$$= \textbf{4}a^\textbf{2} + \textbf{5}a - \textbf{21}$$

30. **A)**

$$6.5 \text{ ft} \times \frac{0.3048 \text{ m}}{1 \text{ ft}} = \textbf{1.98 m}$$

31. **B)**

$$2x - 3y = -7$$

$$2x = 3y - 7$$

$$x = \frac{\textbf{3}y - \textbf{7}}{\textbf{2}}$$

32. **A)**

Let x equal the amount of money Rosie needs to save each week.

$$145 + 5x = 520$$

$$5x = 375$$

x = 75

33. **C)**

$$65 \text{ kg} \times \frac{2.2 \text{ lb}}{1 \text{ kg}} = \textbf{143 lb}$$

34. **B)**

$$\text{whole} = \frac{\text{part}}{\text{percent}}$$

$$\frac{36}{0.75} = \textbf{48}$$

35. **C)**

1 year = 12 months

$$\$1530 \div 12 = \textbf{\$127.50}$$

36. **B)**

$$7x + 3 = 38$$

$$7x = 35$$

x = 5

37. **D)**

$$\$3.49 \times 6 = \$20.94$$

$$\$10.49 \times 3 = \$31.47$$

$$\$20.94 + \$31.47 = \$52.41$$

$$\$100.00 - \$52.41 = \textbf{\$47.59}$$

38. **C)**

$$3 \times 6\frac{2}{5} = \frac{3}{1} \times \frac{32}{5} = \frac{96}{5} = 19\frac{1}{5}$$

$$100 - 19\frac{1}{5} = \frac{500}{5} - \frac{96}{5} = \frac{404}{5} = \textbf{80}\frac{\textbf{4}}{\textbf{5}}$$

39. D)

$$\frac{10}{21} \times \frac{14}{25} = \frac{2}{3} \times \frac{2}{5} = \frac{4}{15}$$

40. D)

Multiply coefficients, add exponents.

$6a^3b^2(5a^2b^5c) = \mathbf{30a^5b^7c}$

41. B)

percent = $\frac{part}{whole}$

$\frac{88}{160} = 0.55 = \mathbf{55\%}$

42. C)

$8 \div 1\frac{1}{3} = \frac{8}{1} \div \frac{4}{3} = \frac{8}{1} \times \frac{3}{4} = \mathbf{6}$

43. D)

$2.7 \times \$5.40 = \mathbf{\$14.58}$

44. C)

$6.2 \times 8.5 = \mathbf{52.7}$

45. A)

$24\frac{1}{2} \div 3\frac{1}{2} = \frac{49}{2} \div \frac{7}{2} = \frac{49}{2} \times \frac{2}{7} = \frac{49}{7} = \mathbf{7}$

46. B)

Multiply by the least common denominator to clear the fractions.

$(12)\frac{x}{3} + (12)\frac{7}{6} = (12)\frac{5}{2}$

$4x + 14 = 30$

$4x = 16$

$\mathbf{x = 4}$

47. D)

$\frac{2}{175} = \frac{5}{x}$

$2x = 875$

$\mathbf{x = 437.5}$

48. B)

$2 \div 3 = 0.\overline{6} \approx \mathbf{0.67}$

49. C)

$\frac{1.50}{100} = \frac{x}{85,000}$

$100x = 127,500$

$\mathbf{x = 1275}$

50. C)

$100\% - 10\% = 90\%$

whole = $\frac{part}{percent}$

$\frac{171}{0.90} = \mathbf{190}$

51. B)

$0.8 + 0.49 + 0.89 = 2.18$

$2.5 - 2.18 = \mathbf{0.32}$

52. B)

$2112 \div 11 = \mathbf{192}$

53. C)

$4.6 + 4.8 + 5.3 + 5.2 + 6 = 25.9$

$25.9 \div 5 = \mathbf{5.18}$

54. A)

$5.63 > 5.627 > 5.6$

$5.63 + 5.627 - 5.6 = \mathbf{5.657}$

55. D)

$3 \div 16 = \mathbf{0.1875}$

1. **C)**

In the second paragraph, the author writes, "In 1896, Italian physician Scipione Riva-Rocci ... created what we still recognize as a sphygmomanometer, the conventional blood pressure meter that we use today."

2. **B)**

In the third paragraph, the author writes, "The cuff of the sphygmomanometer is placed around the patient's upper arm and tightened enough to stop the blood flow."

3. **D)**

The last sentence provides an adequate summary of the passage. The other sentences provide specific details from the passage.

4. **B)**

The author writes, "Even though we now also have digital methods that do not use mercury, blood pressure is still described in millimeters of mercury (mm Hg)." There are no sentences supporting the other claims.

5. **C)**

In the first paragraph, the author describes an invasive procedure used to measure animals' blood pressure. In the second paragraph, the author writes, "Fortunately, we no longer have to use such invasive methods to study blood pressure." The author thinks it is a good thing that blood pressure can be measured less invasively.

6. **B)**

Beginning in 1733 and continuing through the present day, the author explains how blood pressure measuring techniques and instruments have evolved.

7. **C)**

The author writes, "This new device is a pain-free vaccination tool that does not need refrigeration like some vaccines delivered via syringe. The tiny patch ... injects medications into the body's cells without injuring patients like hypodermic needles do." Readers can infer from this that using a patch is more convenient than using a hypodermic syringe needle for two reasons: 1) the patch does not need

refrigeration, and 2) the patch is not painful, so it does not scare patients. The passage does not mention cost.

8. **C)**

The author seems excited about the new pain-free vaccination tool that biotechnology has produced. The passage is not primarily cautionary or advisory. The author does not tell a story about a specific doctor.

9. **C)**

The passage is mainly about the "new, transdermal vaccine delivery system." The other sentences give details from the passage.

10. **A)**

In the second paragraph, the author writes, "Scientists believe transdermal vaccines may be able to supplant hypodermic needles for medical practitioners carrying out vaccination efforts in developing nations. While diseases like polio have been eradicated in the United States, they still affect populations in developing nations. This new technology could change the lives of millions of people around the globe."

11. **D)**

In the second paragraph, the author writes, "[T]he creation of a new, transdermal vaccine delivery system may make the needle obsolete .... The tiny patch ... latches on to human skin via a spring-loading mechanism." Readers can infer that *trans* means "across or through," and *dermal* refers to human skin.

12. **B)**

In the first and second paragraphs, the author writes, "Now biotechnologists are taking aim at one of the most fear-inducing medical instruments in history: the hypodermic syringe needle. The hypodermic syringe needle has been sticking patients since the 1850s, but the creation of a new, transdermal vaccine delivery system may make the needle obsolete." Readers can infer that the author thinks the "new, transdermal vaccine delivery system" will replace—or supplant—the hypodermic syringe needle, making the scary needle outdated and no longer necessary.

13.   A)

The first paragraph explains "how vital blood is for the human body." The word *vital* means "essential, necessary."

14.   D)

The primary purpose of the essay is to inform; its focus is the importance and composition of blood. It is not persuasive, and it does not give advice. It does not mention blood diseases.

15.   C)

In the second paragraph, the author writes, "Plasma, a pale, yellowish fluid, makes up about 55 percent of the volume of our blood. It contains proteins, salts, hormones, glucose, and other elements. Plasma is the liquid that transports the cells of the blood." Readers can infer from this that the other components of blood (cells) need liquid to move around the body.

16.   D)

In the last sentence, the author writes, "[B]lood [adds] up to an average of about five liters of fluid in an adult human, making blood not only a vital component of the human body but a plentiful one as well."

17.   D)

In the second paragraph, the author writes, "[P] latelets are cells that are essential for blood clotting. Without platelets, we would not be able to stop bleeding once injured." The other sentences describe other components of blood: plasma and red and white blood cells.

18.   B)

In the last sentence, the author writes, "Together, these major components of the blood add up to an average of about five liters of fluid in an adult human, making blood not only a vital component of the human body but a plentiful one as well." Readers can infer that the author means that five liters is a lot—in other words, plentiful.

19.   C)

In the first paragraph, the author states that "recent research is changing [the perception that bacteria causes diseases and attacks the immune system]; plenty of scholarly articles point to the benefits of

healthy bacteria that actually reinforce the immune system."

20.   D)

The first sentence reads, "The word *bacteria* typically conjures images of disease-inducing invaders that attack our immune systems." Readers can infer that by "conjures images," they author means "brings up images" (in other words, causes people to imagine).

21.   B)

As this sentence shows, the passage is mainly about healthy bacteria. The other sentences provide details from the passage.

22.   D)

In paragraph 3, the author writes, "Children who live with pets and play outdoors seem to have lower rates of allergies, attention deficit disorder, and obesity."

23.   B)

Readers can infer that bacteria affects the immune system and the digestive system more than other systems in the body.

24.   C)

In the first paragraph, the author writes, "New research indicates that the 'microbiome'—that is, the resident bacteria in your digestive system—may impact your health in multiple ways. Scientists who have been studying microbial DNA now believe that internal bacteria can influence metabolism, mental health, and mood." Readers can infer that "resident bacteria" and "internal bacteria" both refer to bacteria that lives in people's bodies.

25.   D)

In the second sentence, the author writes, "Every winter, US citizens are bombarded with stories about flu outbreaks; stories about the flu have become as common as headlines about holiday discounts." The context shows that the author uses the phrase "are bombarded with stories" to mean "are overwhelmed by a great number of disturbing news stories."

26.   D)

The passage does not contain this detail. The passage says that the H5N1 strain of avian flu is "devastating to bird populations" but "difficult to pass to humans (and among humans)." However, in the rare cases in which this flu strain *does* pass from birds to humans, "it can be deadly."

27. B)

The passage is mainly about the dangers posed by constantly changing strains of the influenza virus. The other sentences give details from the passage.

28. B)

The passage is primarily informative, but there is an underlying cautionary message to take flu epidemics seriously: the flu kills many thousands of people each year. The passage is not reassuring or persuasive, and it does not tell a story about a specific person who caught swine flu from a pig.

29. C)

In the first sentence of the last paragraph, the author writes, "Strains of swine flu and avian flu have wreaked havoc on farms all over the world in the recent past." Readers can infer that swine flu and avian flu kill many farm animals (and even some people), so in this sentence, "wreaked havoc" means "caused devastation."

30. B)

In the last paragraph, the author writes, "[S]cientists are scrambling to develop a universal antivirus for all influenza strains. They are hoping that a universal vaccine can save millions of human lives." Readers can infer that a universal antivirus has not yet been discovered or developed.

31. C)

The first sentence in the second paragraph states the paragraph's main idea: "Men are more likely to exhibit riskier behaviors than women, especially between the ages of fifteen and twenty-four, when testosterone production is at its peak."

32. B)

The primary purpose of the essay is to explain or give reasons; its focus is the gender gap in life expectancy. It is not advisory or cautionary, and it does not express the author's hopes.

33. C)

In the second paragraph, the author implies that young women do not behave as riskily as young men do. In the fourth paragraph, the author states

that men "may be less likely to eat as many fruits and vegetables as their female counterparts. And [men] may be more likely to consume more red meat, including processed meat. These types of meats have been linked to high cholesterol, hypertension, and cancer." In general, the author describes women as more sensible than men when it comes to physical safety and a healthy lifestyle.

34. A)

In the third paragraph, the author writes, "Estrogen ... seems to be correlated with cholesterol levels: an increase in estrogen is accompanied by a decrease in 'bad' cholesterol." Readers can infer that *correlated* means "linked or associated."

35. D)

In the first paragraph, the author writes, "Across the globe, women are, on average, outliving their male counterparts. Although this gender gap has shrunk over the last decade, ... women are still expected to live four and a half years longer than men." The passage does not support any of the other statements.

36. C)

In the first paragraph, the author writes that the "gender gap has shrunk over the last decade thanks to medical improvements and lifestyle changes." Readers can infer from this that the average man has a healthier lifestyle than he did over ten years ago.

37. A)

The first sentence provides an adequate summary of the passage overall. The other choices provide specific details from the passage.

38. A)

In the first paragraph, the author writes, "People with severe cases of autism ... need lifelong support."

39. C)

The primary purpose of the essay is to inform; its focus is on ways that people with autism behave. It is not primarily persuasive, cautionary, or advisory, although the last paragraph gives advice about interacting with people with autism spectrum disorder.

40. C)

In the last sentence, the author writes that "it is best for teachers, employers, coworkers, and friends to collaborate with [people with autism] on a case-by-case basis." Readers can infer that by "collaborate with," the author means "work with" or "interact with."

41. C)

In the second paragraph, the author writes that "people at the mild end of the spectrum ... may have extremely focused interests and require routines to stay on an even keel."

42. D)

In the last paragraph, the author writes, "There is not a one-size-fits-all way to interact with people with autism spectrum disorder, so it is best for teachers, employers, coworkers, and friends to collaborate with these unique learners on a case-by-case basis."

43. A)

In the last paragraph, the author states, "Empathy is crucial for being able to respond properly in social settings." The reader can infer from this information that empathy is a positive quality that people need in order to treat others in a socially acceptable manner.

44. D)

In the last paragraph the author writes, "[S]ome people with very strong cognitive empathy may abuse their social understanding as a means to take advantage of others." Earlier the author defines "cognitive empathy" as "the ability to identify and understand the emotions, mental state, or perspective of others."

45. A)

The primary purpose of the essay is to inform; its focus is on the definition of empathy. It is not persuasive or advisory. The author does not set out to show that one quality is better than another.

46. D)

In the second paragraph, the author defines compassionate empathy as "the ability to control your own emotions while helping others deal with theirs." Readers can infer that this kind of empathy would be useful to medical professionals who have

to remain calm in emergencies (when patients and bystanders are often upset).

47. C)

In the first paragraph, the author writes that epilepsy "is one of the most common neurological disorders, affecting millions of people across the globe." There is no support for any of the other claims.

48. C)

The primary purpose of the essay is to explain; its general focus is on epilepsy. It is not primarily cautionary or advisory. The author does not focus on unexplained causes of epilepsy, though he or she does mention that "an electrical abnormality in the brain" causes seizures, and "[i]n about half the people diagnosed with epilepsy, there is no apparent cause for these abnormalities."

49. D)

The passage tells how common epilepsy is and describes its causes, symptoms, and treatment. The other sentences give details from the passage.

50. C)

In the last sentence, the author writes, "Most people with epilepsy function normally in society without much support." Readers can use context to infer that by the phrase "function normally in society," the author means "lead normal lives" or "act as others [who do not have epilepsy] do."

51. D)

In the first paragraph, the author writes, "Ancient people saw epilepsy as a supernatural phenomenon—a divine punishment or possession by gods or demons—and feared and sometimes cast out people who exhibited frequent seizures." Readers can infer that by "a supernatural phenomenon," the author means an occurrence involving supernatural beings such as gods or demons.

52. A)

In the second paragraph, the author writes, "The cause of [epilepsy's] telltale seizures is an electrical abnormality in the brain. In about half the people diagnosed with epilepsy, there is no apparent cause for these abnormalities. Among the other half, epilepsy is associated with genetics, brain tumors, head trauma, infections, strokes, and other diverse causes."

53. B)

The passage is primarily informative. However, the author uses humorous language like "floppy satellite dishes" and "the deafening reverberations of the top forty" to entertain readers.

54. A)

The author is referring to the fact that our ears have another purpose in addition to hearing.

55. C)

In the second paragraph, the author writes, "[Y]ou have five balance receptors. Two receptors detect linear motion .... The other three receptors ... work together to detect head rotation."

1. **D)**

Palliative care is administered for the relief of pain and easing of symptoms.

2. **A)**

Delevery should be spelled "delivery."

3. **A)**

Expanded means "to increase in extent, bulk, or amount."

4. **A)**

Standard means "normal, regular, or widely used."

5. **C)**

Absorb means "to take in or assimilate."

6. **A)**

Bias is "a general unfair preference or dislike."

7. **A)**

Occlude means "to shut in or out; to close; obstruct passage."

8. **C)**

Latent means "hidden or dormant."

9. **B)**

Etiology means "the cause of a disease or condition."

10. **B)**

Oral means "spoken, not written; pertaining to the mouth."

11. **A)**

Gastric means "pertaining to the stomach."

12. **B)**

Inflammation is a cellular response to injury that leads to swelling, redness, and heat in the area of injury.

13. **D)**

A preexisting condition is one that is "already in place; already occurring."

14. **A)**

Equilibrium means "sense of balance."

15. **B)**

Primary means "first or most important."

16. **D)**

Hepatic means "relating to the liver."

17. **B)**

Renal means "pertaining to the kidneys."

18. **D)**

Palliate means "to lessen symptoms without treating the underlying cause"; palliative care is that which is administered at an end-state illness.

19. **B)**

Culture means "the growth of microorganisms in an artificial environment."

20. **C)**

Innocuous takes its origins from the Latin in–, meaning "not," and nocuus, meaning "injurious." Hence, the word means "not injurious or not harmful."

21. **B)**

Depress means "weaken or lower."

22. **D)**

Imminent means "about to happen in the very near future."

23. **B)**

Chronic means "persistent or recurring over a long period of time."

24. **B)**

Neurologic means "dealing with the nervous system."

25. A)

Ephemeral means "transitory" or "lasting only a short while."

26. D)

Longevity means "having a long life."

27. A)

Therapeutic means "having a beneficial or healing effect."

28. C)

Something that is *primary* is "first in order of importance."

29. C)

An *anomaly* is "a deviation from the norm or an irregularity."

30. D)

Renal means "pertains to the kidneys."

31. D)

Enhance means "to improve."

32. D)

A *compromise* is "an agreement reached by mutual concessions."

33. C)

Lethargic means "sluggish or sleepy."

34. A)

A *prognosis* is "a forecast or prediction of an outcome."

35. B)

Exogenous means "something produced outside the body."

36. B)

The prefix *uni–* means "one." *Unilateral* means "referring only to one side."

37. C)

Void means "to empty or evacuate."

38. B)

Vital means "pertaining to life; essential to existence or well-being."

39. C)

Deteriorating means "becoming worse."

40. A)

Subtle means "understated; not obvious" and therefore barely perceptible or barely able to be noticed.

41. C)

The *transmission* of a disease means "the act or result of sending (passing) something along or onward to a recipient or destination."

42. A)

Dementia is a neurological disorder characterized by confusion and loss of memory. *Vascular* means "pertaining to blood vessels." *Vascular dementia* results from blood flow to the brain being constricted or cut off.

43. C)

An *analgesic* is a drug used to reduce pain without loss of consciousness.

44. A)

Supress should be spelled "suppress."

45. A)

Diligence is the noun form of *diligent,* which means "persistent and hardworking."

46. B)

Dermal means of "or relating to the skin."

47. D)

Discrete means "separate or discontinuous."

48. D)

Seek means "to look for."

49. A)

Discreet means "careful in speech or action to avoid causing offense or injury."

50. B)

A *precaution* is "an action in advance to ensure safety or benefit; a safeguard."

51. C)

Deter means "to prevent or discourage."

52. A)

Contraindication means "discouragement of the use of a treatment" due to possible side effects.

53. C)

Volume means "the amount of space occupied by a substance."

54. A)

In medical terms, *succumb* is used to indicate death due to disease or injury.

55. A)

Ingest means "to take into the body for digestion."

1.   B)

In choice B, the singular masculine proper noun *Pablo* correctly agrees with the singular masculine pronoun *he*. Choices A and C both incorrectly use *good* instead of *well*. Choice D incorrectly uses the adjective *diligent* instead of the adverb *diligently*.

2.   B)

The correct answers are *you're* and *your*. The contraction *you're* ("you are") correctly completes the phrase "if you're ready." The possessive pronoun *your* correctly completes the phrase "please get your coat."

3.   C)

Choice C is correct. To agree with the plural noun *dresses*, the singular verb *was* should be replaced with the plural verb *were* to indicate all the dresses were torn and dirty.

4.   C)

The correct answers are *yet* and *for*. The conjunction *yet* correctly completes the phrase "nervous yet happy," expressing a contrast between the two feelings. The coordinating conjunction *for* (which means "because" or "since") correctly connects the two independent clauses in the sentence ("I felt nervous yet happy" and "I was about to . . . my life").

5.   C)

Choice C correctly uses the word *stairs* to refer to the steps leading up to a higher elevation. Choice A incorrectly uses the homophone *stares*, meaning "to look intensely." Choice B incorrectly uses *steers*, meaning "cows." Choice D incorrectly uses *stars*, meaning "celestial objects," which is a nonsensical choice in the context of this sentence.

6.   D)

Choice D is correct. The comparative adjective *prettier* compares two people (Heidi and Adelaide). Choice A, *truly*, is an adverb; choice B, *believe*, is a verb; and choice C, *Heidi*, is a proper noun.

7.   B)

Choice B is correct. In the proper noun *Los Angeles*, both words should be capitalized.

8.   A)

Choice A is correct. The correct answers are an opening quotation mark and a period. Correctly completed, the sentence looks like this: *Older sister Hollie said she didn't like the way Katrina always answered "No!" whenever Mom asked the little girl to do something.* The quotation must have an opening quotation mark to indicate that Katrina is speaking. The sentence ends with a period because it is declarative. Choice B does not provide the opening quotation mark that is needed to match the closing quotation mark, and a question mark is incorrect because the sentence is a statement, not a question. Choice C might be possible, but the sentence does not deliver a specifically emotional or startling exclamation, so a period is more appropriate than an exclamation point. Choice D does not provide opening quotation marks to match the closing quotation marks, and a semicolon would incorrectly separate the speaker and the quotation.

9.   B)

Choice B correctly pairs the plural noun *parents* with the plural verb *pick* and correctly pairs *either* with *or*. Choice A incorrectly pairs the plural noun *parents* with the singular verb *picks*. Choice C incorrectly pairs *either . . . nor*, and choice D incorrectly pairs *neither . . . or*.

10.   A)

Choice A is correct. The dependent clause "When I offered her a ride" begins the sentence. "Mazie accepted gratefully" is an independent clause.

11.   C)

The correct answers are *died* and *dyeing* in choice C. The verb *died* is the past tense of *to die* and means "perished" or "been killed." The gerund *dyeing* comes from the infinitive *to dye* and means "coloring [something] with dye." Choice A incorrectly switches the two root infinitives (*to dye* and *to die*). Choice B incorrectly switches the two root infinitives and uses the present-tense form rather than the past-tense and gerund forms. Choice D incorrectly uses the present-tense form rather than the past-tense and gerund forms.

12. C)

Choice C is correct. The coordinating conjunction *yet* joins the two independent clauses. Choice A, *dislike*, is a verb; choice B, *wars*, is a plural noun; and choice D, *I*, is a subject pronoun.

13. A)

Choice A is correct. The homophones *bare* and *bear* should be transposed: *That bear in the circus is wearing a funny costume, but I'm sure the poor animal would rather go bare.* The noun *bear* means "a large, furry mammal," and the adverb *bare* means "without clothing."

14. D)

Choice D uses the following punctuation marks correctly: an opening quotation mark, a comma, an exclamation point, a closing quotation mark, another comma, and a period. In choice A, the question mark after *Matty* should be changed to an exclamation point or a comma. In choice B, the semicolon following *cat* should be changed to a comma. In choice C, the period following *Matty* should be changed to an exclamation point or a comma, and the colon following *cat* should be changed to a comma.

15. B)

Choice B is correct. The future-tense verb *will realize* shows that one future event ("whenever I think about my mom") will have happened before a second future event ("I will realize . . . hero"). None of the other choices use the correct future tense.

16. C)

Choice C is correct. The colon should be replaced with a comma or an exclamation point: *"What a wonderful time we're going to have next weekend," Ana said.* Or: *"What a wonderful time we're going to have next weekend!" Ana said.*

17. A)

Choice A is correct. The correct answers are *fewer* and *less*. The comparative adjective *fewer* describes a smaller number of items (such as "fewer teaspoons" or "fewer corn kernels"). *Less* describes a smaller amount of something that cannot be counted (such as jitteriness or happiness). Choice B incorrectly transposes *fewer* and *less*. Choices C and D would each result in a nonsensical sentence (consuming more sugar makes people feel more jittery, not less).

18. B)

Choice B is correct. The comparative adjective *warmest* should not be combined with *most*—the writer should leave out the word *most*.

19. C)

The correct answers are *allowed* and *aloud* in choice C. The verb *allowed* means "given permission," and the adverb *aloud* means "out loud." The past-tense verb *alloyed* means "to mix metals," and the adjective *aglow* means "shining or lit up." Neither makes sense in the sentence.

20. D)

Choice D is correct. The adjective *loose* should be replaced with the verb *lose*: *Oh wow, I hope we don't lose the game! Lose* means the opposite of *win*, and *loose* means the opposite of *tight. Loose* can also be a verb that means "to set free," as in "Loose the guard dogs!"

21. C)

Choice C is correct. The sentence's predicate is as follows: "is conducting a seminar on toxic chemicals." Its subject is "A professor from the chemistry department." Choice A, *A*, begins the sentence. Choice B, *from*, and choice D, *on*, are prepositions; each begins a prepositional phrase. "From the chemistry department" modifies the noun *professor*, and "on toxic chemicals" modifies the noun *seminar*.

22. D)

Choice D correctly uses the verb *accept*, which means "to agree to take [something]." In choice A, *except* is incorrectly used instead of its homophone *accept*. Choice B incorrectly uses *accede*, which means "consent" or "allow"; also, the verb *accede* is almost always used with *to*, as in "I cannot accede to your request." Choice C incorrectly uses *expect* instead of its near-homophone *accept*.

23. C)

Choice C is correct. The plural helping verb *have* does not agree with the singular noun *everybody*. *Have applied* should be replaced with *has applied*.

24. A)

The correct choice is A. The verb *define* explains how researchers would characterize a generation. Choice B, *defend*, meaning "to protect or drive danger away from," does not make sense here; there is no danger. Choice C, *defer*, meaning "to postpone or delay," also does not make sense. Choice D, *differ*, means "to be unlike" someone or something and is nonsensical in the context of the sentence.

25. **B)**

Choice B is correct. "Lots of people" is a plural subject, so the singular verb *agrees* should be replaced with the plural verb *agree*.

26. **D)**

The comparative adjective *healthier* compares two dogs' health. Choice A, *two*, is an adjective (but not a comparative one); choice B, *dogs*, is a plural noun; and choice C, *seems*, is a present-tense verb.

27. **B)**

Choice B is correct. *Could* is a helping verb, and it must be followed by the verb *have* for the entire phrase to make sense. Using choice A, *of*, is a common mistake in English grammar. However, it is incorrect; *of* is a preposition that indicates relationships, origin, and other functions. In choice C, the verb *had* does not match the helping verb *could*. Choice D, *ave*, is incorrect; to form the contraction, both the *h* and the *a* should be removed from *have* and an apostrophe added: *could've*.

28. **C)**

Choice C is correct. Even though the holiday name *Easter* is capitalized, the word *morning* should be lowercased—it is a common noun and not part of the holiday's name. The word *Day* in *Valentine's Day* is capitalized because it is part of the holiday name and thus a proper noun.

29. **D)**

Choice D correctly pairs two past-tense verbs, *left* and *walked*. Choice A incorrectly pairs a present-tense verb, *leaves*, with a past-tense verb, *walked*. Choice B incorrectly pairs a past-tense verb, *left*, with a future-tense verb, *will walk*. Choice C incorrectly pairs a past-tense verb, *left*, with a conditional past-tense verb, "would have walked."

30. **A)**

The correct answers are *poor* and *pour* in choice A. The adjective *poor* correctly modifies the noun *family* by describing them as "lacking sufficient money

to live comfortably." The verb *pour* (meaning "to dispense") correctly completes the phrase "would carefully pour a small portion of milk." The verb *purr* means "to make a purring sound, like a cat" and the adjective *pure* means "wholesome and clean." None of the other pairs of words make sense in the sentences.

31. **B)**

Choice B is correct. The contraction *can't* means "cannot." Choice A, *if*, is a subordinating conjunction. Choices C and D (*heat* and *kitchen*) are common nouns.

32. **B)**

Choice B correctly capitalizes the proper nouns *British Columbia, Canada*; it also correctly lowercases the common nouns *aunt, mom's*, and *husband*. In choice A, the common nouns *mom's* and *husband* are incorrectly capitalized. Choice C incorrectly lowercases *Columbia* (in the proper noun *British Columbia*) and incorrectly capitalizes the common noun *aunt*. Choice D incorrectly capitalizes the common nouns *aunt, mom's*, and *husband*.

33. **D)**

Choice D is correct. *Manner* and *manor* sound alike but have different spellings and meanings, which makes them a homophone pair. Choices A (*new/stew*), B (*member/mumble*), and C (*has/hiss*) are not homophone pairs because they do not sound enough alike.

34. **B)**

Choice B correctly uses the verb *bring*, which means "fetch" or "get." Choice A incorrectly uses *take*, a verb synonymous to *grab, seize*, or *remove*, in place of *bring*. Choice C incorrectly uses the verb *prepare* ("cook"); this word does not make sense in the sentence, because customers do not cook their own food at restaurants. Choice D incorrectly uses the verb *eat*, meaning "consume" or "gobble up" in place of *bring*. *Eat* sounds nonsensical in the sentence: the speaker wants the listener to *bring* the speaker something to eat. The speaker does *not* want the listener to eat the take-out dinner. The phrase "eat me a dinner" is not idiomatic in English.

35. **C)**

Choice C is correct. *Piece* should be replaced with its homophone, *peace*: *During the 1960s, many college students marched in peace marches to protest the Vietnam War. Piece is a noun, synonymous to portion, bit, and chunk. Peace is a noun that is an antonym for war.*

36. D)

Choice D correctly capitalizes *We're* (because it begins the sentence) and *New Mexico* (because it is a proper noun, the name of a state). In choice A, *new* is incorrectly lowercased. Choice B incorrectly capitalizes *desert*, a common noun. Choice C incorrectly lowercases *Mexico*.

37. A)

The correct answers are *and* and *although* in choice A. The conjunction *and* correctly completes the phrase "angers and depresses me." By implying contrast, the subordinating conjunction *although* correctly connects the opening independent clause, "Watching TV news usually angers and depresses me," to the dependent clause, "although it occasionally interests me very much." Any of the other choices would provide incorrect relationships, rendering the sentence nonsensical, unidiomatic, or both.

38. A)

Choice A is correct; the subordinating conjunction *because* links the opening dependent clause ("Because . . . city") to the independent clause ("tourists flock there all year long"). Choice B, *San Francisco*, is a proper noun; choice C, *tourists*, is a common noun; and choice D, *flock*, is a verb.

39. D)

Choice D is correct. The adjective *illicit* means "unlawful"—the test revealed that the patient had taken, or somehow been exposed to, illegal drugs. *Unjust* means "unfair," and *injust* is a misspelling of *unjust*—it is not a word. *Elicit* is a verb that means "to draw from" or "to bring out." It is commonly confused with *illicit*.

40. A)

Choice A is correct. The noun phrase "who works at our school" tells more about the noun *janitor*. Choice B, "has a very difficult job," is the predicate of the sentence. Choice C, *very difficult*, contains the adjective *difficult*, which modifies the noun *job* and the adverb *very*, which modifies *difficult*. Choice D,

"has a . . . job," is the same as Choice B, except it uses an ellipsis to remove two words.

41. B)

Choice B correctly uses the noun *piece* (meaning "slice") in the phrase "piece of cake." None of the other choices is correct in the sentence: *peace* means "the opposite of war"; *peas* are a vegetable; and *place* means "a location."

42. B)

Choice B is correct. The comma should be replaced with a question mark: *"At what time do you want to eat dinner?"* The speaker in the sentence (*she*) is asking a question.

43. C)

Choice C is correct. The speaker is talking about something he or she *will* do in the future: *invite* the brownie baker to a birthday party. Choices A and B are present-tense verbs. Choice D is a two-word noun.

44. B)

Choice B is correct. The place name *Seattle* (a city in the state of Washington) should be capitalized—it is a proper noun.

45. A)

Choice A is correct. The correct answers are *have* and *has*. The other helping-verb choices all create incorrect, ungrammatical phrases such as "I was always wanted to stay" and "my great-aunt is generously offered to take me."

46. B)

Choice B is correct. The homophones *through* and *threw* should be transposed: *I accidentally threw my baseball through my neighbor's window, and it shattered.* The past-tense verb *threw* means "hurled or pitched," and the preposition *through* (which begins the prepositional phrase "through my neighbor's window") means "in one side and out the other."

47. A)

Choice A correctly compares three people using the suffix *–est*. Choice B incorrectly compares three people using the suffix *–er*. Choice C incorrectly uses *most* with a one-syllable adjective, *smart*. Choice D incorrectly uses *more* with a one-syllable adjective, *smart*.

48. **B)**

Choice B is correct. The homophones *write* and *right* should be transposed: *Yes, you're right: we should always try hard to write sentences that are grammatically correct.* The verb *write* means "to compose text," and the adjective *right* is a synonym for *correct, true,* and *accurate*.

49. **B)**

Choice B correctly pairs the plural noun *members* with the plural verb *arrive* and correctly pairs the present-tense verb *arrive* with the present-tense verb *hang*. Choice A incorrectly pairs the plural noun *members* with the singular verb *arrives*. Choice C uses a past-tense verb, *arrived*, in the first clause, and incorrectly pairs this with a present-tense verb, *hang*, in the second clause. Choice D includes a similar error: it pairs a past-perfect verb, *had arrived*, with a present-tense verb, *hang*.

50. **A)**

Choice A is correct. It contains the proper noun *August* and the common nouns *sister* and *college*. The three incorrect choices (B, C, and D) contain the following common nouns: *bread, bakery, street, door, car*. None contain proper nouns.

51. **A)**

Choice A is correct. The verb *laid* is the past tense of *lay*, which means "to set or put down." Choice B, *lied*, is the past tense of the verb *lie*, meaning "to assert something that is untrue." *Ley* is a noun that refers to pasture, and a *lei* is a wreath made of flowers. None of these answer choices make sense in the context of the sentence.

52. **A)**

Choice A is correct. *Ball* and *bawl* sound alike but have different spellings and meanings, which makes them a homophone pair. Choices B (*following/ flowing*), C (*wedding/winding*), and D (*groom/grim*) are not homophone pairs because they do not sound enough alike.

53. **D)**

Choice D correctly uses the noun *suite*, which is pronounced like *sweet* and means "a group of connecting rooms." In choice A, the adjective *sweet* means "sugary" or "kind and loving." In choice B, a *Swede* is a Swedish person. In choice C, *sweat* (which rhymes with *get*) means "to perspire" or "perspiration."

54. **C)**

Choice C contains the correctly paired conjunctions *either . . . or*. In choice A, *either* is incorrectly paired with *nor*. Choice B includes a double negative (*can't . . . neither*), and choice D has a verb error (*can having*).

55. **B)**

Choice B is correct. *Aloud* (an adverb meaning "out loud or audibly") should be replaced with its homophone, *allowed*: *Are you allowed to stay out later on weekend nights than on school nights? Allowed* is a verb that means "given permission to."

1. A)

Adding heat breaks hydrogen bonds, which decreases cohesion (the attraction of water molecules to each other). This, in turn, decreases surface tension.

2. D)

A monomer is a building block used to build large molecules such as proteins. Amino acids are the monomers used to build proteins.

3. A)

Water moves from areas of low concentration to areas of high concentration. Because the concentration of salt is higher inside of the cell, water will move into the cell.

4. A)

The Calvin cycle is the biochemical pathway that converts CO_2 into sugar.

5. C)

Telomeres—the repetitive sequences of DNA at the end of chromosomes—can be elongated by DNA telomerase.

6. B)

The process where genetic information is exchanged between homologous chromosomes (one maternal and one paternal) is called crossing over.

7. C)

Messenger RNA (mRNA) carries the nucleotide code for a specific protein to the ribosome.

8. C)

Point mutations result from single nucleotide changes in the DNA sequence. The change may be the result of nucleotide replacement, deletion, or insertion. In the case of mitochondrial myopathy, a single nucleotide was replaced.

9. B)

Two chromatids are held together by a centromere.

10. B)

Water is polar and can only dissolve polar substances. Since oils are not polar, oils do not mix with water.

11. B)

The mice are neither black nor white, so fur color is not a Mendelian trait. Because the mice have black and white fur, both traits are being expressed and the alleles are codominant.

12. A)

Every amino acid has an amino and a carboxyl group. The group that identifies the amino acid is called the R group.

13. B)

Cyclic AMP (cAMP) is the molecule responsible for intracellular communication. When hormones bind to receptors in the cell membrane, cAMP activates the necessary chemical pathways within the cell.

14. C)

During photosynthesis, 6 CO_2 and 6 H_2O are converted to 1 molecule of $C_6H_{12}O_6$ (glucose) and 6 O_2.

15. B)

There are 20 amino acids that are encoded in human DNA and thus can be synthesized by the human body.

16. A)

DNA polymerase adds complementary bases to the parent strands to form new strands. Enzymes are often named for their function: DNA polymerase joins monomers (nucleotides) to form a polymer (DNA).

17. B)

Phenotype is how genotype is expressed as physical features.

18. C)

Nucleic acids (DNA and RNA) are composed of nucleotides. Each nucleotide is composed of a 5-carbon sugar, a nitrogenous base, and a phosphate group.

19. A)

Insulin regulates the absorption of glucose from the blood into other tissues, where it is either used for respiration or stored.

20. B)

Fermentation occurs when oxygen levels are low.

21. D)

There are four nucleotides, and each codon is three nucleotides long, so there are $4 \times 4 \times 4 = 64$ possible codons.

22. D)

Telophase is the final phase of mitosis.

23. C)

Cells spend 90 percent of their lifetime in interphase. When it does occur, mitosis is a comparatively short process. In the student's sample, most cells will be in the G1 phase of interphase.

24. B)

Translation will end when the ribosome encounters a stop codon. The stop codons activate a protein called release factor, which will bind to the ribosome and release the protein.

25. B)

Hormones allow cells and tissues that are far apart in the body to communicate.

26. B)

Fermentation is used in cells to produce energy when oxygen levels are low.

27. A)

If an allele shows dominance, it will mask the presence of a recessive allele. If a person is heterozygous for a dominant trait, he or she will resemble a person who is homozygous for a dominant trait. Recessive traits don't mask dominant traits in Mendelian genetics. In both incomplete dominance and codominance, the heterozygous individual would not resemble a homozygous individual.

28. A)

Okazaki fragments are generated because DNA polymerase can only be synthesized in the 5' to 3' direction and requires a free 3' end. Since DNA is anti-parallel, one strand has to wait until the 3' end is unwound before the DNA can be replicated.

29. D)

Metaphase is the phase of the cell cycle where chromosomes align at the center of the cell.

30. B)

Gametes are produced by meiosis, which results in four haploid (1n) cells that each have half the chromosomes of a somatic cell. If the organism has 36 chromosomes, its gametes will have $36 \div 2 = 18$ chromosomes.

CHEMISTRY

1. C)

Atoms are most stable when their valence shell is full. The noble gases, which have full valence shells, are almost completely inert.

2. B)

Ionization energy increases from the lower left to the upper right of the periodic table. Silicon (Si) is the element farthest down and left, so it will have the smallest ionization energy.

3. A)

London dispersion forces occur between two neon (Ne) atoms as the result of temporary dipoles within the atom.

4. D)

Sublimation of iodine (I_2) can occur at room temperature when solid iodine (I_2 (s)) converts to gaseous iodine (I_2 (g)). Phase changes are always physical changes because the chemical structure of the substance is unchanged.

5. A)

Nitrogen (N) is the largest component of the mixture and therefore is considered the solvent.

6. D)

Bleach is highly basic and has a pH around 13.

7. A)

Hydrogen (H) always has an oxidation number of +1. To create a neutral molecule, the sulfur (S) must then have an oxidation number of −2.

8. D)

The answer is 8 moles of H_2O. Set up railroad tracks using the conversion factor given by the chemical equation.

8 mol H_2	2 mol H_2O	= **8 mol H_2O**
	2 mol H_2	

9. C)

Valence electrons can be lost, gained, or shared to produce chemical bonds. These electrons are found in the outermost shell of an atom.

10. C)

Ionization energy increases from the lower left to the upper right of the periodic table. Carbon (C) is the element farthest up and right, so it will have the largest ionization energy.

11. A)

Phosphoric acid (H_3PO_4) is a strong acid used in soda to prevent bacteria growth; its presence makes soda acidic. Bleach and baking soda are both bases, and pure water is neutral (not an acid or a base).

12. A)

The nucleus contains protons and neutrons. All electrons are found outside the nucleus, and photons are packets of electromagnetic waves that can be emitted or absorbed by an electron.

13. C)

The list of metalloids or semi-metallic elements includes boron (B), silicon (Si), germanium (Ge), arsenic (As), antimony (Sb), tellurium (Te), and astatine (At). To determine the metalloids on the periodic table, move along the diagonal from B to At and from Ge to Sb.

14. D)

The arrow points from gas to solid, which depicts the process of deposition.

15. C)

Metals have an oxidation number equal to their group number. Sodium (Na), which is in group 1, will have an oxidation number of +1.

Because the oxidation number of oxygen (O) in a compound is −2, the oxidation number of Na can also be found by setting up an equation:

The charge on Na_2O is zero.

$Na_2 + O = 0$

$2(Na) + O = 0$

$2(Na) + (-2) = 0$

$Na = 1$

16. C)

HCl is a polar molecule; permanent dipole-dipole forces occur between two polar molecules.

17. A)

An Arrhenius acid is a species or substance that produces H^+ ions. Strong acids such as hydrochloric acid (HCl) produce hydrogen ions (H^+).

18. C)

Mixing sugar in coffee creates a solution. Because the amount of sugar cane added is less than the amount of coffee, it is considered the minority component and thus termed the solute. Sugar is a neutral substance that does not have properties of acids or bases.

19. B)

Oxygen (O) belongs to group 16 and has six electrons. It will need to add two electrons to fill its valence shell with eight total electrons. The two extra electrons will give it a charge of O^{2-}.

20. B)

Hydrogen bonding occurs between the hydrogen atom (H) of one molecule of ethanol (bonded to an electronegative atom such as O) and the lone pair of electrons of oxygen on another molecule of ethanol.

21. C)

Sulfur (S) is in group 16 and has six valence electrons. Thus, it needs two electrons to fill its valence shell with eight total electrons.

22. A)

The arrow points from solid to gas, which depicts the process of sublimation.

23. C)

Nitrogen (N) is in group 15 and has five valence electrons.

24. B)

Metals have an oxidation number equal to their group number. Potassium (K) will have an oxidation

number of +1. Use this information to set up an equation:

The charge on K_2O_2 is zero.

$$K_2 + O_2 = 0$$
$$2(K) + 2(O) = 0$$
$$2(1) + 2(O) = 0$$
$$O = -1$$

25. A)

Alpha decay produces a particle with two protons and two neutrons, usually written as ^4_2He.

26. D)

The reaction of KI and $Pb(NO_3)_2$ creates a solid precipitate, $PbI_2(s)$, in aqueous solution.

27. B)

Elements in group 16 such as oxygen (O) and sulfur (S) typically form two bonds according to the octet rule. These elements start with six valence electrons and gain two electrons by forming covalent bonds in order to satisfy the octet rule.

28. B)

The freezing point of water is 0°C. When the temperature is raised from −5°C to 10°C, solid ice will melt into liquid water.

29. C)

The answer is 3 moles of $Pb(NO_3)_2$. Set up railroad tracks using the conversion factor given by the chemical equation.

$$6 \text{ mol KNO}_3 \times \frac{1 \text{ mol } Pb(NO_3)_2}{2 \text{ mol KNO}_3} = \textbf{3 mol } Pb(NO_3)_2$$

30. A)

The oxidation number of solid zinc (Zn) is zero (0) because the reactant is a solid. The oxidation number of Zn in zinc nitrate ($Zn(NO_3)_2$) is +2:

$$Zn(NO_3)_2 = 0$$
$$Zn + 2(NO_3) = 0$$
$$Zn + 2(-1) = 0$$
$$Zn = +2$$

Zn moved from an oxidation number of 0 to +2, meaning it lost electrons, or was oxidized.

1. **C)**

   The abdominal cavity holds organs involved in urinary and digestive function, including the appendix.

2. **C)**

   Short bones are present in the foot and the wrist.

3. **D)**

   The vibration from the mucous membrane folds, or vocal folds, produces sound when air passes through them.

4. **D)**

   Sunlight helps the skin produce vitamin D.

5. **B)**

   Antibodies bind to the antigen on the pathogen, neutralizing the pathogen and attracting phagocytes.

6. **C)**

   Adrenal glands are found on top of each kidney.

7. **A)**

   The bones and joints store iron, calcium, and fat.

8. **D)**

   The mucosa is the innermost layer of the stomach; it secretes hydrochloric acid and digestive enzymes.

9. **B)**

   The right ventricle pumps deoxygenated blood from the heart to the lungs for gas exchange.

10. **D)**

    Mature sperm are stored in the epididymis.

11. **A)**

    The nephrons are the functional unit of the kidneys. They filter metabolic wastes and electrolytes from the blood.

12. **B)**

    When the elbow is flexed, the biceps is contracted while the triceps is relaxed. Thus, the biceps is the agonist while the triceps is the antagonist.

13. **A)**

    Schwann cells secrete myelin, which forms a sheet around the neuron and allows the electrical signal to travel faster.

14. **B)**

    Single, short nerve impulses produce a twitch contraction.

15. **C)**

    Lactic acid is elevated in the blood when prolonged muscle contraction causes muscle fatigue.

16. **D)**

    The collecting ducts are located in the renal medulla.

17. **C)**

    The cerebellum coordinates movement, increasing the precision and accuracy of voluntary muscle actions.

18. **A)**

    The femur, or thigh bone, is the largest bone in the human body.

19. **D)**

    The fallopian tubes are the passages through which eggs travel from the ovaries to the uterus.

20. **C)**

    Capillaries enable the exchange of nutrients, gases, and waste on the cellular level.

21. **C)**

    The caudate lobe spirals around the vena cava while the quadrate lobe is located around the gallbladder.

22. **B)**

    Dentin is the component of teeth that looks like bone and is covered by the enamel.

23. C)

Ventricles are the hollow spaces in the brain where cerebrospinal fluid can be found.

24. A)

The ovaries produce progesterone, one of the hormones responsible for menstruation and pregnancy.

25. B)

The diaphragm contracts during inspiration, or inhalation, to provide space for air to move into the lungs.

26. D)

The tibia is a bone in the lower leg.

27. D)

The left ventricle pumps oxygenated blood into the aorta and throughout the rest of the body.

28. D)

The sympathetic nervous system is responsible for the fight-or-flight response.

29. C)

The pancreas produces and secretes insulin, a hormone that plays a role in maintaining blood sugar level.

30. C)

The gastrocnemius is located in the lower leg.

1.   B)

X-rays are electromagnetic waves.

2.   B)

Plug the variables into the appropriate formula and solve.

$N = mg$ and $F_f = \mu_k N$

$F_f = \mu_k mg$

$F_f = 0.3(100 \text{ kg})(9.8 \text{ m/s}^2) = \textbf{294 N}$

3.   B)

Sonar waves are mechanical sound waves that require a medium through which to propagate.

4.   B)

Plug the variables into the appropriate formula and solve.

$W = Fd$

$F = \dfrac{W}{d}$

$F = \dfrac{850 \text{ J}}{100 \text{ m}} = \textbf{8.5 N}$

5.   B)

Plug the variables into the appropriate formula and solve.

$KE = \dfrac{1}{2}mv^2$

$KE = \dfrac{1}{2}(9.1 \times 10^{-31} \text{ kg})(1 \times 10^6 \text{ m/s})^2$

$= \textbf{4.55} \times \textbf{10}^{-19} \textbf{ J}$

6.   D)

Plug the variables into the appropriate formula and solve.

$v_f = v_i + at$

$-14.9 = -5 - 9.8t$

$t = \dfrac{-14.9 + 5}{-9.8} = \textbf{1.01 s}$

7.   B)

Plug the variables into the appropriate formula and solve.

$v_f^2 = v_i^2 + 2ad$

$v_f^2 = 0^2 + 2(3.8 \text{ m/s}^2)(2 \text{ m})$

$v_f = \sqrt{2(3.8 \text{ m/s}^2)(2 \text{ m})} = \textbf{3.9 m/s}$

8.   B)

Convert 100 miles per hour to meters per second.

$\dfrac{100 \text{ mi}}{\text{hr}} \times \dfrac{1609 \text{ m}}{\text{mi}} \times \dfrac{1 \text{ hr}}{3600 \text{ s}} = 44.7 \text{ m/s}$

Plug the variables into the appropriate formula and solve.

$KE = \dfrac{1}{2}mv^2$

$KE = \dfrac{1}{2}(0.145 \text{ kg})(44.7 \text{ m/s})^2 = \textbf{145 J}$

9.   A)

$KE = \dfrac{1}{2}mv^2$

Kinetic energy does not depend on the acceleration due to gravity.

10.   B)

Plug the variables into the appropriate formula and solve.

$V = IR$

$I = \dfrac{V}{R}$

$I = \dfrac{15 \text{ V}}{15 \text{ }\Omega} = \textbf{1 A}$

11.   C)

Plug the variables into the appropriate formula and solve.

$\dfrac{1}{R_t} = \dfrac{1}{2} + \dfrac{1}{5} + \dfrac{1}{10} = \dfrac{5}{10} + \dfrac{2}{10} + \dfrac{1}{10} = \dfrac{8}{10} = \dfrac{4}{5}$

$R_t = \dfrac{5}{4}\Omega = \textbf{1.25 }\Omega$

12.   B)

Plug the variables into the appropriate formula and solve.

$F = ma$

$a = \dfrac{F}{m}$

$a = \dfrac{15 \text{ N}}{10 \text{ kg}} = \textbf{1.5 m/s}^2$

13.   A)

Convert 3 grams to 0.003 kilograms.

Plug the variables into the appropriate formula and solve.

$p = mv$

$p = (0.003 \text{ kg})(300 \text{ m/s}) = \textbf{0.9 kg m/s}$

14. C)

Plug the variables into the appropriate formula and solve.

$V = IR$

$V = (1 \text{ A})(1 \times 10^5 \ \Omega)= 1 \times 10^5 \text{ V} = \textbf{100,000 V}$

15. D)

Plug the variables into the appropriate formula and solve.

$a_{rad} = 3g = 3(9.8 \text{ m/s}^2) = \textbf{29.4 m/s}^2$

16. B)

Plug the variables into the appropriate formula and solve.

$KE_1 = \frac{1}{2}mv^2 = \frac{1}{2}(1200 \text{ kg})(11.2 \text{ m/s})^2 = 75,264 \text{ J}$

$KE_2 = \frac{1}{2}mv^2 = \frac{1}{2}(1200 \text{ kg})(29.1 \text{ m/s})^2 = 508,086 \text{ J}$

$\Delta KE = KE_2 - KE_1$

$508,086 \text{ J} - 75,264 \text{ J} = \textbf{432,822 J}$

17. A)

Plug the variables into the appropriate formula and solve.

$m_1v_{1i} + m_2v_{2i} = m_1v_{1f} + m_2v_{2f}$

$0 + 0 = m_1v_{1f} + m_2v_{2f}$

$v_{1f} = \frac{-m_2}{m_1} v_{2f} = \left(\frac{-0.003 \text{ kg}}{5 \text{ kg}}\right)(300 \text{ m/s})$

$= -0.18 \text{ m/s} = \textbf{-18 cm/s}$

18. D)

Work is a scalar without a direction.

19. B)

Plug the variables into the appropriate formula and solve.

$\omega_f = \omega_i + at$

$\omega_f = 0 \text{ rad/s} + (1.5 \text{ rad/s}^2)(5s) = \textbf{7.5 rad/s}$

20. C)

The pitch is directly proportional to frequency, so the pitch decreases. A 1000 hertz sound is still audible to humans.

21. C)

Plug the variables into the appropriate formula and solve.

$v = \lambda f$

$\lambda = \frac{v}{f} = \frac{343 \text{ m/s}}{600 \text{ Hz}} = \textbf{0.57 m}$

22. D)

Plug the variables into the appropriate formula and solve.

$N = \frac{Q_{TOT}}{q}$

$r = \sqrt{9 \times 10^9 \frac{(1.602 \times 10^{-19})^2}{1}} = \textbf{1.51} \times \textbf{10}^{-14} \textbf{ m}$

23. B)

Plug the variables into the appropriate formula and solve.

$F_g = \frac{GM_{Earth}M_{Moon}}{R^2}$

$F_g = \frac{(6.67 \times 10^{11})(6 \times 10^{24} \text{ kg})(7.4 \times 10^{22} \text{ kg})}{(3.84 \times 10^8 \text{ m})^2}$

$= \textbf{2} \times \textbf{10}^{20} \textbf{ N}$

24. C)

The minimum possible amplitude is the difference of the maximum amplitudes of the two waves.

$2.5 \text{ m} - 0.3 \text{ m} = \textbf{2.2 m}$

25. A)

$v = \frac{\lambda}{T}$

$c = \frac{\lambda}{T}$

For c to remain constant, as the wavelength increases, the period must also increase.

26. A)

Plug the variables into the appropriate formula and solve.

$\tau = rF\sin\theta$

$\tau = (0.20 \text{ m})(15 \text{ N})\sin\pi = \textbf{0 N m}$

27. **A)**

$n_1 \sin\theta_1 = n_2 \sin\theta_2$

Snell's Law says that the transmitted light ray will be deflected toward the normal.

28. **C)**

Plug the variables into the appropriate formula and solve.

$F = qE$

$F = (7 \times 10^{-3}\,\text{C})(3 \times 10^4\,\text{N/C}) = \mathbf{210\,N}$

29. **A)**

Plug the variables into the appropriate formula and solve.

$V_t = V_1 + V_2 = 9\,\text{V} + 9\,\text{V} = 18\,\text{V}$

$V = IR$

$I = \dfrac{18\,\text{V}}{200\,\Omega} = \mathbf{0.09\,A}$

30. **D)**

The object is dropped from rest, so the initial velocity is zero in both locations. Because the objects were dropped from the same height, d will be the same in both locations as well. The acceleration due to gravity is different on the earth and the moon, so both a and the final velocity (v_f) will be different.

FOUR: PRACTICE TEST FOUR

Mathematics

Directions: Work the problem carefully, and choose the best answer.

1. One foot is approximately how many centimeters?

    A) 30.5 cm

    B) 5.08 cm

    C) 100 cm

    D) 45 cm

2. Evaluate the following expression for $r = 315$ and $t = -2$: $\frac{r}{5} - 10t$

    A) 59

    B) 83

    C) 64

    D) 43

3. Danika bought two packages of ground beef weighing 1.73 pounds and 2.17 pounds. What was the total weight of the two packages?

    A) 0.44 lb

    B) 3.81 lb

    C) 3.9 lb

    D) 4.2 lb

4. Solve: $-4x + 2 = -34$

    A) 8

    B) -8

    C) -9

    D) 9

5. Find the difference between $\frac{2}{3}$ and $\frac{1}{4}$.

    A) $\frac{11}{12}$

    B) $\frac{5}{24}$

    C) $\frac{3}{7}$

    D) $\frac{5}{12}$

6. Morris went shopping with four $20 bills. He spent $24.17 at the hardware store and $32.87 on clothes. How much money did he have left?

    A) $22.96

    B) $42.96

    C) $57.04

    D) $23.04

7. A 24-hour clock reads 1945. What is the equivalent time on a 12-hour clock?

A) 7:45 p.m.

B) 9:45 a.m.

C) 9:45 p.m.

D) 7:45 a.m.

8. Frank and Josh need 1 pound of chocolate to bake a cake. If Frank has $\frac{3}{8}$ pound of chocolate, and Josh has $\frac{1}{2}$ pound, how much more chocolate do they need?

A) $\frac{3}{5}$ lb

B) $\frac{7}{8}$ lb

C) $\frac{1}{8}$ lb

D) $\frac{1}{10}$ lb

9. How much alcohol by volume is in a 500 milliliter bottle of 70% isopropyl alcohol?

A) 35 ml

B) 50 ml

C) 400 ml

D) 350 ml

10. Simplify the following expression:
$(5 - 2)^3 - 14 \div 7$

A) 2

B) 25

C) $-\frac{5}{7}$

D) 7

11. In their first year of business, a small company lost $2100. The next year, the company recorded a profit of $11,200. What was the company's average profit over the two years?

A) $5650

B) $4550

C) $9100

D) $11,300

12. Sally has $127 in her checking. An automatic draft takes out $150 for her electric bill. What is her balance after the automatic draft?

A) $23

B) –$123

C) –$23

D) –$277

13. Simplify the following expression:
$2(7 - 9) + 4 \times 10$

A) 36

B) 44

C) 0

D) 160

14. The property tax on a boat valued at $30,000 is $270. Find the tax rate.

A) 0.9%

B) 90%

C) 2.7%

D) 3%

15. John's rain gauge recorded rain on three consecutive days: $\frac{1}{2}$ inch on Sunday, $\frac{2}{3}$ inch on Monday, and $\frac{1}{4}$ inch on Tuesday. What was the total amount of rain received over the three days?

A) $\frac{17}{36}$ in

B) $1\frac{5}{12}$ in

C) $\frac{4}{9}$ in

D) $1\frac{1}{2}$ in

16. Find the product of 0.4 and 0.2.

A) 0.6

B) 0.8

C) 0.08

D) 0.06

17. A bridge is 119.7 meters long in the summer. In the winter, the metal contracts, and the bridge shrinks by 1.05 meters. How long is the bridge in winter?

A) 118.65 m

B) 120.75 m

C) 109.2 m

D) 130.2 m

18. A medication's expiration date has passed. The label says it contains 600 milligrams of ibuprofen, but it has lost 125 milligrams of ibuprofen. How much ibuprofen is left in the tablet?

A) 475 mg

B) 525 mg

C) 425 mg

D) 125 mg

19. If the average person drinks ten 8-ounce glasses of water each day, how many ounces of water will she drink in a week?

A) 80 oz

B) 700 oz

C) 560 oz

D) 70 oz

20. The cost of 2.4 yards of lumber is $24.96. What is the cost per yard?

A) $5.99

B) $10.40

C) $22.46

D) $27.36

21. An emergency surgery begins at 2300 hours. The surgery is expected to last 3 hours. At what time is the surgery likely to end?

A) 0300

B) 0200

C) 2600

D) 1400

22. Find the batting average of a baseball player who get 14 hits in 52 at-bats. (Divide the number of hits by the number of at-bats. Round to the nearest thousandth.)

A) 0.145

B) 3.714

C) 0.269

D) 0.380

23. Dashawn is baking two desserts for Thanksgiving dinner. One recipe calls for $2\frac{1}{2}$ cups of flour and the other recipe calls for $1\frac{1}{3}$ cups of flour. If the flour canister had 8 cups of flour before he started baking, how much flour is left?

A) $4\frac{3}{5}$ c

B) $5\frac{5}{6}$ c

C) $4\frac{1}{6}$ c

D) $5\frac{2}{5}$ c

24. Solve for y: $6x - 2y = 10$

A) $6y + 10$

B) $5 - 3x$

C) $10 - 6y$

D) $3x - 5$

25. Julie ran 5.5 kilometers. How many meters did she run?

A) 5500 m

B) 550 m

C) 55,000 m

D) 55 m

26. Solve the proportion: $\frac{5}{x} = \frac{7}{14}$

A) 70

B) 10

C) 2.5

D) 25

27. Yuri's cell phone bill is computed using the formula $A = 50 + 0.15(x - 750)$, where x is the number of texts he sends for the month. Find the amount of Yuri's bill when he sends 820 texts.

   A) $173
   B) $60.50
   C) $123
   D) $39.50

28. Put the following numbers in order from least to greatest: $-0.31, 0.25, -\frac{2}{5}, \frac{1}{3}$

   A) $0.25, -0.31, \frac{1}{3}, -\frac{2}{5},$
   B) $-0.31, -\frac{2}{5}, \frac{1}{3}, 0.25$
   C) $\frac{1}{3}, 0.25, -0.31, -\frac{2}{5}$
   D) $-\frac{2}{5}, -0.31, 0.25, \frac{1}{3}$

29. If one serving of milk contains 280 milligrams of calcium, how much calcium is in 1.5 servings?

   A) 187 mg
   B) 295 mg
   C) 420 mg
   D) 200 mg

30. How many meters long is a 100-yard dash?

   A) 109.4 m
   B) 9.14 m
   C) 1094 m
   D) 91.4 m

31. Solve: $3(2y + 1) + 3 = 4(y - 2)$

   A) -7
   B) 7
   C) -1
   D) -6

32. A snail moves about 0.029 miles per hour. Convert its speed to inches per second.

   A) 0.23 in/sec
   B) 0.51 in/sec
   C) 5 in/sec
   D) 2 in/sec

33. Simplify the following expression:
   $2x - 3xy + 4x - 9y + 2xy$

   A) $-4xy$
   B) $6x - xy - 9y$
   C) $-4x4y$
   D) $6x^2 - x^2y^2 - 9y$

34. Find the product of $\frac{4}{5}$ and $\frac{9}{10}$.

   A) $\frac{13}{15}$
   B) $\frac{18}{25}$
   C) $\frac{13}{50}$
   D) $\frac{8}{9}$

35. Sarah works $22\frac{1}{2}$ hours per week, which she splits between two departments. Sarah spends $\frac{1}{3}$ of her hours working for the marketing department. How many hours per week does Sarah work for marketing?

   A) $6\frac{1}{3}$ hr
   B) 7 hr
   C) $7\frac{1}{2}$ hr
   D) $8\frac{2}{3}$ hr

36. There were 135 people in an auditorium. If the auditorium was 45% full, how many seats are in the auditorium?

   A) 300 seats
   B) 608 seats
   C) 180 seats
   D) 500 seats

37. Solve the following proportion:

$$\frac{2}{0.5} = \frac{7}{x}$$

A) 3.5

B) 35

C) 28

D) 1.75

38. Write 2.75 as a mixed number in lowest terms.

A) $2\frac{3}{4}$

B) $2\frac{5}{7}$

C) $2\frac{1}{5}$

D) $2\frac{3}{5}$

39. Two out of three dental patients request fluoride treatment after their dental cleanings. If 147 patients get their teeth cleaned this week, how many will probably choose to have fluoride treatment?

A) 98 patients

B) 22 patients

C) 49 patients

D) 125 patients

40. Chan owes his parents $2500. So far he has paid back $800. What percent of the original loan has Chan paid back?

A) 68%

B) 32%

C) 16%

D) 8%

41. Simplify the following expression: $\frac{4x^6y^2}{3x^2y^4}$

A) x^3y^2

B) $\frac{4x^3}{y^2}$

C) $\frac{4x^4}{3y^2}$

D) $12x^4y^2$

42. The distance from Boston to New York City is 215 miles. Convert the distance to kilometers. Round to the nearest whole number.

A) 108 km

B) 134 km

C) 400 km

D) 346 km

43. Simplify the following expression:

$2(3x + 4y) + 7(2x - 2y)$

A) $20x - 6y$

B) $5x + 2y$

C) $20x^2 - 6y^4$

D) $20x + 22y$

44. The bill for a gallbladder surgery was $9400. Insurance paid $6580, and the patient was responsible for the rest. What percent of the bill did the patient have to pay?

A) 70%

B) 80%

C) 20%

D) 30%

45. Solve the following proportion:

$$\frac{25}{100} = \frac{12}{x}$$

A) 48

B) 3

C) 1200

D) 300

46. An investor believes she will make $12 for every $100 she invests. How much would she expect to make on a $1500 investment?

A) $125

B) $112

C) $180

D) $120

47. A hospital delivered 2213 babies last year, and 44% of those babies were boys. How many boys were born in that hospital last year? Round the answer to the nearest whole number.

A) 1239 boys
B) 1170 boys
C) 974 boys
D) 503 boys

48. A recipe calls for $1\frac{3}{4}$ cups sugar. How much sugar is needed to triple the recipe?

A) $3\frac{3}{4}$ c
B) $\frac{7}{12}$ c
C) $5\frac{1}{4}$ c
D) $4\frac{1}{5}$ c

49. The average rainfall in May for Austin, Texas, is 4.5 inches. In July, the average rainfall is 1.67 inches. How much more precipitation falls on average in May than in July?

A) 1.22 in
B) 2.97 in
C) 2.83 in
D) 6.17 in

50. Simplify the following expression:
$20 \times 2 \div 2^2 + 5(-2)$

A) 0
B) 10
C) −50
D) 140

51. Simplify the following expression:
$15 \div 3 \times 5 - 10$

A) −15
B) −9
C) −25
D) 15

52. How much saline solution is needed to fill 24 bottles that each hold 0.75 liters?

A) 18 L
B) 32 L
C) 24 L
D) 6 L

53. Which decimal number is approximately $\frac{5}{6}$?

A) 0.083
B) 0.056
C) 0.83
D) 0.56

54. How many $\frac{1}{3}$-cup servings can be poured from $5\frac{2}{3}$ cups of juice?

A) 17 servings
B) $1\frac{1}{9}$ servings
C) 51 servings
D) $15\frac{1}{3}$ servings

55. Solve: $6x - 7 = 5(2x + 1)$

A) −3
B) −2
C) 4
D) 3

Reading

Directions: Read the passage carefully, and then read the questions that follow and choose the most correct answer.

The discovery of penicillin by Alexander Fleming in 1928 revolutionized medical care. The widespread use of penicillin and other antibiotics has saved millions of people from the deadliest bacterial infections known to humans and prevented the spread of bacterial diseases. But we have relied on antibiotics too heavily, which has undermined their effectiveness as bacteria evolve resistance to these drugs.

To add to the problem, factory farms across the United States are inundating pigs, cattle, chickens, and turkeys with cocktails of antibiotics to prevent diseases from proliferating among their tightly packed livestock. Because livestock manure is used as fertilizer, drug-resistant bacteria are spreading within the soils and waterways of farms, contaminating even plant-producing environments. The result: a dramatic rise in drug-resistant bacterial infections, sickening two million people per year and killing 23,000 in the United States alone.

1. Which sentence best summarizes the passage's main idea?

   A) "The discovery of penicillin by Alexander Fleming in 1928 revolutionized medical care."

   B) "The widespread use of penicillin and other antibiotics has saved millions of people from the deadliest bacterial infections known to humans and prevented the spread of bacterial diseases."

   C) "But we have relied on antibiotics too heavily, which has undermined their effectiveness as bacteria evolve resistance to these drugs."

   D) "Because livestock manure is used as fertilizer, drug-resistant bacteria are spreading within the soils and waterways of farms, contaminating even plant-producing environments."

2. Readers can infer from reading this passage that the author feels _____ about the "dramatic rise in drug-resistant bacterial infections."

   A) relieved
   B) concerned
   C) infuriated
   D) enthralled

3. What is the meaning of the word *revolutionized* in the first sentence?

   A) rebelled and rejected authority
   B) protested unfair treatment
   C) inspired hopeful thoughts
   D) transformed and modernized

4. Which of the following is NOT listed as a detail in the passage?

   A) Factory farms give antibiotics to pigs, cattle, chickens, and turkeys.

   B) Factory farmers give their animals "cocktails of antibiotics"—more than one kind of antibiotics.

   C) On factory farms, livestock are packed closely together.

   D) On some farms, free-range chickens and turkeys can wander about the property.

5. What is the author's primary purpose in writing this essay?

   A) to suggest changing the ways we use antibiotics

   B) to suggest that people need to stop taking so many antibiotics

   C) to honor Alexander Fleming's groundbreaking discovery of penicillin

   D) to suggest that factory farmers need to start treating their animals more humanely

6. In the last sentence, what does the word *dramatic* mean?

    A) theatrical

    B) impressive

    C) thrilling

    D) striking

Studies by the American Medical Association and the American Cancer Society link the prevalence of over a dozen types of cancer to smoking cigarettes: colon cancer, pancreatic cancer, kidney cancer, liver cancer, stomach cancer, throat cancer, lung cancer, and leukemia, among others, are believed to be related to heavy tobacco smoking. Even though cigarette use has been plummeting in the United States, close to 40 million people continue to smoke. This number is troubling, especially when one considers that nearly 30 percent of all cancer-related deaths in the United States can be tied to smoking. To make matters worse, cigarette-linked cancers disproportionately affect men of color, especially if they come from lower-income communities. This means that smoking continues to be not only an issue of public health, but also one of social equity.

    Smoking is linked to other health problems as well. Heart disease and stroke are among the most visible, but cigarette smoke affects nearly every organ in the human body. It is correlated with birth defects, lower sperm counts, diabetes, lower bone density, tooth loss and gum disease, and more.

    Continuing research reinforces the necessity of anti-smoking campaigns, both government funded and grassroots. The numbers show that such campaigns work, encouraging people to quit smoking. For the moment, however, the United States still has a long road of anti-smoking campaigning ahead.

---

7. Which sentence best summarizes the passage's main idea?

    A) "Studies ... link the prevalence of over a dozen types of cancer to smoking cigarettes."

    B) "Even though cigarette use has been plummeting in the United States, close to 40 million people continue to smoke."

    C) "This number [40 million smokers] is troubling, especially when one considers that nearly 30 percent of all cancer-related deaths in the United States can be tied to smoking."

    D) "[The fact that 'cigarette-linked cancers disproportionately affect men of color'] means that smoking continues to be not only an issue of public health, but also one of social equity."

8. Which of the following is NOT listed as a detail in the passage?

    A) The American Medical Association and the American Cancer Society have sponsored studies that show smoking cigarettes causes cancer.

    B) Studies show that more than a dozen kinds of cancer can be caused by cigarette smoking.

    C) Cigarette smoking is also linked to heart disease, strokes, birth defects, and diabetes.

    D) Tobacco companies advertise cigarettes on billboards and smaller signs in low-income neighborhoods.

9. Which phrase from the passage has about the same meaning as "are believed to be related to" in the first paragraph?

   A) "can be tied to" (paragraph 1)

   B) "disproportionately affect" (paragraph 1)

   C) "are among the most visible" (paragraph 2)

   D) "still has a long road ... ahead" (paragraph 3)

10. What is the author's primary purpose in writing this essay?

   A) to suggest "the necessity of anti-smoking campaigns"

   B) to scare smokers into quitting cigarette smoking immediately

   C) to honor the research done by the American Medical Association and the American Cancer Society

   D) to express anger at big tobacco companies that continue to target people who do not realize how harmful smoking can be

11. Readers can infer from reading this passage that the author thinks all cigarette smokers _____.

   A) are uneducated

   B) should quit smoking

   C) are low-class people

   D) should stop smoking near their children

12. In the last sentence, what does the phrase "still has a long road ... ahead" mean?

   A) People should not smoke on public transportation.

   B) A cancer patient has a long, grueling treatment program to suffer through.

   C) Anti-smoking campaigns still have a lot more work to do in the United States.

   D) Even if you drive with the window open, you should not smoke while driving.

While smoking remains a public health concern for politicians and medical practitioners, a new epidemic has entered the media's sights: drug overdoses. Over 70,000 people in the United States died from drug overdoses in 2017; 68 percent of those involved opioids. This epidemic began in the late 1990s with the overprescription of legal drugs for pain management—pharmaceutical companies downplayed their addictive qualities—and their subsequent misuse.

In particular, one extremely powerful opioid has raised the concerns of law enforcement officials and medical professionals: fentanyl. Fentanyl and its close cousins, oxycodone (commonly known by its brand name, Oxycontin, or just "oxy") and methadone, have made the leap from prescription drugs to street fare. Now add drugs such as heroin into the mix. Fentanyl, which is fifty times more potent than heroin, is mixed with heroin for sale on the street, leading to more overdoses from street drugs than ever before.

The impact of the opioid epidemic has been so devastating that the life expectancy for men—who disproportionately die from overdoses—has decreased in recent years. In particular, the number of deaths between the ages of twenty-five and fifty-four has increased, largely because this is the prime age range for risky drug use. White people account for the majority of opioid-related deaths, and the epidemic has hit hard in rural communities and among veterans. Government officials are focusing on drug prevention and rehabilitation programs, and the epidemic has been declared a public health emergency.

13. Which sentence best summarizes the passage's main idea?

   A) In the United States there is an epidemic of opioid drug overdoses.

   B) The majority of users who die from opioid drug overdoses are white people.

   C) Politicians and medical practitioners still consider smoking a public health concern.

   D) The US government has declared opioid drug use a public health emergency.

14. What is the meaning of the word *concern* in the first sentence?

   A) distressed state

   B) fretfulness

   C) worrisome matter

   D) establishment or business

15. Which of the following is NOT listed as a detail in the passage?

   A) In 2017 in the United States, over 70,000 people died from drug overdoses.

   B) Of the 70,000 drug overdoses in 2017, 68 percent were related to opioids.

   C) Fentanyl and Oxycontin, once available only by prescription, are now sold illegally on the street.

   D) Drug companies that manufacture opioids are taking responsibility for the opioid epidemic.

16. What is the author's primary purpose in writing this essay?

   A) to reassure readers that public health officials have the opioid crisis well in hand

   B) to inform readers that opioid drug overdoses are a serious problem in the United States

   C) to persuade opioid drug users to enter treatment as soon as possible

   D) to tell a story about a drug dealer who mixed fentanyl with heroin, which caused users to overdose

17. Readers can infer from reading this passage that public health officials have not yet _____.

   A) learned what causes drug overdoses in the United States

   B) gotten the opioid drug overdose epidemic under control

   C) studied pharmaceutical drug companies' role in selling addictive pain killers

   D) figured out which types of people have been hit hardest by the opioid drug crisis

18. In the last paragraph, what does the word *prime* mean in the phrase "prime age range"?

   A) superior

   B) first-rate

   C) primary

   D) best

Chronic traumatic encephalopathy (CTE) is a degenerative brain disease that has garnered the attention of the media in recent years. Medical studies have indicated that American football players have a higher chance of developing CTE than many other athletes because of the repeated brain trauma that results from helmet-to-helmet collisions on the field. Some studies have found that nearly 87 percent of all football players show signs of CTE. This is a troubling statistic, considering that CTE has been linked to memory loss, mood disorders, and even dementia. There is also a strong correlation with CTE and suicide, and it may be the high percentage of suicides among former NFL players that has shed light on the troubling symptoms of chronic head trauma.

Many organizations, colleges, and high schools have responded by introducing stricter standards for concussion protocols and head-to-head collisions. However, even these protocols have done little to mitigate the traumatic consequences of accidental helmet-to-helmet collisions that occur on a daily basis on football fields across the country.

Many concerned parents have begun to ask if football is too violent a sport for their children. It may be too early for Americans to honestly answer this question, but there is certainly room for growing concern. Recent statistics show a decline in enrollment in youth football programs across the country, and for good reason: head trauma—no matter how many times or how often—appears to have long-term effects on the brain and the mind.

19. Which sentence best summarizes the passage's main idea?

A) CTE is a degenerative brain disease that a large percentage of American football players develop.

B) CTE has been linked to memory loss, mood disorders, dementia, and suicide among former NFL players.

C) Many organizations, colleges, and high schools have introduced stricter standards for concussion protocols and head-to-head collisions.

D) Stricter protocols have done little to alleviate the results of accidental helmet-to-helmet collisions that occur on football fields.

20. What is the meaning of the word *garnered* in the first sentence?

A) harvested

B) gotten

C) stored

D) accumulated

21. What is the author's primary purpose in writing this essay?

A) to reassure readers that football players' brains can heal from CTE

B) to suggest that, following any kind of head trauma, an athlete should take several months off to heal

C) to suggest that football may be too violent a sport for children and teenagers to play

D) to persuade readers not to allow their children to play high school sports such as football

22. Which of the following is NOT listed as a detail in the passage?

A) Studies have shown that American football players have a higher chance of developing CTE than other athletes do.

B) When playing football, players sustain repeated brain trauma from helmet-to-helmet collisions.

C) Studies have shown that nearly 87 percent of all football players show signs of CTE.

D) Professional football organizations across the United States are taking responsibility for the high incidence of CTE among players.

23. In the second paragraph, the author writes, "It may be too early for Americans to honestly answer this question, but there is certainly room for growing concern." To which question does the author refer?

A) Is playing professional football worth suffering memory loss, mood disorders, and dementia?

B) Should football fans stop attending games and watching football on television?

C) Is CTE so painful that it causes sufferers to commit suicide?

D) Is tackle football too violent a sport for children?

24. Readers can infer from reading this passage that professional football's future _____.

A) may be threatened

B) will not be affected by CTE studies

C) will definitely be threatened

D) should be threatened, due to suicides among former players

Inflammation is a word that resonates throughout the health and wellness industries today. Though seemingly pervasive, inflammation is hardly ever explicitly defined. What is the medical definition of inflammation? What are some of its causes?

We typically think of inflammation as the swelling and soreness of an injured or infected part of the body. That part of the body may also appear red and be hot to the touch. But, at a biological level, inflammation is caused by the aggressive chemical signals sent by immune cells calling on other cells and substances to converge on the injury or infection to protect and heal it. Blood flow is increased, causing the heat and redness, and fluids can leak into the surrounding tissue, causing the swelling and soreness.

Although inflammation is, first and foremost, one of the body's most vital forms of defense, it can also be detrimental if it does not "turn off" or if it rushes to the aid of otherwise healthy tissue. Inflammatory diseases such as inflammatory bowel disease (IBD) or rheumatoid arthritis can have debilitating effects. Chronic inflammation can cause pain, fatigue, gastrointestinal problems, and other symptoms. Anti-inflammatory medications and certain steroids can lessen the inflammation and relieve some of the symptoms.

25. Which of the following statements can the reader infer from the passage?

   A) Inflammation is mainly detrimental to the body.

   B) Inflammation is caused by the body's own immune system.

   C) Inflammation is always a good sign: it means the immune system is working well.

   D) When a body part becomes too inflamed, the immune system rushes to heal that body part.

26. In the second paragraph, what does the word *aggressive* mean?

   A) violent

   B) destructive

   C) forceful

   D) hardline

27. What is the author's primary purpose in writing this essay?

   A) to advise readers on ways to treat patients with IBD or rheumatoid arthritis

   B) to warn readers with inflammatory diseases not to take too many steroids

   C) to define inflammation and inform readers about its causes and effects

   D) to point out that research scientists are still searching for the causes of inflammation

28. Which sentence best summarizes the passage's main idea?

   A) "Inflammation is a word that resonates throughout the health and wellness industries today."

   B) "[A]t a biological level, inflammation is caused by the aggressive chemical signals sent by immune cells calling on other cells and substances to converge on the injury or infection to protect and heal it."

   C) "Inflammatory diseases such as inflammatory bowel disease (IBD) or rheumatoid arthritis can have debilitating effects."

   D) "Anti-inflammatory medications and certain steroids can lessen the inflammation and relieve some of the symptoms."

29. In the last paragraph, what does the word *debilitating* mean?

   A) devastating and unbearable

   B) inconvenient and bothersome

   C) medicating and healing

   D) weakening or incapacitating

30. According to the passage, what causes inflammation?

   A) "swelling and soreness of an injured or infected part of the body"

   B) "chemical signals sent by immune cells calling on other cells ... to converge"

   C) "heat and redness, and fluids [leaking] into the surrounding tissue"

   D) "pain, fatigue, gastrointestinal problems, and other symptoms"

Have you ever wondered why exactly we feel pain when we get hurt? Or why some patients feel phantom pain even in the absence of a real trauma or damage? Pain is a highly sophisticated biological mechanism, one that is often downplayed or misinterpreted. Pain is much more than a measure of tissue damage—it is a complex neurological chain reaction that sends sensory data to the brain. Pain is not produced by the toe you stubbed; rather, it is produced once the information about the "painful" incident reaches the brain. The brain analyzes the sensory signals emanating from the toe you stubbed, but the toe itself is not producing the sensation of pain.

In most cases, the brain offers accurate interpretations of the sensory data that is sent to it via the neurological processes in the body. If you hold your hand too close to a fire, for instance, the brain triggers pain that causes you to jerk your hand away, preventing further damage.

Phantom pain, most commonly associated with the amputation or loss of a limb, on the other hand, is triggered even in the absence of any injury. One possible explanation is that the spinal cord is still processing sensations from that area.

The science of pain management is complex and still poorly understood. However, anesthetics or anti-inflammatory medications can reduce or relieve pain by disrupting the neurological pathways that produce it. The absence of pain, however, is a double-edged sword—sometimes pain is the only clue to an underlying injury or disease. Likewise, an injury or disease can dull or eliminate pain, making it impossible to sense when something is actually wrong.

31. Readers can infer from the passage that pain is _____.

   A) simple: pain is painful

   B) more complicated than most people know

   C) caused by the body's system of endocrine glands

   D) often exaggerated in patients' minds

32. What does the term "phantom pain" mean in the first and third paragraphs?

   A) ghostly pain

   B) pain that is *not* the result of an injury

   C) mild pain

   D) pain that is "a double-edged sword"

33. According to the passage, what is true of phantom pain?

   A) It is psychological, not physical; in other words, it is not real.

   B) Biologists are mystified by this kind of pain.

   C) It occurs because the body remembers how painful it felt when a limb was severely injured.

   D) It may happen because the spinal cord is still processing sensations from an amputated limb.

34. On which system of the human body does the author focus in this passage?

   A) the neurological system

   B) the immune system

   C) the circulatory system

   D) the cardiovascular system

35. Which sentence best summarizes the passage's main idea?

A) Many people wonder why we feel pain when we are injured, or why some patients feel phantom pain.

B) Pain is a complicated biological process, one that many people misjudge or do not understand.

C) When you stub your toe, your brain analyzes the sensory signals coming from your injury.

D) Anti-inflammatory medications can lessen or ease pain by affecting neurological processes.

36. In the last paragraph, the phrase "a double-edged sword" means that the absence of pain can be _____.

A) positive or negative

B) mild or unbearable

C) caused by knife wounds

D) even more painful than pain

In the digital age, with all its technological advances, it is hard to imagine a world without modern medical breakthroughs. But what we now consider "modern" medicine is still a relatively new phenomenon, having truly begun to develop in the nineteenth century. Many historians look to the scientific and technological advancements that followed the Industrial Revolution in the late eighteenth century and the Civil War in the nineteenth century as the beginnings of modern medicine.

Before the 1840s, surgery did not include the use of anesthesia. But on October 16, 1846, the first public demonstration of using ether to render a patient unconscious and immune to pain during surgery made waves throughout the medical community. Before the discovery of anesthesia, patients had to merely endure as doctors sliced into their bodies with scalpels. The types of surgeries that could be performed remained limited because it was nearly impossible to carry out more advanced operations or research while patients were writhing in pain.

Just twenty years later, the unprecedented bloodshed of the Civil War resulted in many medical innovations. Although many of the battlefield practices seem barbaric by today's standards, the sheer volume of medical need encouraged medical personnel, public health advocates, scientists, and inventors to seek more effective and humane treatment. Advances in amputation techniques, infection control, and transport of patients all stem from Civil War medicine. In addition, plastic surgery and prosthetics design took turns for the better after the war. As a result, the late nineteenth and early twentieth centuries witnessed a wave of new medicines, tools, and technologies.

37. What is the author's primary purpose in writing this passage?

A) to inform readers about the latest breakthroughs in surgical techniques

B) to give a history of modern medicine from the 1840s through the early 1900s

C) to inform readers about "barbaric" medical practices that occurred in army hospitals during the Civil War

D) to convince readers that the Civil War was mainly good for the United States, even though many thousands died

38. The author writes that "plastic surgery and prosthetics design took turns for the better" after the Civil War ended. Readers can infer that this occurred because so many soldiers _____ as a result of the war.

A) suffered post-traumatic stress disorder

B) dreamed of going to medical school

C) died of injuries and diseases

D) lost limbs and were disfigured

39. Which of the following statements can the reader infer from the passage?

A) During the Civil War, army doctors performed so many surgeries that they often ran out of ether.

B) After the Civil War there was a shortage of men, so United States medical schools began accepting women.

C) During the Civil War there was little money available to buy ether, and surgeons stopped using it for a few years.

D) Years after the Civil War was over, surgical patients benefitted from the sheer number of surgeries army doctors performed during the war.

40. According to the passage, how did the Civil War affect modern medicine?

A) The war caused advancements in medicine to cease for a few years.

B) The war did not greatly affect modern medicine.

C) The war caused advancements in many branches of medicine.

D) The war encouraged surgeons to use ether as an anesthetic.

41. Which sentence best summarizes the passage's main idea?

A) "In the digital age ... it is hard to imagine a world without modern medical breakthroughs."

B) "[T]he scientific and technological advancements that followed the Industrial Revolution in the late eighteenth century and the Civil War in the nineteenth century [were] the beginnings of modern medicine."

C) "[O]n October 16, 1846, the first public demonstration of using ether to render a patient unconscious and immune to pain during surgery made waves throughout the medical community."

D) "[T]he unprecedented bloodshed of the Civil War resulted in many medical innovations."

42. In the second paragraph, what does the word *endure* mean?

A) bear the pain

B) brave the hardships

C) survive the shortages

D) continue living

Aside from the uterus itself, the placenta is, perhaps, the most important organ directly involved with pregnancy. It is an organ that only exists during pregnancy; it is delivered after birth. Connected to the fetus through the umbilical cord, the placenta is a nutrient-rich organ attached to the wall of the uterus. It not only nourishes the fetus with crucial gases (i.e., oxygen), but it also protects the fetus by carrying away wastes.

Some scientists describe the placenta as a kind of "trading post." It exchanges nutrients between the blood supplies of the mother and the fetus—although the blood supplies do not intermingle throughout this process. Nutrients from the fetal blood and maternal blood are instead exchanged and regulated via blood vessels that filter each source without bringing them in direct contact. Since the maternal blood delivers nutrients to the fetus, pregnant people should strive for a healthy lifestyle. Certain substances can pass through the placenta, causing problems for the developing fetus. Alcohol, tobacco, and drugs are among the products that can cause lifelong medical complications or disorders.

43. Which of the following is NOT listed as a detail in the passage?

A) The placenta is delivered after the baby is born.

B) The placenta is attached to the uterine wall.

C) Some scientists call the placenta a "trading post."

D) The placenta protects the fetus from alcohol, tobacco, and drugs.

44. Which sentence best summarizes the passage's main idea?

   A) "Aside from the uterus itself, the placenta is, perhaps, the most important organ directly involved with pregnancy."

   B) "Some scientists describe the placenta as a kind of 'trading post.'"

   C) "Nutrients from the fetal blood and maternal blood are instead exchanged and regulated via blood vessels that filter each source without bringing them in direct contact."

   D) "Alcohol, tobacco, and drugs are among the products that can cause lifelong medical complications or disorders."

45. What is the author's primary purpose in writing this essay?

   A) to persuade pregnant women to avoid alcohol, tobacco, and drugs

   B) to inform readers about the placenta functions during pregnancy

   C) to explain the "trading post" metaphor that some scientists use

   D) to advise women to have their placentas checked regularly

46. What is the meaning of the word *intermingle* in the second paragraph?

   A) intermix

   B) interact

   C) amalgamate

   D) fuse

47. In the last sentence the author writes, "Alcohol, tobacco, and drugs are among the products that can cause lifelong medical complications or disorders." For whom or what can these substances cause "lifelong complications or disorders"?

   A) the uterus

   B) the placenta

   C) the mother

   D) the baby

48. Readers can infer from reading this passage that during pregnancy, the placenta is second in importance to the _____.

   A) mother

   B) fetus

   C) uterus

   D) blood

A devastating condition known as microcephaly has been affecting newborn babies across the world. Microcephaly literally means "small head." It can occur when a fetus's brain stops developing in utero. There is no known cure, and many babies born with microcephaly have other problems as a result, such as developmental delays or loss of hearing or vision. This microcephaly epidemic is strongly correlated with the mosquito-borne disease known as the Zika virus. As government authorities look to resolve this public health risk, scientists are working hard in their laboratories to better understand the connection between the Zika virus and microcephaly.

Thus far, evidence has shown that if a mother contracts Zika, either by being bitten by an infected mosquito or engaging in sexual activity with someone infected, the virus has the ability to cross the placental barrier between the mother and fetus. While Zika causes only mild symptoms—or more commonly, none—in the mother, it has more detrimental effects on the developing fetus. While researchers are rushing to find a cure or a vaccine, health officials are worried that the Zika virus might eventually mutate, making a cure even more elusive. Americans who are pregnant or planning to become pregnant have been advised not to travel to areas where Zika is known to be present, or if they must, to take great care to avoid mosquito bites.

49. What is the meaning of the word *devastating* in the first sentence?

A) demolishing

B) very harmful

C) confounding

D) very disturbing

50. Which of the following is NOT listed as a detail in the passage?

A) The word *microcephaly* means "small head."

B) Microcephaly causes a fetus's brain to stop developing.

C) Babies born with microcephaly may have developmental delays, hearing loss, or blindness.

D) The Zika virus has been reported in northwest India.

51. Which sentence best summarizes the passage's main idea?

A) Microcephaly, a terrible condition that affects newborns, is caused by the Zika virus.

B) Public health authorities are trying to resolve the microcephaly epidemic.

C) Research scientists are striving to better understand the link between the Zika virus and microcephaly.

D) The Zika virus causes only mild symptoms in the mother, but it stops her baby's brain from developing properly.

Instances of vector-borne illnesses are on the rise around the world. Government officials and scientists are concerned that climate change—specifically, the recent rises in temperatures and rainfall—is contributing to this increase in insect- and tick-borne disease, exacerbating these public health threats. Pathogens like the Zika, West Nile, Heartland, Lyme, dengue, chikungunya, and Bourbon viruses have been spreading throughout communities across the globe. Transmission of these viruses depends on the vector populations, which are in turn affected by numerous factors including not just climate but also the built environment, land use, pest control, and global commerce and travel. These environmental factors have changed the breeding and biting habits of ticks, fleas, and mosquitoes, which are now spreading illnesses at a more rapid rate. Warmer conditions are more hospitable to such species and have made it virtually impossible to eliminate these pests.

Recent research released by the US Centers for Disease Control and Prevention (CDC) shows that cases of vector-borne illnesses in the United States tripled between 2004 and 2016. Additionally, the CDC found nine new germs in mosquitoes and ticks in the United States in that time period. The media, the government, and researchers fear that we may be woefully unprepared to face what some have called a vector-borne crisis.

52. What is the author's primary purpose in writing this passage?

A) to advise readers on ways to immunize patients against vector-borne illnesses

B) to warn readers that vector-borne illnesses are on the rise worldwide

C) to tell readers some exciting news about new pesticides that kill vectors

D) to tell a story about a government agency that copes with epidemics

53. Which of the following is NOT a vector that carries illnesses?

A) Zika

B) ticks

C) fleas

D) mosquitoes

54. Which sentence best summarizes the passage's main idea?

A) "Instances of vector-borne illnesses are on the rise around the world."

B) "Government officials and scientists are concerned that climate change ... is contributing to this increase in insect- and tick-borne disease, exacerbating these public health threats."

C) "Pathogens like the Zika, West Nile, Heartland, Lyme, dengue, chikungunya, and Bourbon viruses have been spreading throughout communities across the globe."

D) "Recent research released by the US Centers for Disease Control and Prevention (CDC) shows that cases of vector-borne illnesses in the United States tripled between 2004 and 2016."

55. Which of the following statements can the reader infer from the passage?

A) Halting or slowing down climate change might also slow down the rise in vector-borne diseases.

B) Climate change has already reached its peak; global weather patterns are slowly returning to normal.

C) A number of people in the United States do not believe that climate change is real.

D) We can stop the rise in vector-borne diseases by eliminating pests such as fleas and ticks.

Vocabulary

Directions: Read the question and then choose the most correct answer.

1. Select the meaning of the underlined word in the sentence.

The MRI revealed a tumor in the child's naval cavity that the parents hoped was not <u>malignant</u>.

A) harmful

B) mobile

C) growing

D) large

2. Which word is not spelled correctly in the context of this sentence?

Several years after having eye surgery, the woman found her night vision impared.

A) several

B) surgery

C) vision

D) impared

3. Select the meaning of the underlined word in the sentence.

The patient's digestive tract was <u>intact</u> despite the intensive surgery he went through.

A) overactive

B) inflamed

C) ruptured

D) functional

4. Select the word that means "related to sound or hearing."

The acoustics in the auditorium were superb, allowing the audience to relish every note.

A) acoustics

B) auditorium

C) superb

D) relish

5. Select the meaning of the underlined word in the sentence.

The experienced nurse <u>demonstrated</u> a depth of knowledge that inspired confidence in the patient.

A) showed

B) questioned

C) withheld

D) intended

6. Select the word that best completes the sentence.

The interns had been at the conference all day and were relieved when the closing speech was _____.

A) expanded

B) boring

C) pedantic

D) concise

7. Select the meaning of the underlined word in the sentence.

Physicians who lack <u>compassion</u> usually have a poor bedside manner.

A) training

B) experience

C) sympathy

D) awareness

8. Select the meaning of the underlined word in the sentence.

<u>Chronic</u> pain can be treated through a combination of medications and physical therapy.

A) difficult

B) periodic

C) secondary

D) persistent

9. What best describes the term *supplement*?
    A) to add to
    B) to make darker
    C) to misunderstand
    D) to follow closely

10. Select the meaning of the underlined word in the sentence.
    Chronic <u>cephalic</u> pain often proves debilitating.
    A) heart
    B) head
    C) abdominal
    D) joint

11. What best describes the term *deficit*?
    A) a lack
    B) a theft
    C) a correction
    D) a mistake

12. Select the meaning of the underlined word in the sentence.
    Foods in the red and purple color group, such as berries, contain <u>potent</u> antioxidants.
    A) powerful
    B) weak
    C) detrimental
    D) nutritional

13. Select the meaning of the underlined word in the sentence.
    Bed rest can <u>impair</u> respiratory function and lead to pneumonia in elderly patients.
    A) concentrate
    B) allow
    C) increase
    D) weaken

14. What best describes the term *virulent*?
    A) pertaining to mental alertness
    B) opening easily
    C) severe and destructive
    D) loud and unexpected

15. Which word means to "diminish the seriousness of something"?
    A) extenuate
    B) interrogate
    C) incur
    D) interfere

16. What best describes the term *exogenous*?
    A) related to the blood vessels
    B) caused by bacterial pathogens
    C) regulated by hormones
    D) produced outside the body

17. Which word is not spelled correctly in the context of this sentence?
    Even healthy women often discover that incontinence encreases with age.
    A) healthy
    B) discover
    C) incontinence
    D) encreases

18. Select the meaning of the underlined word in the sentence.
    The mother experienced postpartum complications that required <u>prompt</u> medical intervention.
    A) complex
    B) immediate
    C) normal
    D) helpful

19. Select the word that means "a surface curved inward."

The young man's anorexia led to anemia and a prominently concave abdomen.

A) anorexia

B) anemia

C) prominently

D) concave

20. Select the meaning of the underlined word in the sentence.

The nurse <u>counseled</u> the patient to schedule a follow-up appointment with her primary care doctor.

A) ordered

B) advised

C) allowed

D) prevented

21. Select the word that best completes the sentence.

The kind-hearted nurse was always _____ when dealing with her patient.

A) indifferent

B) amused

C) compassionate

D) impatient

22. Select the meaning of the underlined word in the sentence.

Emergency rooms have seen more <u>abrasions</u> and broken bones since skateboarding became popular.

A) concussions

B) bruises

C) scrapes

D) rashes

23. Which word means "to open to the external environments"?

A) recur

B) expose

C) accept

D) degrade

24. What word best describes the term *abrasion*?

A) a corrosive element

B) a damaged area of skin

C) a compress applied to a wound

D) an infected wound

25. Select the meaning of the underlined word in the sentence.

All notes in a patient's medical record should be both accurate and <u>concise</u>.

A) factual

B) brief

C) consistent

D) recorded

26. Select the meaning of the underlined word in the sentence.

Muffled behind his surgical mask, the surgeon's words were barely <u>audible</u> to the intern.

A) understood

B) spoken

C) perceptible

D) clarified

27. Select the meaning of the underlined word in the sentence.

Documentation requirements exist to promote <u>accountability</u> for hospital employees.

A) responsibility

B) accuracy

C) compliance

D) confidence

28. Select the meaning of the underlined word in the sentence.

The posterior view of the injury showed further damage to his organs.

A) rear
B) front
C) side
D) top

29. Which word means "causing death or ruin"?

A) collapse
B) internal
C) fatal
D) detrimental

30. Select the word that means "to follow a command; acquiesce to another's wishes."

The students complied reluctantly with the burdensome rules in the class syllabus.

A) complied
B) reluctantly
C) burdensome
D) syllabus

31. Select the meaning of the underlined word in the sentence.

Women over sixty do not have the resilience following surgery that men of the same age have.

A) risk factors
B) rapid recovery
C) positive results
D) rapid heartbeat

32. Occult blood in the stool is

A) absent.
B) abnormal.
C) hidden.
D) moderate.

33. Select the word that best completes the sentence.

The Heimlich maneuver is used on someone who is choking and whose airway is

_____.

A) depressed
B) constricted
C) aggravated
D) hepatic

34. Which word is not spelled correctly in the context of this sentence?

The nursing student always studeed all night before an important test.

A) always
B) studeed
C) important
D) test

35. Select the meaning of the underlined word in the sentence.

In a child, a cough followed by a wheezing intake of air may be a symptom of whooping cough.

A) diagnosis
B) treatment
C) indication
D) sickness

36. Select the meaning of the underlined word in the sentence.

Patients on bed rest are told to restrict activity and only move around when absolutely necessary.

A) study
B) limit
C) anticipate
D) integrate

37. Select the word that means "abundant and plentiful."

Her copious notes helped her prepare for the difficult and technical final exam.

A) copious

B) difficult

C) technical

D) final

38. Select the meaning of the underlined word in the sentence.

Vigorous hand-washing is the best method for preventing the spread of <u>infection</u>.

A) disease

B) inflammation

C) irritation

D) dirt

39. Select the meaning of the underlined word in the sentence.

The blood test confirmed the nurse's <u>intuition</u> that her patient was regressing.

A) knowledge

B) hope

C) fear

D) instinct

40. Select the meaning of the underlined word in the sentence.

New nurses go through the <u>novice</u> stage and gradually become more competent and efficient.

A) beginner

B) difficult

C) knowledgeable

D) cautious

41. To assign priority to a patient is to

A) provide treatment.

B) triage the patient.

C) make a diagnosis of the patient's disorder.

D) ensure the patient is attended to first.

42. Select the word that best completes the sentence.

Patients with swelling in their feet are advised to _____ their feet above their heart.

A) restrict

B) elevate

C) accelerate

D) lower

43. The watery diarrhea of cholera victims is pathogenic because it

A) carries and causes disease.

B) causes dehydration.

C) is the most common symptom of cholera.

D) requires immediate medical attention.

44. What word best describes the term *ambulatory*?

A) not able to move

B) able to be transported

C) having the ability to walk

D) missing a limb

45. Select the meaning of the underlined word in the sentence.

The son wanted a genetic test to determine if he had inherited the same <u>malady</u> as his father.

A) eye color

B) intelligence

C) height

D) disease

46. Select the meaning of the underlined word in the sentence.

The employee break room serves as the <u>nexus</u> for informal communication in many offices.

A) space

B) source

C) conduit

D) center

47. Select the meaning of the underlined word in the sentence.

Hypotension can cause low <u>perfusion</u> of oxygen into tissues, leading to tissue damage.

A) spread

B) usage

C) adjustment

D) loss

48. A patient who wants to make a prudent choice should

A) decide quickly.

B) act carefully and sensibly.

C) think about the needs of others.

D) consider his or her own needs first.

49. A patient whose condition is labile is

A) improving.

B) undergoing treatment.

C) unstable.

D) lethargic.

50. Select the meaning of the underlined word in the sentence.

The <u>laceration</u> from the vertical saw required numerous sutures.

A) bruise

B) tear

C) abrasion

D) contusion

51. Women in more developed countries have increased longevity over men, meaning that

A) women will live longer.

B) men will live longer.

C) women will be healthier than men in old age.

D) men will be healthier than women in old age.

52. What best describes the term *compliant*?

A) following the rules

B) working together to achieve a goal

C) depending on someone else

D) asking for advice

53. Which word is not spelled correctly in the context of this sentence?

Everyone was delayed and working late accept for the lead nurse.

A) delayed

B) working

C) accept

D) lead

54. Which word is not spelled correctly in the context of this sentence?

The supervisor resinded the regulations pertaining to using cell phones at work.

A) supervisor

B) resinded

C) regulations

D) pertaining

55. Which word is not spelled correctly in the context of this sentence?

Some patients taking this medication have a tendincy to speak with slurred speech.

A) patients

B) tendincy

C) slurred

D) speech

Grammar

Directions: Read the question and then choose the most correct answer.

1. Which of the following sentences is grammatically correct?

    A) They are standing right over they're with their brother.

    B) They're standing right over their with there brother.

    C) Their standing right over there with their brother.

    D) They're standing right over there with their brother.

2. Which of the following sentences contains a plural subject?

    A) My brother's college graduation is on May 19th.

    B) I bought him a gift that I know he will like.

    C) The ceremony will begin at 11:00 in the morning.

    D) My parents and I will fly to Austin, Texas, on May 18th.

3. Select the best word for the blank in the following sentence.

    I can eat neither strawberries _____ tree nuts such as walnuts—I'm allergic to both.

    A) so

    B) yet

    C) or

    D) nor

4. Select the best word for the blank in the following sentence.

    What _____ does too much sunlight have on indoor plants?

    A) affect

    B) effect

    C) efficient

    D) affection

5. Which of the following sentences is grammatically correct?

    A) Brenda and Pauletta are working late because the deadline was tomorrow.

    B) Brenda and Pauletta were working late because the deadline was tomorrow.

    C) Brenda and Pauletta are working late because the deadline is tomorrow.

    D) Brenda and Pauletta is working late because the deadline is tomorrow.

6. Which of the following sentences contains a <u>coordinating</u> conjunction?

    A) I'll never again fly long distance in coach, nor will I ever again fly when I have a cold.

    B) Because the seats are so uncomfortable, it is impossible to sleep on a long-distance flight.

    C) If you fly when you are sick, you run the risk of infecting the other passengers.

    D) Although I love to travel, I dislike long plane rides—they are just too tiring.

7. Select the best word for the blank in the following sentence.

    Queen Elizabeth II has _____ over the United Kingdom for over sixty-five years (since 1952, when her father died).

    A) reined

    B) rained

    C) rayon

    D) reigned

8. Which word is used incorrectly in the following sentence?

Speaker Paul Ryan, the leader of the House of representatives, met with President Trump.

A) leader
B) representatives
C) President
D) Trump

9. Which of the following sentences contains a comparative adjective?

A) Of all the students in our class, Pablo was the only one who earned an *A* grade.
B) Of the two top students, Pablo earned an *A* and Emma earned an *A-minus*.
C) Of all the students in our class, Pablo is the most intelligent.
D) Emma and Pablo are both very intelligent.

10. Select the best word for the blank in the following sentence.

Rather than wear cute costumes forced upon them by humans, most animals would rather go _____.

A) bear
B) bare
C) beer
D) boar

11. Which of the following sentences contains two independent clauses?

A) Before I feed the cats, I need to finish my essay on responsibility.
B) Whenever the cats get hungry, they meow for food.
C) I'm willing to feed them, but I need to finish my essay first.
D) When a cat eats too fast, its stomach becomes upset.

12. Which word is used incorrectly in the following sentence?

Of the many art works on display, Peter's was the impressivest.

A) art
B) works
C) Peter's
D) impressivest

13. Which of the following sentences uses punctuation correctly?

A) My cat (Jack) likes the following items in this order: food, affection, and lying in the sunlight.
B) My cat Jack likes the following items in this order; food, affection, and lying in the sunlight.
C) My cat Jack likes the following items in this order: food, affection, and lying in the sunlight.
D) My cat Jack likes the following items in this order: food, affection, and lying in the sunlight?

14. Which of the following sentences contains an adverb that modifies an adjective?

A) Even in California, January can be a cold month.
B) In California, December and January are the coldest months.
C) Even in California, January can be an excruciatingly cold month.
D) Last January it was cold in Northern California.

15. Select the best word for the blank in the following sentence.

Mr. Henderson, a kind, fair _____, coached us in physical education at recess time.

A) Man
B) men
C) man
D) main

16. Which word is used incorrectly in the following sentence?

    If you brake that expensive glass vase, Dad will be very angry with you.

    A) If

    B) brake

    C) expensive

    D) angry

17. Select the best word for the blank in the following sentence.

    At the track _____, our team won two first-place medals.

    A) meat

    B) meet

    C) mete

    D) mate

18. Which word or phrase is used incorrectly in the following sentence?

    Because temperatures will drop below freezing tonight, we couldn't drive on the icy city streets.

    A) Because temperatures

    B) tonight

    C) couldn't drive

    D) icy city streets

19. Select the best punctuation mark for the blank in the following sentence.

    I felt like asking, "What are we doing here, anyway____"

    A) .

    B) !

    C) ?

    D) ;

20. Which of the following is a simple sentence?

    A) We stayed at the Palace Hotel in San Francisco, and we had a wonderful time.

    B) If you ever visit San Francisco, I highly recommend this hotel.

    C) San Francisco, in Northern California, is one of the most beautiful cities in the world.

    D) While we were at the hotel, we went swimming every day, and we ate many calories' worth of rich food.

21. Which word is used incorrectly in the following sentence?

    My twin cousins Sue and Sandy are the older cousins I have.

    A) twin

    B) are

    C) older

    D) cousins

22. Select the best word for the blank in the second sentence.

    Do you know the Raymer twins? _____ standing over there with their parents.

    A) They

    B) There

    C) Their

    D) They're

23. Select the best word for the blank in the following sentence.

    The experienced nurse was _____ by the grisly wound on the patient's leg.

    A) unphased

    B) unfazed

    C) unplaced

    D) unfaced

24. Which of the following sentences is grammatically correct?

A) Neither the administrative assistant nor her boss were scheduled to take a vacation.

B) Neither the administrative assistant or her boss was scheduled to take a vacation.

C) Either the administrative assistant nor her boss was scheduled to take a vacation.

D) Neither the administrative assistant nor her boss was scheduled to take a vacation.

25. Which of the following sentences contains a verbal phrase that modifies a proper noun?

A) Danny, smelling his favorite dish in the oven, smiled as he entered the kitchen.

B) Danny smelled his favorite dish in the oven, and he entered the kitchen.

C) Danny entered the kitchen, where his favorite dish cooked in the oven.

D) As he entered the kitchen, Danny smiled.

26. Select the best word for the blank in the following sentence.

I can't believe that you ate the _____ pie! Don't you feel sick?

A) hole

B) whole

C) howl

D) hall

27. Which punctuation mark is used incorrectly in the following sentence?

"Do you want to join us!" Adelaide asked.

A) " (opening quotation mark)

B) ! (exclamation point)

C) " (closing quotation mark)

D) . (period)

28. Which two words are used incorrectly in the following sentence?

Let's meat at my house for a barbecue; I've been marinating some meet in a spicy sauce.

A) Let's, I've

B) meat, meet

C) house, sauce

D) barbecue, spicy

29. Which of the following sentences contains an apostrophe that shows possession?

A) My sister Lani won't be starting college until next January.

B) She completed her applications too late to enter college in the fall.

C) It's too bad, because most of her friends will be leaving town in August or September.

D) Lani's mistake was dawdling during the months when she should have been paying attention to application deadlines.

30. Select the best word for the blank in the following sentence.

I don't plan to visit Russia ever again, _____ do I recommend that you go—we were robbed there.

A) but

B) so

C) yet

D) nor

31. Which of the choices is a homophone for a word in the sentence below?

The new member of the royal family has a sweet smile and a poised manner.

A) mambo

B) funnily

C) suite

D) pursed

32. Which <u>two</u> words are used incorrectly in the following sentence?

I want to where my fancy new dress, but I don't know wear I can do so—it is too fancy for most occasions.

A) I want

B) where, wear

C) fancy, dress

D) most occasions

33. Which of the following sentences uses capitalization and lowercasing correctly?

A) Cousin Sue will be at the Lake, and so will my cousins Sandy, Bonny, and Jack.

B) Cousin Sue will be at the lake, and so will my Cousins Sandy, Bonny, and Jack.

C) Cousin Sue will be at the lake, and so will my cousins Sandy, Bonny, and Jack.

D) Cousin Sue will be at the lake, and so will my cousins sandy, Bonny, and Jack.

34. Which of the following sentences is grammatically correct?

A) I'm having a hard time deciding what to were where.

B) I'm having a hard time deciding what to wear weird.

C) I'm having a hard time deciding what to wear where.

D) I'm having a hard time deciding what to wire which.

35. Which of the following sentences is grammatically correct?

A) If we loose the game, we won't go on to the semifinals.

B) If we lose the game, we won't go on to the semifinals.

C) If we louse the game, we won't go on to the semifinals.

D) If we lice the game, we won't go on to the semifinals.

36. Select the best word for the blank in the following sentence.

In _____ we always go camping in Yosemite National Park.

A) sooner

B) summer

C) sunner

D) sunnier

37. Which word is used incorrectly in the following sentence?

I lead the horse to water, but it refused to drink.

A) lead

B) water

C) but

D) drink

38. Which of the following sentences is grammatically correct?

A) My sister keeps dying her hair different neon colors like lime green and electric blue.

B) My sister keeps dyeing her hair different neon colors like lime green and electric blue.

C) My sister keeps dye her hair different neon colors like lime green and electric blue.

D) My sister keeps died her hair different neon colors like lime green and electric blue.

39. Which word is used incorrectly in the following sentence?

Please poor me a glass of lemonade.

A) Please

B) poor

C) glass

D) lemonade

40. Which word from the following sentence is a coordinating conjunction?

Imani offered to help Jake study for the quiz, but he said he prefers studying alone.

A) offered

B) quiz

C) but

D) prefers

41. Which of the following sentences uses capitalization correctly?

A) The Automobile industry earned more than Microsoft did last year.

B) The automobile industry earned more than microsoft did last year.

C) The Automobile Industry earned more than Microsoft did last year.

D) The automobile industry earned more than Microsoft did last year.

42. Which of the following sentences is grammatically correct?

A) The hurricane and the damaged levy flooded New Orleans, Slidell, and other places.

B) The hurricane and the damaged levy flooded New Orleans, Slidell, but other places.

C) The hurricane and the damaged levy flooded New Orleans, Slidell, yet other places.

D) The hurricane and the damaged levy flooded New Orleans, Slidell, for other places.

43. Which of the following sentences is grammatically correct?

A) Everyone want to succeed in business.

B) Everybody want to succeed in business.

C) None of us wants to owe a lot of money.

D) Nobody want to owe a lot of money to the bank.

44. Which punctuation mark is used incorrectly in the following sentence?

Here is how I answered her question; "Let's not eat early, because I'm still full from lunch."

A) ; (semicolon)

B) " (opening quotation mark)

C) ' (apostrophe)

D) . (period)

45. Which word from the following sentence is a conjunction?

I told my mom I would make dinner for everyone, but she said I should study instead.

A) told

B) dinner

C) but

D) instead

46. Which word is incorrectly capitalized or lowercased in the following sentence?

Mr. Yetto, my third-grade Teacher, used to do magic tricks for the class.

A) Mr.

B) Yetto

C) third

D) Teacher

47. Which of the following sentences is grammatically correct?

A) To insure that order is preserved, the mayor will order the police to keep the two groups of protesters apart.

B) To reassure that order is preserved, the mayor will order the police to keep the two groups of protesters apart.

C) To ensure that order is preserved, the mayor will order the police to keep the two groups of protesters apart.

D) To rest assured that order is preserved, the mayor will order the police to keep the two groups of protesters apart.

48. Select the best word or phrase for the blank in the following sentence.

My dog _____ me happy every day.

A) make

B) makes

C) will have made

D) should have make

49. Which of the following sentences is grammatically correct?

A) Please read allowed the first paragraph on page 143.

B) Please read aloud the first paragraph on page 143.

C) Please read aloft the first paragraph on page 143.

D) Please read about the first paragraph on page 143.

50. Which of the following sentences is grammatically correct?

A) Of the four paintings, Stanley's was the most beautiful.

B) Of the four paintings, Stanley's was more beautiful.

C) Of the four paintings, Stanley's was the beautifulest.

D) Of the four paintings, Stanley's was beautifuler.

51. Which word is used incorrectly in the following sentence?

Since our school colors are orange and black, I'm going to die a few of my white T-shirts orange.

A) our

B) colors

C) black

D) die

52. Select the best word for the blank in the following sentence.

I don't want to _____ my keys, so I put them in the same place every night.

A) loosen

B) loose

C) lose

D) lost

53. Which word is used incorrectly in the following sentence?

Please don't stair at strangers; it is rude and can make people feel uncomfortable.

A) Please

B) don't

C) stair

D) uncomfortable

54. Which of the following sentences is grammatically correct?

A) Mario realized he had burned the soup by leaving it on the stove for too long.

B) Left on the stove for too long, Mario realized he had burned the soup.

C) Burning on the stove, Mario realized he had left the soup on for too long.

D) Realizing that Mario had burned it, the soup stayed on the stove for too long.

55. Which of the following sentences contains a comparative adjective or adverb?

A) I have a terrible cold today.

B) I've been sneezing and coughing nonstop.

C) I'm very sorry to hear that, Pablo.

D) I hope your cold gets better by tomorrow.

Biology

Directions: Read the question carefully, and then choose the most correct answer.

1. A polar molecule always has:

   A) an overall negative charge.

   B) more than four shared electrons.

   C) a covalent bond.

   D) at least one hydrogen atom.

2. Which property of RNA makes it different from DNA?

   A) RNA contains cytosine.

   B) RNA carries the code for producing proteins.

   C) RNA contains uracil.

   D) RNA forms a helix.

3. Which of the following requires active transport to enter a cell?

   A) water

   B) sodium

   C) glucose

   D) carbon dioxide

4. What kind of gradient is formed by the movement of electrons across the electron transport chain?

   A) ATP

   B) oxygen

   C) proton

   D) NADH

5. A strand of DNA includes the nucleotide sequence ATGCTGG, but after replication the new strand has the sequence ATGCCTGG. What type of mutation occurred during replication?

   A) insertion

   B) deletion

   C) frameshift mutation

   D) chromosome inversion

6. What is produced when a sperm and an egg combine?

   A) zygote

   B) gamete

   C) somatic cell

   D) daughter cell

7. What is the function of ribosomes during protein synthesis?

   A) Ribosomes transcribe DNA into mRNA.

   B) Ribosomes replicate DNA.

   C) mRNA is translated into proteins on ribosomes.

   D) DNA is translated into carbohydrates on ribosomes.

8. Within the nucleus, DNA is tightly wound around histones. How does this arrangement regulate gene transcription?

   A) Enzymes are only able to reach regions of DNA where the chromatin has unwound.

   B) Histones are able to modify the DNA sequence of genes.

   C) DNA replication cannot occur while the chromatin is tightly wound.

   D) The tightly wound structure of chromatin prevents it from being carried out of the nucleus.

9. A scientist does a monohybrid cross to determine how a trait is inherited and finds that the trait is mostly seen in male offspring. What type of inheritance pattern does this gene show?

   A) dominant

   B) recessive

   C) X-linked

   D) gene linkage

10. What is the complementary DNA strand for 5'ATGCTGGGA3'?

   A) 5'GCAGCCAAT3'

   B) 3'TACGACCCT5'

   C) 5'TACGACCCT3'

   D) 3'CGTCGGTTA'3

11. Why do hydrogen bonds form in water?

   A) The negative charge on the oxygen atoms in one water molecule is attracted to the positive charge of a hydrogen atom in another water molecule.

   B) Electrons are shared equally between two molecules of water.

   C) Covalent bonds form between the oxygen of one water molecule and the hydrogen of another water molecule.

   D) Negatively charged hydrogen atoms bond with positively charged hydrogen atoms.

12. Which sugar is found in DNA?

   A) ribose

   B) deoxyribose

   C) glucose

   D) hexose

13. Cyanide inhibits the production of ATP. Which method of cellular transport would be affected by the presence of cyanide?

   A) active transport

   B) osmosis

   C) facilitated diffusion

   D) passive transport

14. In which biochemical pathway is pyruvate converted to CO_2?

   A) glycolysis

   B) fermentation

   C) Krebs cycle

   D) electron transport chain

15. What is the complementary DNA strand for 5'TTGGCCTTA3'?

   A) 3'AACCGGAAT5'

   B) 3'TAATGGTCA5'

   C) 3'ATTACCAGT5'

   D) 3'TTGGCCTTA5'

16. How does meiosis increase genetic variability in offspring?

   A) The chance of a mutation in DNA is increased during meiosis.

   B) Chromosomes are sorted independently during meiosis.

   C) New and unique chromosomes are added to the cell during meiosis II.

   D) Meiosis prevents mutations in DNA from being passed down to offspring.

17. Genes controlled by the trp operon are only expressed when tryptophan is absent. The trp operon is an example of:

   A) negative regulation.

   B) positive regulation.

   C) chromatin modification.

   D) promoter binding.

18. An individual who is heterozygous for a dominant trait is mated with an individual who is homozygous for the trait. What percentage of the offspring will be heterozygous for the trait?

   A) 25 percent

   B) 50 percent

   C) 75 percent

   D) 100 percent

19. To regulate gene transcription, a repressor binds to which part of an operon?

   A) promoter

   B) operator

   C) histone

   D) mutation

20. An organism's genotype is:
    A) the number of chromosomes in its somatic cells.
    B) the number of chromosomes in its gametes.
    C) the organism's physical traits.
    D) the organism's complete genetic code.

21. Which molecule is formed by joining monomers?
    A) glucose
    B) ribose
    C) DNA
    D) thymine

22. In which energy-producing pathway is pyruvate generated?
    A) glycolysis
    B) fermentation
    C) Krebs cycle
    D) electron transport chain

23. What is the mRNA strand for the DNA sequence TTGGCCTTA?
    A) UAAUGGUCA
    B) AACCGGAAT
    C) TTGGCCTTA
    D) UUGGCCUUA

24. A function of microtubules during the cell cycle is to:
    A) stop homologous chromosomes from attaching to each other.
    B) prevent the telomeres from becoming shorter in S phase.
    C) help separate chromosomes during anaphase.
    D) control crossing over between chromosomes during metaphase.

25. Where is mRNA translated into a protein?
    A) nucleus
    B) ribosomes
    C) vacuoles
    D) Golgi apparatus

26. During which phase of the cell cycle does the nuclear envelope dissolve?
    A) prophase
    B) prometaphase
    C) anaphase
    D) interphase

27. Which of the following molecules are embedded in the plasma membrane to facilitate the transport of molecules into or out of the cell?
    A) carbohydrates
    B) ATP
    C) lipids
    D) proteins

28. Which molecule is used as the final electron acceptor during fermentation?
    A) glucose
    B) pyruvate
    C) oxygen
    D) carbon dioxide

29. An individual who is heterozygous for a recessive trait is mated with an individual who is homozygous for the trait. What percentage of offspring will express the recessive trait?
    A) 25 percent
    B) 50 percent
    C) 75 percent
    D) 100 percent

30. In RNA, the nucleotide guanine binds to:

A) adenine.

B) cytosine.

C) thymine.

D) uracil.

Chemistry

Directions: Read the question carefully, and then choose the most correct answer.

1. How many protons does selenium (Se) have?

   A) 16

   B) 79

   C) 34

   D) 8

2. Which of the following elements has a full valence shell?

   A) fluorine (F)

   B) carbon (C)

   C) radon (Rn)

   D) sodium (Na)

3. Which of the following compounds contains an ionic bond?

   A) glucose ($C_6H_{12}O_6$)

   B) potassium nitrate (KNO_3)

   C) nitrate (NO_3^-)

   D) carbon tetrachloride (CCl_4)

4. In the following acid-base reaction, which species acts as a Brønsted-Lowry base?

   $HCl(aq) + H_2O\ (l) \rightarrow Cl^-\ (aq) + H_3O^+\ (aq)$

   A) HCl

   B) H_2O

   C) Cl^-

   D) H_3O^+

5. The solubility of sugar sucrose in water at 25°C is about 200 grams per 100 mL of water. If 205 grams of sugar is added to 100 mL of water so that some sugar is not dissolved, what type of mixture would be produced?

   A) saturated solution

   B) unsaturated solution

   C) supersaturated solution

   D) homogeneous mixture

6. When the temperature drops below 0°C (32°F), liquid water undergoes a phase transition. Which of the following describes this phase transition and energy change?

   A) Evaporation of water occurs, and energy is released to the surroundings.

   B) Freezing of water occurs, and energy is released to the surroundings.

   C) Evaporation of water occurs, and energy is absorbed from the surroundings.

   D) Freezing of water occurs, and energy is absorbed from the surroundings.

7. Which species is the oxidizing agent in the following reaction?

   $Zn(s) + 2AgNO_3(aq) \rightarrow 2Ag(s) + Zn(NO_3)_2(aq)$

   A) zinc (Zn)

   B) silver (Ag)

   C) silver nitrate ($AgNO_3$)

   D) zinc nitrate ($Zn(NO_3)_2$)

8. What type of radioactive decay produces a high-energy electron from the decomposition of a neutron?

   A) alpha decay

   B) beta decay

   C) gamma decay

   D) positron emission

9. In the following acid-base reaction, which pair of species acts as a Brønsted-Lowry acid?

   $NH_3(aq) + H_2O(l) \rightarrow NH_4^+(aq) + HO^-(aq)$

   A) NH_3 and H_2O

   B) NH_3 and NH_4^+

   C) H_2O and NH_4^+

   D) NH_4^+ and HO^-

10. Tungsten (W) is found in which group?

   A) group 4

   B) group 5

   C) group 6

   D) group 7

11. Which of the following organic molecules will have the highest boiling point?

   A) ethane (CH_3CH_3)

   B) propane ($CH_3CH_2CH_3$)

   C) n-butane ($CH_3CH_2CH_2CH_3$)

   D) n-pentane ($CH_3CH_2CH_2CH_2CH_3$)

12. How many electrons does a neutral atom of vanadium (V) have?

   A) 20

   B) 21

   C) 22

   D) 23

13. Which of the following elements has a full valence shell?

   A) hydrogen (H)

   B) helium (He)

   C) lithium (Li)

   D) nitrogen (N)

14. The solubility of sugar sucrose in water at 25°C is about 200 grams per 100 mL of water. If 250 g of sugar are fully dissolved in a glass containing 100 mL of water at 80°C, what type of mixture will be produced?

   A) saturated solution

   B) unsaturated solution

   C) supersaturated solution

   D) heterogeneous mixture

15. Which of the following elements is most likely to form a covalent bond with a nonmetal?

   A) boron (B)

   B) barium (Ba)

   C) potassium (K)

   D) calcium (Ca)

16. Which phase transition occurs when water vapor from the air forms liquid drops on the outside of a cold glass?

   A) sublimation

   B) freezing

   C) condensation

   D) deposition

17. What type of reaction is shown below?
    $$Cu(OH)_2(s) \rightarrow CuO(s) + H_2O(g)$$

   A) decomposition

   B) synthesis

   C) single displacement

   D) double displacement

18. Which of the following ionic substances has the greatest bond polarity?

   A) potassium chloride (KCl)

   B) rubidium chloride (RbCl)

   C) cesium chloride (CsCl)

   D) lithium chloride (LiCl)

19. Tin-112 (Sn-112) is the most abundant isotope of tin (Sn) and has a mass number of 112. How many neutrons does Sn-112 have?

   A) 62

   B) 60

   C) 58

   D) 50

20. Which of the following elements is NOT a transition metal?

A) gold (Au)

B) radium (Ra)

C) silver (Ag)

D) chromium (Cr)

21. Which of the following covalent bonds is the most polar?

A) C-O

B) C-B

C) C-F

D) C-N

22. The list below describes the relative strength of the intermolecular forces for several substances.

Intermolecular force strength:
$H_2O > CH_3CH_2OH > CH_4 > He$
Which of the substances will have the lowest boiling point?

A) water (H_2O)

B) ethanol (CH_3CH_2OH)

C) methane (CH_4)

D) helium (He)

23. What type of reaction is shown below?
$2AgNO_3(aq) + Zn(s) \rightarrow 2Ag(s) + Zn(NO_3)_2(aq)$

A) decomposition

B) synthesis

C) single displacement

D) double displacement

24. Which of the following elements is most likely to form a cation?

A) iodine (I)

B) calcium (Ca)

C) fluorine (F)

D) carbon (C)

25. If 8 moles of iron (Fe) react with unlimited oxygen gas (O_2), how many moles of iron (III) oxide (Fe_2O_3) are produced?
$4Fe(s) + 3O_2(g) \rightarrow 2Fe_2O_3(s)$

A) 1 mole

B) 2 moles

C) 3 moles

D) 4 moles

26. Which of the following elements is most likely to lose an electron to form a charge of 1+?

A) magnesium (Mg)

B) boron (B)

C) barium (Ba)

D) francium (Fr)

27. What type of reaction is shown below?
$KOH(aq) + HCl(aq) \rightarrow H_2O(l) + KCl(aq)$

A) decomposition

B) synthesis

C) single displacement

D) double displacement

28. Silver (Ag) is found in which period of the periodic table?

A) two

B) three

C) four

D) five

29. Which reactant is the limiting reactant if 6 moles of hydrogen gas (H_2) react with 1 mole of nitrogen gas (N_2) to produce ammonia gas (NH_3)?
$3 H_2(g) + N_2(g) \rightarrow 2 NH_3(g)$

A) hydrogen gas (H_2)

B) nitrogen gas (N_2)

C) ammonia (NH_3)

D) No limiting reactant exists.

30. Strontium (Sr) is likely to form an ion with which of the following charges?

  A) Sr^{2+}

  B) Sr^+

  C) Sr^-

  D) Sr^{2-}

Anatomy and Physiology

Directions: Read the question carefully, and then choose the most correct answer.

1. Which of the following organs does food pass through during digestion?
   A) pharynx
   B) gall bladder
   C) epiglottis
   D) pancreas

2. Which of the following refers to the large amount of air moved during a deep breath?
   A) vital signs
   B) vital capacity
   C) vital volume
   D) vital respiration

3. Which of the following terms best describes the position of the bladder relative to the uterus?
   A) inferior
   B) anterior
   C) distal
   D) lateral

4. The incus, stapes, and malleus play an important role in which sense?
   A) vision
   B) taste
   C) hearing
   D) smell

5. Which type of cell is NOT part of the antibody-mediated response to pathogens?
   A) cytotoxic T-cells
   B) B-cells
   C) plasma cells
   D) memory cells

6. Which of the following attaches skeletal muscle to bone?
   A) ligaments
   B) cartilage
   C) tendons
   D) nerves

7. A disruption in which of the following glands is most likely to cause a growth disorder?
   A) pituitary
   B) pineal
   C) parathyroid
   D) thyroid

8. Which of the following correctly describes the flow of food through the gastrointestinal tract?
   A) mouth → pyloric sphincter → esophagus
   B) esophagus → jejunum → stomach
   C) pylorus → duodenum → ileum
   D) stomach → ileum → duodenum

9. Which of the following protects the spinal cord?
   A) rib cage
   B) vertebral cavity
   C) sternal notch
   D) pelvic cavity

10. Which of the following is a sesamoid bone?
    A) hip bone
    B) sacrum
    C) patella
    D) sternum

11. Which of the following describes a function of cilia in the trachea?

   A) They keep the windpipe clear by moving mucus up.

   B) They prevent food from entering the trachea.

   C) They produce mucus to trap contaminants.

   D) They produce sound as air moves over them.

12. Which of the following does NOT contribute to semen?

   A) seminal vesicle

   B) prostate gland

   C) vas deferens

   D) Cowper's gland

13. Which of the following does the placenta develop from?

   A) blastocyst

   B) trophoblast

   C) ovule

   D) oocyte

14. Which of the following is a waste product that results from protein catabolism?

   A) uric acid

   B) urea

   C) nitrates

   D) phosphates

15. Synovial joints—gaps between bones—are filled with which of the following substances?

   A) air

   B) marrow

   C) fluid

   D) cartilage

16. Which division of the nervous system controls the digestive system?

   A) central

   B) sympathetic

   C) somatic

   D) enteric

17. Which of the following is true of a muscle that is fatigued?

   A) Very little ADP remains.

   B) There is a large amount of available glucose.

   C) The lactic acid level is high.

   D) Myoglobin releases carbon dioxide.

18. A patient arrives in the emergency room complaining of shortness of breath. A blood test shows that her iron level is low. Which of the following will likely also be decreased?

   A) hemoglobin

   B) plasma

   C) white blood cells

   D) platelets

19. In which part of a long bone is red marrow found?

   A) above the compact bone

   B) at the ends of the bone

   C) within the periosteum

   D) outside and around the trabecula

20. What structure drains the urine into the bladder?

   A) ureter

   B) urethra

   C) nephron

   D) glomerulus

21. Which of the following is the connective tissue that surrounds fascicles in the peripheral nervous system?

A) fascia

B) epineurium

C) meninges

D) myelin

22. Serosa, one of the layers of the stomach, secretes a serous fluid. What is the function of this fluid?

A) It protects the stomach from the acidity of its contents.

B) It prevents friction from the organs around the stomach.

C) It enables the stomach to stretch and relax.

D) It maintains a moist environment in the stomach.

23. The nervous system is responsible for gathering, transporting, and reacting to information. Which of the following parts of the nervous system transports information back and forth?

A) brain

B) spinal cord

C) nerves

D) sensory organs

24. In males, what happens to the external sphincter of the bladder during sexual activity?

A) It closes to prevent seminal fluid from entering the bladder.

B) It opens to facilitate flow of seminal fluid to the vas deferens.

C) It spasms to help create pressure to ejaculate the semen.

D) It retracts to push urine back to the ureters.

25. What role do the sinoatrial (SA) and atrioventricular (AV) nodes play in the circulatory system?

A) They control the amount of blood that enters the heart's chambers.

B) They produce fluid to lubricate the heart's muscles.

C) They coordinate the contraction of the atria and ventricles.

D) They repair injured muscle tissue around the heart.

26. What is one role of the eccrine glands in the integumentary system?

A) They collect excess water from the blood vessels.

B) They secrete hormones that regulate sweating.

C) They release sweat to maintain electrolyte balance.

D) They absorb urea and lactic acid from the skin.

27. Which of following best describes the function of white matter?

A) It gathers signals from the sensory organs.

B) It protects the brain from injury.

C) It transmits information between regions of the brain.

D) It secretes hormones that regulate the nervous system.

28. Which digestive enzyme breaks down fat molecules into monoglycerides and fatty acids?

A) pancreatic amylase

B) trypsin

C) pancreatic lipase

D) chymotrypsin

29. A male teenager develops a deep voice and hair on his chest. Which hormone is responsible for these secondary sex characteristics?

A) oxytocin

B) dopamine

C) testosterone

D) estrogen

30. Which of the following is NOT one of the four lobes of the cerebrum?

A) frontal

B) lateral

C) occipital

D) temporal

Physics

Directions: Work the problem carefully, and choose the best answer.

1. A ball is thrown straight in the air with a velocity of 12 meters per second. How high does it go?

   A) 7.35 m

   B) 9.80 m

   C) 17.35 m

   D) 22.0 m

2. What is the kinetic energy of a 3 gram bullet fired at 300 meters per second?

   A) 135 J

   B) 145 J

   C) 450 J

   D) 135,000 J

3. A rope with one end attached to a wall is shaken up and down. Visually, this is an example of what type of wave?

   A) mechanical

   B) electromagnetic

   C) longitudinal

   D) transverse

4. What is the mass of an elephant with momentum 12,000 kilogram meters per second walking at 2 meters per second?

   A) 600 kg

   B) 2400 kg

   C) 6000 kg

   D) 24,000 kg

5. Sound propagating through air is what kind of wave?

   A) transverse

   B) longitudinal

   C) electromagnetic

   D) water

6. A neutral particle is placed at rest directly between a north and south magnetic pole. In what direction does the particle move?

   A) It moves up.

   B) It moves down.

   C) It moves right.

   D) It does not move.

7. A force meter reads that a constant 2000 newtons of force is required to move an 800 kilogram sofa across a room. What is the coefficient of friction between the sofa and the floor?

   A) 0.26

   B) 0.32

   C) 0.56

   D) 1.32

8. If it takes 1 hour to push a 500 kilogram treasure chest 400 meters applying a constant 45 newtons of force, how much power was exerted to accomplish this task?

   A) 5 W

   B) 36 W

   C) 2500 W

   D) 18,000 W

9. A 2000 ohm and a 3000 ohm resistor are attached in parallel. What is the total resistance of the circuit?

   A) 1.5 Ω

   B) 1200 Ω

   C) 3000 Ω

   D) 5000 Ω

10. It is observed that on Planet X a known 60 kilogram mass exerts a 370 newton force on a scale. What is the acceleration due to gravity on Planet X?

A) 0.16 m/s^2

B) 0.62 m/s^2

C) 6.2 m/s^2

D) 18.5 m/s^2

11. How many electrons are contained in a group of charge equal to 1 coulomb?

A) 1.602×10^{-19}

B) 6.24×10^{-18}

C) 6.24×10^{18}

D) 1.602×10^{19}

12. A radio wave with wavelength of 1 meter propagates at the speed of light ($c = 3 \times 10^8$ meters per second). What is the frequency of this radio wave?

A) $0.33 \times 10^{-8} \text{ Hz}$

B) $3 \times 10^{-8} \text{ Hz}$

C) $0.33 \times 10^8 \text{ Hz}$

D) $3 \times 10^8 \text{ Hz}$

13. If unlimited 1800 ohm resistors are available, how many are needed to reach 3600 ohms?

A) one

B) two

C) three

D) four

14. The frequency of a wave increases by a factor of four. By what factor does the period change?

A) $\frac{1}{4}$

B) $\frac{1}{2}$

C) 2

D) 4

15. A washing machine draws 20 amperes from the wall socket at 120 volts. What is the electrical resistance of the washer?

A) $0.6 \, \Omega$

B) $6 \, \Omega$

C) $12 \, \Omega$

D) $240 \, \Omega$

16. An amusement park Gravitron ride presses riders against the wall with three times their weight. What is the centripetal force on an 80 kilogram rider in the ride?

A) 80 N

B) 784 N

C) 2352 N

D) 5352 N

17. Scientists measure the speed of light in a new material as 2.11×10^8 meters per second. What is the index of refraction of this new material?

A) 0.70

B) 1.21

C) 1.42

D) 2.11

18. A clay block with a mass of 2 kilograms moving to the left at 4 meters per second collides head-on with another clay block with a mass of 5 kilograms moving to the right at 1 meter per second. If they stick together after the collision, with what speed and in what direction do they move?

A) 0.43 m/s to the left

B) 0.43 m/s to the right

C) 1.86 m/s to the left

D) 1.86 m/s to the right

19. A car battery produces a voltage of 12 volts. If the battery leads are separated by 20 centimeters, what is the electric field between the leads?

    A) 0.6 N/C
    B) 6 N/C
    C) 60 N/C
    D) 600 N/C

20. A proton ($mp = 1.67 \times 10^{-27}$ kilograms) moves at 90% of the speed of light ($c = 3 \times 10^8$ meters per second) in a particle accelerator. What is the kinetic energy of the proton?

    A) 2.3×10^{-19} J
    B) 6.1×10^{-12} J
    C) 6.1×10^{-11} J
    D) 7.5×10^{-11} J

21. A hockey puck with a mass of 0.3 kilograms on ice slides at 2 meters per second and collides with another identical puck at rest. They stick together and continue sliding in the same direction as the first puck. What is the speed of these two pucks stuck together?

    A) 0.5 m/s
    B) 0.6 m/s
    C) 1 m/s
    D) 4 m/s

22. A laser beam is measured to be reflected off a mirror at an angle of 31 degrees. What was the beam's incident angle to the normal surface?

    A) 0°
    B) 29°
    C) 31°
    D) 59°

23. A merry-go-round accelerates at a constant 1.5 radians per second squared starting from rest. How many radians does the merry-go-round rotate through in the first 5 seconds?

    A) 3.75 rad
    B) 7.5 rad
    C) 18.75 rad
    D) 28.75 rad

24. The acceleration due to gravity on an object on the surface of Earth is 9.8 meters per second squared and exerts a force $F_g = mg$. What is the mass of Earth if its radius is 6400 kilometers?

    A) 6×10^{21} kg
    B) 6×10^{22} kg
    C) 6×10^{23} kg
    D) 6×10^{24} kg

25. A 12 kilogram rock is hanging from a light rope off the end of a circular pulley with a radius of 25 centimeters. What torque is applied by this rock as it hangs?

    A) 0 N m
    B) 3 N m
    C) 29.4 N m
    D) 2940 N m

26. What is the difference in gravitational potential energy of a 1 kilogram mass at the top of a 1000 meter mountain on Earth ($g_E = 9.8$ m/s^2) and Mars ($g_M = 3.8$ m/s^2)?

    A) 600 J
    B) 3800 J
    C) 6000 J
    D) 9800 J

27. If light is to be slowed to a speed equal to the speed of sound in air (v_s = 340 meters per second) inside a material, what must be the index of refraction of the material?

A) 0.88

B) 8.8

C) 3×10^5

D) 8.8×10^5

28. If the distance between two charges is doubled, by what factor is the magnitude of the electric force between them changed?

A) $\frac{1}{2}$

B) $\frac{1}{4}$

C) 2

D) 4

29. How far must a bowling ball with a mass of 5 kilograms fall to gain 100 joules of kinetic energy?

A) 2.04 m

B) 12.1 m

C) 25 m

D) 100 m

30. A parallel circuit has two identical resistors. If the resistance of each resistor suddenly doubles, what happens to the current through the circuit?

A) It goes to zero.

B) It halves.

C) It doubles.

D) It does not change.

ANSWER KEY

MATHEMATICS

1. **A)**

    $1 \text{ ft} \times \frac{12 \text{ in}}{\text{ft}} \times \frac{2.54 \text{ cm}}{\text{in}} = 30.48 \text{ cm} \approx \textbf{30.5 cm}$

2. **B)**

    $\frac{315}{5} - 10(-2) = 63 + 20 = \textbf{83}$

3. **C)**

    $1.73 + 2.17 = \textbf{3.9}$

4. **D)**

    $-4x + 2 = -34$

    $-4x = -36$

    $\boldsymbol{x = 9}$

5. **D)**

    $\frac{2}{3} - \frac{1}{4} = \frac{8}{12} - \frac{3}{12} = \boldsymbol{\frac{5}{12}}$

6. **A)**

    $4 \times \$20 = \$80$

    $\$24.17 + \$32.87 = \$57.04$

    $\$80.00 - \$57.04 = \textbf{\$22.96}$

7. **A)**

    Military times greater than 1200 are p.m. on the 12-hour clock. 1945 − 1200 = 745, which means it is **7:45 p.m.**

8. **C)**

    $\frac{3}{8} + \frac{1}{2} = \frac{3}{8} + \frac{4}{8} = \frac{7}{8}$

    $1 - \frac{7}{8} = \frac{8}{8} - \frac{7}{8} = \boldsymbol{\frac{1}{8}}$

9. **D)**

    part = whole × percent

    $500 \times 0.70 = \textbf{350}$

10. **B)**

    $(5 - 2)^3 - 14 \div 7 = 3^3 - 14 \div 7$

    $= 27 - 2 = \textbf{25}$

11. **B)**

    $-2100 + 11,200 = \$9100$

    $\$9100 \div 2 = \textbf{\$4550}$

12. **C)**

    $\$127 - \$150 = 127 + (-150) = \textbf{−23}$

13. **A)**

    $2(7 - 9) + 4 \times 10 = 2(-2) + 4 \times 10$

    $= -4 + 4 \times 10 = -4 + 40 = \textbf{36}$

14. **A)**

    $\text{percent} = \frac{\text{part}}{\text{whole}}$

    $\frac{270}{30,000} = 0.009 = \textbf{0.9\%}$

15. **B)**

    $\frac{1}{2} + \frac{2}{3} + \frac{1}{4}$

    $\frac{6}{12} + \frac{8}{12} + \frac{3}{12} = \frac{17}{12} = \boldsymbol{1\frac{5}{12}}$

16. **C)**

    $0.4 \times 0.2 = \textbf{0.08}$

17. **A)**

    $119.7 - 1.05 = \textbf{118.65}$

18. **A)**

    $600 - 125 = \textbf{475}$

19. **C)**

    1 week = 7 days

    $10 \times 8 \times 7 = \textbf{560}$

20. **B)**

    $\$24.96 \div 2.4 = \textbf{\$10.40}$

21. **B)**

    At 2400 hours, the 24-hour clock restarts at 0, so adding 3 hours to 2300 would be **0200 hours**.

22. **C)**

$14 \div 52 \approx \mathbf{0.269}$

23. **C)**

$2\frac{1}{2} + 1\frac{1}{3} = 2\frac{3}{6} + 1\frac{2}{6} = 3\frac{5}{6}$

$8 - 3\frac{5}{6} = \frac{48}{6} - \frac{23}{6} = \frac{25}{6} = \mathbf{4\frac{1}{6}}$

24. **D)**

$6x - 2y = 10$

$-2y = -6x + 10$

$\mathbf{y = 3x - 5}$

25. **A)**

$5.5 \text{ km} \times \frac{1000 \text{ m}}{1 \text{ km}} = \mathbf{5500 \text{ m}}$

26. **B)**

$\frac{5}{x} = \frac{7}{14}$

$7x = 70$

$\mathbf{x = 10}$

27. **B)**

$50 + 0.15(820 - 750)$

$50 + 0.15(70)$

$50 + 10.50 = \mathbf{60.50}$

28. **D)**

$-\frac{2}{5} = -0.4$

$\frac{1}{3} = 0.\overline{3}$

$\mathbf{-0.4 < -0.31 < 0.25 < 0.3}$

29. **C)**

$\frac{1}{280} = \frac{1.5}{x}$

$\mathbf{x = 420}$

30. **D)**

$100 \text{ yd} \times \frac{0.914 \text{ m}}{1 \text{ yd}} = \mathbf{91.4 \text{ m}}$

31. **A)**

$3(2y + 1) + 3 = 4(y - 2)$

$6y + 3 + 3 = 4y - 8$

$6y + 6 = 4y - 8$

$6y = 4y - 14$

$2y = -14$

$\mathbf{y = -7}$

32. **B)**

$\frac{0.029 \text{ mi}}{\text{hr}} \times \frac{5280 \text{ ft}}{\text{mi}} \times \frac{12 \text{ in}}{\text{ft}} \times \frac{1 \text{ hr}}{3600 \text{ sec}}$

$\approx \mathbf{0.51 \text{ in/sec}}$

33. **B)**

$2x - 3xy + 4x - 9y + 2xy$

$= 2x + 4x - 3xy + 2xy - 9y = \mathbf{6x - xy - 9y}$

34. **B)**

$\frac{4}{5} \times \frac{9}{10} = \frac{2}{5} \times \frac{9}{5} = \mathbf{\frac{18}{25}}$

35. **C)**

$22\frac{1}{2} \times \frac{1}{3} = \frac{45}{2} \times \frac{1}{3} = \frac{15}{2} = \mathbf{7\frac{1}{2}}$

36. **A)**

$\text{whole} = \frac{\text{part}}{\text{percent}}$

$\frac{135}{0.45} = \mathbf{300}$

37. **D)**

$\frac{2}{0.5} = \frac{7}{x}$

$2x = 3.5$

$\mathbf{x = 1.75}$

38. **A)**

$2\left(\frac{75 \div 25}{100 \div 25}\right) = \mathbf{2\frac{3}{4}}$

39. **A)**

$\frac{2}{3} = \frac{x}{147}$

$3x = 294$

$\mathbf{x = 98}$

40. **B)**

$\text{percent} = \frac{\text{part}}{\text{whole}}$

$\frac{800}{2500} = 0.32 = \mathbf{32\%}$

41. **C)**

Reduce coefficients, subtract exponents.

$$\frac{4x^6y^2}{3x^2y^4} = \frac{4x^4}{3y^2}$$

42. D)

$215 \text{ mi} \times \frac{1.61 \text{ km}}{1 \text{ mi}} \approx \textbf{346 km}$

43. A)

$2(3x + 4y) + 7(2x - 2y)$

$6x + 8y + 14x - 14y$

$6x + 14x + 8y - 14y$

$\textbf{20x} - \textbf{6y}$

44. D)

$9400 - 6580 = 2820$

$\text{percent} = \frac{\text{part}}{\text{whole}}$

$\frac{2820}{9400} = 0.3 = \textbf{30\%}$

45. A)

$\frac{25}{100} = \frac{12}{x}$

$25x = 1200$

$\textbf{x = 48}$

46. C)

$\frac{12}{100} = \frac{x}{1500}$

$100x = 18,000$

$\textbf{x = 180}$

47. C)

$\text{part} = \text{whole} \times \text{percent}$

$2213 \times 0.44 = 973.72 \approx \textbf{974}$

48. C)

$3 \times 1\frac{3}{4} = \frac{3}{1} \times \frac{7}{4} = \frac{21}{4} = \textbf{5}\frac{\textbf{1}}{\textbf{4}}$

49. C)

$4.5 - 1.67 = \textbf{2.83}$

50. A)

$20 \times 2 \div 2^2 + 5(-2)$

$= 20 \times 2 \div 4 + 5(-2)$

$= 40 \div 4 + 5(-2)$

$= 10 + 5(-2)$

$= 10 + (-10) = \textbf{0}$

51. D)

$15 \div 3 \times 5 - 10$

$= 5 \times 5 - 10 = 25 - 10 = \textbf{15}$

52. A)

$24 \times 0.75 = \textbf{18}$

53. C)

$5 \div 6 = \textbf{0.8}\overline{\textbf{3}}$

54. A)

$5\frac{2}{3} \div \frac{1}{3} = \frac{17}{3} \times \frac{3}{1} = \frac{17}{3} \times \frac{3}{1} = \textbf{17}$

55. A)

$6x - 7 = 5(2x + 1)$

$6x - 7 = 10x + 5$

$6x = 10x + 12$

$-4x = 12$

$\textbf{x = -3}$

1.   C)

The passage is mainly about ways that the overuse of antibiotics has led drug-resistant bacteria to evolve. The other sentences give details from the passage.

2.   B)

Phrases such as "undermined their effectiveness," "inundating [livestock] with cocktails of antibiotics," "dramatic rise in drug-resistant bacterial infections," and "sickening two million people per year and killing 23,000 in the United States alone" show that the author feels very concerned about the problem described in the passage.

3.   D)

In the first sentence, the author writes, "The discovery of penicillin by Alexander Fleming in 1928 revolutionized medical care. The widespread use of penicillin and other antibiotics has saved millions of people from the deadliest bacterial infections known to humans and prevented the spread of bacterial diseases." The context shows that the author uses the word *revolutionized* to refer to an important discovery that modernized medicine and saved many lives.

4.   D)

The passage does not contain this detail. The passage does not mention other types of farms besides factory farms.

5.   A)

While the author does not explicitly suggest a solution, he or she points out a serious problem that is caused by using antibiotics in harmful ways.

6.   D)

In the last two sentences, the author writes, "Because livestock manure is used as fertilizer, drug-resistant bacteria are spreading within the soils and waterways of farms, contaminating even plant-producing environments. The result: a dramatic rise in drug-resistant bacterial infections, sickening two million people per year and killing 23,000 in the United States alone." Readers can infer that by "a dramatic rise," the author means "a very noticeable or striking rise."

7.   C)

The passage is mainly about the "troubling" fact that 40 million people in the United States still smoke, even though most people know that heavy smoking shortens people's lives. The other sentences give details from the passage.

9.   D)

The passage does not contain this detail. The passage does not mention advertising.

8.   A)

The author uses various phrases to describe the cause-effect relationship between cigarette smoking and serious illnesses. Other words and phrases the author uses include "link," "cigarette-linked cancers," "is linked to," and "correlated with."

10.   A)

In the last paragraph, the author states that "[c]ontinuing research reinforces the necessity of anti-smoking campaigns, both government funded and grassroots. The numbers show that such campaigns work, encouraging people to quit smoking." Clearly, the author is strongly in favor of "anti-smoking campaigns."

11.   B)

Words and phrases such as "40 million people continue to smoke," "troubling," "30 percent of all cancer-related deaths in the United States can be tied to smoking," and "the necessity of anti-smoking campaigns" show that the author thinks all smokers should quit—the sooner the better.

12.   C)

In the last sentence, the author writes, "[T]he United States still has a long road of anti-smoking campaigning ahead." Readers can infer that by "a long road" the author means "a lot of hard work left to do."

13.   A)

The passage is mainly about the epidemic of opioid drug overdoses. The other sentences give details from the passage.

14. C)

In the first sentence, the author writes, "While smoking remains a public health concern for politicians and medical practitioners, a new epidemic has entered the media's sights: drug overdoses." Readers can use context to infer that by "a public health concern," the author means "a public health matter that worries people."

15. D)

The passage does not contain this detail. The passage refers to drug companies in this sentence only: "This epidemic began in the late 1990s with the overprescription of legal drugs for pain management—pharmaceutical companies downplayed their addictive qualities—and their subsequent misuse."

16. B)

The passage is primarily informative, but there is an underlying cautionary message to take the drug overdose epidemic seriously: it kills many thousands of people each year. The passage is not reassuring or persuasive, and it does not tell a story about a specific drug dealer, though it mentions that on the street, fentanyl mixed with heroin is sold.

17. B)

In the last paragraph, the author writes, "Government officials are focusing on drug prevention and rehabilitation programs, and the epidemic has been declared a public health emergency." Readers can infer that government officials are working hard on the problem but have not yet solved it.

18. C)

In the last paragraph, the author writes, "[T]he number of deaths [among men] between the ages of twenty-five and fifty-four has increased, largely because this is the prime age range for risky drug use." Readers can infer that by "prime age range for risky drug use" the author means that when men are between the ages of twenty-five and fifty-four, they are more likely (than younger or older men) to use drugs in a risky manner.

19. A)

The passage is mainly about the large number of American football players who develop CTE. The other sentences give details from the passage.

20. B)

In the first sentence, the author writes, "Chronic traumatic encephalopathy (CTE) is a degenerative brain disease that has garnered the attention of the media in recent years." The context shows that the author uses the phrase "garnered the attention of the media" to mean "gotten the attention of the news media."

21. C)

In the first paragraph, the author points out that studies have shown that the vast majority of professional football players develop CTE, a serious brain illness. The second paragraph deals primarily with implications for younger athletes. The author writes, "Many concerned parents have begun to ask if football is too violent a sport for their children." The evidence in the passage suggests that the author may think that football is too violent for athletes of all ages.

22. D)

The passage does not contain this detail. The passage does not mention what stance professional football organizations are taking regarding CTE.

23. D)

In the second paragraph, the author writes, "Many concerned parents have begun to ask if football is too violent a sport for their children. It may be too early for Americans to honestly answer this question, but there is certainly room for growing concern."

24. A)

The author does not say whether studies on CTE among players have affected professional football one way or another. However, readers can infer that professional football's success may be threatened in the future, depending on public reaction to the studies.

25. B)

In the second paragraph, the author writes that "at a biological level, inflammation is caused by the aggressive chemical signals sent by immune cells calling on other cells and substances to converge on the injury or infection to protect and heal it." In the third paragraph, the author writes, "Although inflammation is ... one of the body's most vital forms of defense, it can also be detrimental if it does not 'turn off' or if it rushes to the aid of otherwise healthy tissue." In other words, inflammation can be either helpful or harmful, and the immune system causes both types. There is no support for the other statements.

26. C)

In the second paragraph, the author writes, "[A]t a biological level, inflammation is caused by the aggressive chemical signals sent by immune cells calling on other cells and substances to converge on the injury or infection to protect and heal it." By "aggressive chemical signals" the author means that the immune system works very quickly and strongly to fight infections and heal injuries.

27. C)

The primary purpose of the essay is to define inflammation and inform readers about its causes and its effects—both beneficial effects and detrimental ones. The passage is not primarily cautionary or advisory. The author does not say that scientists are still trying to figure out what causes inflammation; apparently, biologists already know what causes it: the immune system.

28. B)

The passage is mainly about the fact that the immune system causes inflammation. The other sentences give details from the passage.

29. D)

In the last paragraph, the author writes, "Inflammatory diseases such as inflammatory bowel disease (IBD) or rheumatoid arthritis can have debilitating effects. Chronic inflammation can cause pain, fatigue, gastrointestinal problems, and other symptoms." Readers can infer from context that "pain, fatigue, gastrointestinal problems, and other symptoms" are some of the "debilitating effects" to which the author refers.

30. B)

In the second paragraph, the author writes that "inflammation is caused by the aggressive chemical signals sent by immune cells calling on other cells and substances to converge on the injury or infection to protect and heal it. Blood flow is increased, causing the heat and redness, and fluids can leak into the surrounding tissue, causing the swelling and soreness."

31. B)

In the first paragraph, the author writes, "Pain is a highly sophisticated biological mechanism, one that is often downplayed or misinterpreted. Pain is much more than a measure of tissue damage—it is a complex neurological chain reaction that sends sensory data to the brain."

32. B)

In the third paragraph, the author writes, "Phantom pain, most commonly associated with the amputation or loss of a limb, ... is triggered even in the absence of any injury. One possible explanation is that the spinal cord is still processing sensations from that area."

33. D)

In paragraph 3, the author writes, "Phantom pain [may be caused when] the spinal cord [continues to process] sensations from that area."

34. A)

In the first paragraph, the author writes, "Pain ... is a complex neurological chain reaction that sends sensory data to the brain."

35. B)

The passage is mainly about the fact that pain is a complicated process. The other sentences provide details from the passage.

36. A)

In the last paragraph, the author writes, "The absence of pain ... is a double-edged sword—sometimes pain is the only clue to an underlying injury or disease. Likewise, an injury or disease can dull or eliminate pain, making it impossible to sense when something is actually wrong." Readers can infer that the author is using the metaphor of a double-edged sword to show that the absence of pain is not always positive.

37. B)

The author begins by relating events that happened in the 1840s and ends with "new medicines, tools, and technologies" of the "late nineteenth and early twentieth centuries."

38. D)

In the third paragraph, the author refers to "[a]dvances in amputation techniques" developed during the Civil War. Readers can infer that thousands of soldiers who had had limbs amputated as a result of war injuries needed prosthetics after the war was over.

39. D)

In the third paragraph, the author writes, "[T]he sheer volume of medical need encouraged medical personnel, public health advocates, scientists, and inventors to seek more effective and humane treatment. Advances in amputation techniques, infection control, and transport of patients all stem from Civil War medicine .... As a result, the late nineteenth and early twentieth centuries witnessed a wave of new medicines, tools, and technologies."

40. C)

In the third paragraph, the author writes, "[T]he unprecedented bloodshed of the Civil War resulted in many medical innovations .... [T]he sheer volume of medical need encouraged medical personnel, public health advocates, scientists, and inventors to seek more effective and humane treatment. Advances in amputation techniques, infection control, and transport of patients all stem from Civil War medicine. In addition, plastic surgery and prosthetics design took turns for the better after the war." Readers can infer that, even though the war killed many thousands of people, it was a positive event for modern medicine.

41. B)

The passage is mainly about "the beginnings of modern medicine," which began earlier than most people might think. The other sentences give details from the passage.

42. A)

In the second paragraph, the author writes, "Before the discovery of anesthesia, patients had to merely endure as doctors sliced into their bodies with scalpels .... [I]t was nearly impossible to carry out more advanced [surgery] while patients were writhing in pain." Readers can infer that by "merely endure," the author means that without anesthesia, patients had to just bear the pain "as doctors sliced into their bodies with scalpels."

43. D)

The passage does not contain this detail. The author writes that "[c]ertain substances can pass through the placenta, causing problems for the developing fetus. Alcohol, tobacco, and drugs are among [these harmful] products."

44. A)

The passage is mainly about the importance of the placenta. The other sentences give details from the passage.

45. B)

The passage's primary purpose is informative. It is not persuasive or advisory. The author does mention the "trading post" metaphor, but this is a detail rather than a main idea or purpose for writing.

46. A)

In the second paragraph, the author writes, "[The placenta] exchanges nutrients between the blood supplies of the mother and the fetus—although the blood supplies do not intermingle throughout this process. Nutrients from the fetal blood and maternal blood are instead exchanged and regulated via blood vessels that filter each source without bringing them in direct contact." The context shows that the author uses the word *intermingle* to point out that the mother's blood and the fetus's blood do not come into direct contact—instead, the placenta acts as a "trading post."

47. D)

In the second-to-last sentence, the author writes, "Certain substances can pass through the placenta, causing problems for the developing fetus." Readers can infer that if a mother smokes or consumes alcohol or drugs when she is pregnant, it can harm her baby. The seriousness of the harm probably depends on the amounts and kinds of substances the mother uses.

48. C)

In the first sentence the author writes, "Aside from the uterus itself, the placenta is, perhaps, the most important organ directly involved with pregnancy."

49. B)

In the first paragraph, the author writes, "A devastating condition ... microcephaly ... literally means 'small head.' It can occur when a fetus's brain stops developing in utero. There is no known cure, and many babies born with microcephaly have other problems as a result, such as developmental delays or loss of hearing or vision." Readers can use context to infer that by "a devastating condition," the author means "a condition that causes great harm" to a developing fetus.

50.   D)

The passage does not contain this detail. The author does not list countries or regions where the Zika virus may be found.

51.   A)

The passage is mainly about the link between the Zika virus and microcephaly. The other sentences give details from the passage.

52.   B)

The author seems worried about the recent rise in vector-borne illnesses that are linked to climate change.

53.   A)

The Zika virus is a vector-borne disease, not a vector. The author writes that "not just climate but also the built environment, land use, pest control, and global commerce and travel ... have changed the breeding and biting habits of ticks, fleas, and mosquitoes, which are now spreading illnesses at a more rapid rate."

54.   B)

The passage is mainly about the link between climate change and the rise in vector-borne illnesses. The other sentences give details from the passage.

55.   A)

In the second sentence, the author writes, "Government officials and scientists are concerned that climate change—specifically, the recent rises in temperatures and rainfall—is contributing to this increase in insect- and tick-borne disease." Readers can infer from this that if temperatures and levels of rainfall stopped rising or rose more slowly, "this increase in insect- and tick-borne disease" might stop increasing or increase more slowly.

VOCABULARY

1. A)

The prefix of *malignant* is *mal–*, from the Latin meaning "bad" or "evil." *Malignant* means "harmful."

2. D)

Impared should be spelled "impaired."

3. D)

Intact means "whole or uninjured."

6. A)

Acoustics means "related to sound or hearing."

7. A)

Demonstrate means "to show or make clear."

8. D)

Concise means "brief and to the point."

9. C)

Compassion is "an awareness and sympathy for the experience and suffering of others."

10. D)

Chronic means "persistent or recurring over a long period of time."

11. A)

A *supplement* is "an addition to something substantially complete; to add to."

12. B)

Cephalic means "pertaining to the head."

13. A)

Deficit means "a lack or deficiency."

14. A)

Potent means "wielding power; strong; effective."

15. D)

Impair means "to weaken or damage."

4. C)

Virulent means "rapid, severe, and destructive."

5. A)

Extenuate means "to lessen or diminish the seriousness of something."

16. D)

Exogenous means "relating to or developing from external factors."

17. D)

Encreases should be spelled "increases."

18. B)

Prompt means "performed quickly."

19. D)

Concave means "a surface curved inward."

20. B)

To *counsel* is "to give advice to."

21. C)

To show *compassion* is to demonstrate "an awareness and sympathy for the suffering of others."

22. C)

An *abrasion* is "an area of the skin damaged by scraping or wearing away."

23. B)

Expose means "to open to an external environment." A wound, for example, may be left exposed to heal.

24. B)

An *abrasion* is "an area of skin damaged by scraping or wearing away."

25. B)

Concise means "brief and compact."

26. C)

Audible means "loud enough to be heard."

27. A)

Accountability means "to be responsible for or subject to providing an account."

28. A)

Posterior refers to any location in "the rear or the back."

29. C)

A *fatal* accident or disease is one that causes death or ruination.

30. A)

Complied means "to follow a command; acquiesce to another's wishes."

31. B)

Resilience means "possessing the ability to recover quickly."

33. C)

In medicine, something that is *occult* "does not have clear signs or symptoms."

32. B)

Constricted means "blocked, cramped, or crushed." A constricted airway means the person cannot breathe freely.

34. B)

Studeed should be spelled "studied."

35. C)

A *symptom* is "a sign or indication of a problem or disease."

36. B)

Restrict means to "limit or restrain."

37. A)

Copious means "abundant and plentiful."

38. A)

Infection means "tainted with germs or disease."

40. D)

Intuition is "understanding by instinct or quick insight."

41. A)

A *novice* is someone who "is a beginner or lacks experience."

39. D)

Priority means "order of importance; right of precedence."

42. B)

Elevate means "to raise or lift up."

43. A)

Something that is *pathogenic* causes disease.

44. C)

Ambulatory means "able to walk."

45. D)

A *malady* is a "disease or disorder."

46. D)

Nexus means "a connection between two or more things" or "the central or most important place."

47. A)

Perfusion means "to spread or diffuse, especially through blood vessels."

48. B)

To act in a *prudent* manner is "to act carefully and sensibly or use good judgment."

49. C)

Labile means "unstable; readily or frequently changing."

51. B)

A *laceration* is "a wound caused by tearing."

50. A)

Longevity means "having a long life."

52. A)

Compliant means "conforming or adhering to requirements."

53. C)

Accept should be spelled "except" in this context.

54. B

Resinded should be spelled "rescinded."

55. B

Tendincy should be spelled "tendency."

1. **D)**

   Choice D correctly uses the three homophones *they're* (a contraction meaning "they are"), *there* (a noun meaning "that place"), and *their* (a plural possessive pronoun). In choice A, *they're* is incorrectly used instead of *there*. Choice B incorrectly transposes *their* and *there*, and choice C incorrectly uses *their* in place of *they're* or *they are*.

2. **D)**

   Choice D is correct; it contains a plural subject: "my parents and I." Choices A, B, and C contain singular subjects (*graduation, I,* and *ceremony*).

3. **D)**

   Choice D is correct: it correctly pairs the conjunctions *neither* and *nor*. Completing the sentence with choices A, B, or C would result in a sentence that is not idiomatic in English.

4. **B)**

   The correct choice is B. The noun *effect* means "result" or "a change that happens due to a certain reason or cause." Choice A, *affect*, is a verb that means "to cause a change." Choice C, the adjective *efficient*, means "achieving maximum productivity with minimum waste." Choice D, the noun *affection*, means "positive sentiment or feeling."

5. **C)**

   Choice C correctly pairs the compound subject "Brenda and Pauletta" with the plural verb *are*. The adverb *tomorrow* indicates that the deadline is in the future. Therefore, *deadline* cannot take a past-tense verb, making choices A and B incorrect. Choice D is incorrect because the singular verb *is* cannot be paired with the compound subject "Brenda and Pauletta."

6. **A)**

   Choice A contains the coordinating conjunction *nor*. Choices B, C, and D each contain a subordinating conjunction (*because, if,* and *although*) that joins a dependent clause to an independent one.

7. **D)**

   The correct choice is D. The sentence correctly uses the past-tense verb *reigned* (meaning "ruled").

In choice A, the verb *reined* means "to control or guide an animal such as a horse with leather reins." In choice B, the verb *rained* means "falling down in mass quantities." In choice C, *rayon* is a type of synthetic cloth. None of these other choices make sense in the sentence.

8. **B)**

   Choice B is correct. In the proper noun "House of Representatives," both nouns should be capitalized. The United States Congress, the nation's legislative body, has two chambers: the Senate and the House of Representatives. The leader of the House has the title *Speaker* as in "Speaker Nancy Pelosi."

9. **C)**

   Choice C is correct. The comparative adjective *most intelligent* compares Pablo to the rest of the students in the class. None of the other choices contains a comparative adjective.

10. **B)**

    The correct choice is B. The adverb *bare* means "without clothing." Choice A, *bear*, is "a large heavy animal with thick fur and a short tail." Choice C, *beer*, is "an alcoholic drink made from yeast-fermented malt flavored with hops." Choice D, *boar*, is "a tusked wild pig."

11. **C)**

    Choice C is correct. The conjunction *but* joins the independent clauses "I'm willing to feed them" and "I need to finish my essay first." Choices A, B, and D each have one dependent clause and one independent one.

12. **D)**

    Choice D is correct. If an adjective is three or more syllables long, a suffix like *–est* or *–er* should NOT be added to create a comparative adjective (in fact, there is no such word as *impressivest*). This made-up word should be changed to *most impressive*.

13. **C)**

    Choice C uses the following punctuation marks correctly: a colon, a comma, another comma, and a period. In choice A, the parentheses around the name *Jack* are unnecessary. In choice B, the semicolon following *order* should be changed to a colon. In choice D, the question mark at the end of the sentence should be changed to a period.

14. C)

In the correct answer, choice C, the adverb *excruciatingly* modifies the adjective *cold*. Choice A contains an adverb, *even*, but it does not modify an adjective. Neither choice B nor D contains an adverb.

15. C)

Choice C is correct. Here, the word *man* is a common noun, so it should be lowercased (which is why choice A is incorrect). Choice B incorrectly matches the singular proper noun *Mr. Henderson* with a plural noun, *men*. Choice D, *main* (an adjective meaning "chief in size or importance") does not make sense in the sentence.

16. B)

Choice B is correct. The verb *brake* should be replaced with its homophone, *break: If you break that expensive glass vase, Dad will be very angry with you. Brake* means "to stop or slow down by using a vehicle's brakes," and *break* means "to smash into pieces."

17. B)

The correct choice is B. A track meet happens when *athletes* gather in a particular place to take part in a race or races, as well as in other track-and-field events. In choice A, *meat* is "food made from the tissue of animals." In choice C, the verb *mete* means "to allot justice, a punishment, or cruel treatment"; it is usually used with the preposition *out*, as in "to mete out punishment." In choice D, *mate* means "to join together for breeding purposes." None of these choices make sense in the sentence.

18. C)

Choice C is correct. To agree with the future-tense verb *will drop*, the past-tense verb *couldn't drive* should be replaced with the phrase "will not be able to drive" or with something similar in the future tense.

19. C)

The correct choice is C (a question mark). Correctly completed, the sentence looks like this: *I felt like asking, "What are we doing here, anyway?"* The

sentence indicates a question with the word *asking* in the speaker tag, which means that only a question mark can correctly complete the sentence. None of the other punctuation marks are appropriate to use with an interrogative sentence.

20. C)

The correct answer, choice C, has only one subject (*San Francisco*) and only one verb (*is*), so it is a simple sentence, even though it is very long. Choice A is a compound sentence (two independent clauses joined by the coordinating conjunction *and*). Choice B is a complex sentence (one dependent clause and one independent one, joined by the subordinating conjunction *if*). Choice D is a compound-complex sentence: it has one dependent clause ("While we were at the hotel") and two independent clauses ("we went . . . every day" and "we ate . . . food").

21. C)

Choice C is correct. The writer has at least three cousins, so the comparative adjective *older* should be replaced with *oldest*. Sue and Sandy, who are twins, are the same age as each other.

22. D)

Choice D is correct. The second sentence begins with the contraction *They're*, which means "They are." This contraction correctly completes the phrase "They're standing over there." Each of the other choices forms a grammatically incorrect sentence.

23. B)

Choice B, the verb *unfazed* (meaning "undisturbed" or "undaunted"), is correct. An experienced nurse is unlikely to be put off by a gruesome wound; he or she would set aside any personal discomfort and focus on helping the patient. *Unphased* (meaning "not organized or structured in any chronological order") is a homonym of *unfazed*; the words are frequently confused. *Unplaced* means "not placed" and would not make sense in this context. *Unfaced* means "not having a facing," usually in reference to a wall or other surface, and it would not make sense in the context of this sentence.

24. D)

Choice D correctly pairs the singular noun *boss* with the singular verb *was* and correctly pairs *neither* with *nor*. Choice A incorrectly pairs the singular noun *boss* with the plural verb *were*. Choice B incorrectly pairs neither . . . or, and choice C incorrectly pairs *either. . . nor.*

25. A)

Choice A is correct. The verbal phrase "smelling his favorite dish in the oven" modifies the proper noun *Danny*. Choice B contains a prepositional phrase, "in the oven," which modifies the noun *dish*. Choice C contains a subject (*Danny*), a verb (*entered*), and a direct object (*the kitchen*). It also contains the relative clause "where his favorite dish cooked in the oven," which has a subject (*dish*) and a verb (*cooked*). The prepositional phrase "in the oven" acts as an adverb and modifies *cooking*, but there is no verbal phrase modifying a proper noun. In choice D, the adverbial phrase "As he entered the kitchen" modifies the verb *smiled* (it tells when Danny smiled).

26. B)

Choice B is correct. The phrase "the whole pie" means "the entire pie." Choice A, *hole*, means "an opening or cavity"; choice C, *howl*, means "to wail"; and choice D, *hall*, means "a corridor or passageway between rooms." None of these answer choices would make sense in the context of the sentence.

27. B)

Choice B is correct. The exclamation point should be replaced with a question mark since Adelaide is asking a question: *"Do you want to join us?" Adelaide asked.*

28. B)

Choice B is correct. The homophones *meat* and *meat* should be transposed: *Let's meet at my house for a barbecue; I've been marinating some meat in a spicy sauce.* The verb *meet* means "to gather," and the noun *meat* means "food such as beef, pork, chicken, or lamb."

29. D)

Choice D is correct. *Lani's* contains an apostrophe that shows possession (of the mistake). In choices A and C, the contractions *won't* (*will not*) and *It's* (*it is*) each contains an apostrophe, but neither contraction shows possession. Choice B contains the possessive pronoun *her*, but does not contain any apostrophes.

30. D)

Choice D is correct. The coordinating conjunction *nor* correctly connects the opening independent

clause to the clause "nor do I recommend that you go." It logically explains the connection between the speaker's experience and his or her advice to the reader. Any of the other three conjunctions would render the sentence nonsensical, ungrammatical, or both.

31. C)

Choice C is correct. *Sweet* and *suite* sound alike but have different spellings and meanings, which makes them a homophone pair. Choices A (*member/ mambo*), B (*family/funnily*), and D (*poised/pursed*) are not homophone pairs because they do not sound enough alike.

32. B)

Choice B is correct. The homophones *where* and *wear* should be transposed: *I want to wear my fancy new dress, but I don't know where I can do so—it is too fancy for most occasions.* The verb *wear* means "be dressed in," and the adverb *where* means "in which place."

33. C)

Choice C correctly capitalizes *Cousin* (both because it begins the sentence and because it precedes a name, *Cousin Sue*); it also capitalizes the names *Sandy, Bonny,* and *Jack*. In choice A, common noun *lake* is incorrectly capitalized. Choice B incorrectly capitalizes *cousins*, a common plural noun. Choice D incorrectly lowercases *Sandy*, a person's name.

34. C)

Choice C is correct; the speaker means that he or she is finding it difficult to decide which outfit to wear to a place or event. Choice A incorrectly uses the verb *were*, which means "to be," instead of *wear* (in reference to clothing oneself). Choice B is ungrammatical; the adjective *weird* cannot modify the verb *wear*. Choice D is nonsensical; the verb *to wire* means "to connect, predispose, or provide with electrical wiring." It does not make sense in this context or with the relative pronoun *which*.

35. B)

Choice B correctly uses the verb *lose*, which means "the opposite of win." In choice A, the adjective *loose* means "the opposite of tight." In choice C, a *louse* is a tiny insect, and in choice D, *lice* is the plural form of *louse*.

36. B)

Choice B is correct. The names of seasons are common nouns, so *summer* is correctly lowercased. Choice A, the adverb *sooner*, does not make sense in this context. Choice C, *sunner*, is not a word—it might be a misspelling of the adjective in choice D, *sunnier*, which also does not make sense in the sentence.

37. A)

Choice A is correct. The verb *lead* should be spelled *led*, because the event is taking place in the past.

38. B)

Choice B correctly uses the verb *dyeing*, which means "coloring with dye." Choice A incorrectly uses *dying*, which is a synonym for *perishing* and *deceasing*. Choice C uses the present-tense verb *dye* with the helping verb *keeps*, which is incorrect usage. Choice D uses the past-tense verb *died* (meaning "perished") with the helping verb *keeps*; this is incorrect usage and does not make sense, either.

39. B)

Choice B is correct. *Poor* should be replaced with its homophone, *pour*: *Please pour me a glass of lemonade. Poor* is an adjective, an antonym for *rich. Pour* is a verb that means "to transfer [a liquid] from one container to another."

40. C)

Choice C is correct. The coordinating conjunction *but* joins the two independent clauses ("Imani . . . quiz" and "he said . . . alone"). Choice A, *offered*, is a verb; choice B, *quiz*, is a noun; and choice D, *prefers*, is a verb.

41. D)

Choice D correctly capitalizes the proper noun *Microsoft*, leaving the common nouns *automobile* and *industry* in lower case. Choice A incorrectly capitalizes the common noun *automobile*. In choice B, the proper noun *Microsoft* is incorrectly written in lower case. Choice C incorrectly capitalizes the common nouns *automobile* and *industry*.

42. A)

Choice A contains the correct conjunction, *and*. Choices B, C, and D contain incorrect conjunctions (*but, yet,* and *for*) that should not be used to add items to a list.

43. C)

Choice C correctly pairs the singular subject "none of us" with the singular verb *wants*. Choice A incorrectly pairs the singular subject *everyone* with the plural verb *want*. Choice B incorrectly pairs the singular subject *everybody* with the plural verb *want*. Choice D incorrectly pairs the singular subject *nobody* with the plural verb *want*.

44. A)

Choice A is correct. The semicolon should be replaced with a colon: *"Here is how I answered her question: . . ." "Here is how I answered her question"* introduces the dialogue in the second half of the sentence, so the first half should end with a colon.

45. C)

Choice C is correct. The coordinating conjunction *but* joins the two independent clauses. Choice A, *told*, is a verb; choice B, *dinner*, is a noun; and choice D, *instead*, is a conjunctive adverb.

46. D)

Choice D is correct. The word *teacher* should be lowercased—it is a common noun.

47. C)

Choice C correctly uses the verb *ensure*, which means "to make sure." In choice A, the verb *insure* means "to cover with an insurance policy." In choice B, to *reassure* means "to comfort [someone]." In choice D, the saying "rest assured" means "don't worry—everything is going to be alright."

48. B)

Choice B is correct. The singular present-tense verb *makes* makes sense in the sentence "My dog makes me happy every day." Choice A incorrectly matches a singular subject, *dog*, with a plural verb, *make*. Choice C does not make sense: the future-perfect verb "will have made" clashes with the phrase "every day" (which suggests the present). Choice D is incorrectly written. The conditional past-tense verb should be written "should have *made*," not "should have *make*."

49. B)

Choice B correctly uses the adverb *aloud*, which means "out loud" or "loudly enough to be heard." Choice A incorrectly uses *allowed*, a verb meaning "given permission to," in place of its homophone *aloud*. Choice C incorrectly uses *aloft*, an adverb meaning "up in the sky," in place of *aloud*. Choice D incorrectly uses *about*, meaning "related to" or "concerning," in place of *aloud*.

50. **A)**

Choice A correctly compares four items using *most* with the three-syllable adjective *beautiful*. Choice B incorrectly compares four items using *more* with the adjective (*more* should be used when only two items are being compared). Choice C incorrectly adds the suffix –*est* to a three-syllable adjective (there is no such word as *beautifulest*), and choice D incorrectly adds the suffix –*er* to a three-syllable adjective (there is no such word as *beautifuler*).

51. **D)**

Choice D is correct. *Die* (a verb meaning "to perish or pass away") should be replaced with its homophone, *dye*: *Since our school colors are orange and black, I'm going to dye a few of my white T-shirts orange. Dye* is a verb that means "to color with dye."

52. **C)**

Choice C is correct. The verb *lose* means "to be deprived of [something]" or "to have something go missing." To *loosen* is "to make something less tight," and *loose* is an antonym of *tight*. The verb *lost* is the past tense of *to lose* and does not make sense grammatically in this context because the sentence is written in the present tense.

53. **C)**

Choice C is correct. *Stair* should be replaced with its homophone, *stare*: *Please don't stare at strangers; it is rude and can make people feel uncomfortable. Stair* is a noun that means "one step on a staircase." *Stare* is a verb that means "to gaze fixedly [at someone]."

54. **A)**

Choice A has no misplaced modifiers; this choice makes it clear who burned the soup (Mario) and how he did so (by leaving it on the stove for too long). Choices B and C contain misplaced modifiers that make it seem like Mario was left on the stove for too long. Choice D is incorrectly constructed so that it sounds as if the soup realized that it was burned and Mario was the culprit.

55. **D)**

In choice D, the comparative adverb *better* compares the state of Pablo's health today to the state of his health tomorrow. Choice A contains the adjective *terrible*, choice B contains the adverb *nonstop*, and choice C contains both the adjective *sorry* and the adverb *very*; none of these are comparative.

BIOLOGY

1. C)

Polar bonds occur when one atom in a covalently bonding molecule has more affinity for electrons than the other molecules.

2. C)

RNA uses the nucleotide uracil instead of thymine, which is found in DNA. The other statements are true of both RNA and DNA.

3. C)

Water, small molecules (e.g., sodium), and gases (e.g., carbon dioxide) can freely diffuse through the membrane. Glucose and other large molecules require energy to be moved across the membrane.

4. C)

A hydrogen gradient or proton gradient builds up as protons are passed from one enzyme to the next in the electron transport chain. The hydrogen atoms are used to synthesize ATP by ATP synthase.

5. A)

This is an example of an insertion mutation. A cytosine has been inserted into the sequence in the mutated sequence.

6. A)

Sperm and eggs are the male and female gametes. When a sperm fertilizes an egg, a zygote is formed.

7. C)

Ribosomes are the organelles where protein synthesis occurs. mRNA is transported to the ribosomes, where it is converted to protein with the help of tRNA.

8. A)

Chromatin modification (or remodeling) allows for specific areas of DNA to unwind and become accessible to transcription enzymes. This process allows the cell to control which genes are available for transcription.

9. C)

X-linked traits are mostly seen in males. Females have two chromosomes, meaning a recessive X-linked allele can be masked by a dominant allele. In males, who only have one X chromosome, the X-linked recessive allele will always be expressed.

10. B)

Answers A and D do not complement the DNA strand shown in the question. Additionally, the complementary sequence is in the right direction in strand B.

11. A)

Hydrogen bonds form between two water molecules. The positive charge on the hydrogen atoms in one molecule of water is attracted to the negative charge on the oxygen atom in another molecule of water.

12. B)

DNA stands for deoxyribonucleic acid.

13. A)

Active transport requires energy and would stop if ATP production was inhibited. Osmosis, facilitated diffusion, and passive transport do not require energy.

14. C)

Pyruvate is catabolized, or broken down, to produce $6CO_2$ during the Krebs cycle.

15. A)

Only answer A has a complementary sequence.

16. B)

Genetic variation is increased when chromosomes are individually sorted, meaning each gamete has a random mix of maternal and paternal chromosomes.

17. A)

Tryptophan represses the trp operon. It acts as a repressor and affects the gene in a negative way by turning it off.

18. B)

Fifty percent of the offspring will be heterozygous for the trait.

	D	d
D	DD	Dd
D	DD	Dd

19. B)

Repressors and activators bind to the operator to regulate gene expression.

20. D)

A genotype is all of the genes encoded by DNA in an organism's chromosomes.

21. C)

DNA—a nucleic acid—is formed by joining nucleotides.

22. A)

Two molecules of pyruvate are generated from the catabolism, or breakdown, of glucose during glycolysis.

23. D)

Only answer D has a complementary sequence.

24. C)

Microtubules help move things around the cell. During mitosis, they help separate the chromosomes during anaphase.

25. B)

Proteins are translated on ribosomes that may be located in the endoplasmic reticulum or cytoplasm.

26. B)

The nuclear envelope breaks down during prometaphase.

27. D)

Proteins are embedded in the membrane to allow large molecules to cross the membrane.

28. B)

During fermentation, pyruvate is used as the final electron acceptor when oxygen levels are low.

29. B)

Fifty percent of the offspring will be homozygous recessive for the trait and thus will express the recessive trait.

	D	d
d	dD	dd
d	dD	dd

30. B)

Guanine binds to cytosine in both DNA and RNA.

CHEMISTRY

1. C)

For each element block or cell, the top number corresponds to the atomic number, which is equal to the number of protons. Selenium (Se) has an atomic number (Z) of 34, which means it has thirty-four protons.

2. C)

Radon (Rn) is a noble gas (group 18) with a full valence shell of eight electrons.

3. B)

Ionic bonds form between a cation and an anion. KNO_3 is the result of an electrostatic attraction (or ionic bond) between the cation K^+ and the anion NO_3^-.

4. B)

A Brønsted-Lowry base is a species or substance that accepts a hydrogen ion (H^+). Water can act as a base by taking a H^+ from hydrochloric acid (HCl), to produce a hydronium ion (H_3O^+).

5. A)

The solution is saturated with respect to sugar, meaning no more sugar can be dissolved in the water. The solution is considered a heterogeneous mixture because the excess solid sugar is not uniformly distributed and instead will settle at the bottom of the container.

6. B)

Water freezes at 0°C. When a substance moves from liquid to solid (the state with the lowest energy), energy is released.

7. C)

An oxidizing agent takes electrons (oxidizes), becoming reduced in the process. $AgNO_3$ takes electrons from zinc (Zn), which goes from being neutral to having a positive charge. $Ag^+(aq)$ becomes reduced in the process: .

8. B)

Beta decay produces a high energy electron (written as $_{-1}^{0}e$ or $_{-1}^{0}\beta$).

9. C)

A Brønsted-Lowry acid is a species or substance that donates a hydrogen ion (H^+). In the forward direction, ammonia acts as a weak base and accepts a H^+ from H_2O, which acts as an acid. In the reverse direction, ammonium (NH_4^+) acts as an acid since it donates a H^+ to H_2O. Weak acids and bases partially ionize and are represented by a forward and reverse arrow.

10. C)

The group on the periodic table refers to the column number. Tungsten (W) is in group 6.

11. D)

Longer hydrocarbon chains will have higher boiling points because the intermolecular forces (London dispersion forces) between two different chains increase with chain length.

12. D)

Vanadium (V) has an atomic number of 23, which corresponds to twenty-three protons. For the atom to be neutral, it must also have twenty-three electrons.

13. B)

Helium (He) is a noble gas (group 18) with a full valence shell of eight electrons.

14. C)

A supersaturated solution is created by dissolving the solute (sugar) in the solvent (water) at high temperatures. The high temperature allows more than 200 g of sugar to be dissolved in 100 mL of water.

15. A)

Boron (B) is the only given element that is not considered a pure metal. It is classified as a metalloid and forms covalent bonds by sharing electrons.

16. C)

The transition from gas to liquid is condensation.

17. A)

The reaction is a decomposition reaction that has the form A → B + C. Copper (II) hydroxide ($Cu(OH)_2$) breaks apart into two new compounds.

18. **C)**

The electronegativity of elements in group 1 decreases going down the column. Cesium (Cs) has the lowest electronegativity, and thus will have the largest difference with chlorine (Cl), which has a high electronegativity. This difference will create the greatest bond polarity.

19. **A)**

Mass number is the number of protons plus the number of neutrons. Sn-112 has an atomic number of 50, which means it has fifty protons: $112 - 50 = 62$, so Sn-112 has sixty-two neutrons.

20. **B)**

Radium (Ra) is in group 2, the alkaline earth metals.

21. **C)**

The electronegativity of an element increases from left to right across the periodic table. Fluorine (F) is more electronegative than oxygen (O), boron (B), or nitrogen (N), so it will exert a strong pull on the electrons it shares with carbon (C), resulting a bond that is more polar.

22. **D)**

To boil a substance, molecules of liquid must have enough energy to break free as gas molecules. When the substance has strong intermolecular forces, more energy is needed to break molecules free. Because helium (He) experiences the weakest intermolecular forces, the least amount of energy will be required to bring it to its boiling point.

23. **C)**

The reaction is a single displacement that has the form: $AB + C \rightarrow A + CB$. Silver (Ag) and zinc (Zn) exchange places to form a new compound, $Zn(NO_3)_2$.

24. **B)**

A cation is a positively charged element that has undergone oxidation or electron loss. Calcium (Ca, atomic number of 20) will lose two electrons to form the calcium cation, Ca^{2+}.

25. **D)**

Use dimensional analysis using the coefficients from the equation:

$\dfrac{8 \text{ mol Fe}}{1}$	$\dfrac{2 \text{ mol } Fe_2O_3}{4 \text{ mol Fe}}$	$= \mathbf{4 \text{ mol } Fe_2O_3}$

26. **D)**

Francium (Fr) is an alkali metal (group 1) and has one valence electron. Alkali metals are highly reactive and will lose their one valence electron to form a cation that has a 1+ charge.

27. **D)**

The reaction is a double displacement that has the form: $AB + CD \rightarrow AD + CB$. Potassium (K) and hydrogen (H) swap places to form the two new compounds, H_2O and KCl.

28. **D)**

The period on the periodic table refers to the row number. Silver (Ag) is in period 5.

29. **B)**

Use dimensional analysis using the coefficients from the equation to find the amount of NH_3 produced by each reactant:

$\dfrac{6 \text{ mol } H_2}{}$	$\dfrac{2 \text{ NH}_3}{3 \text{ H}_2}$	$= \mathbf{4 \text{ mol } NH_3}$
$\dfrac{1 \text{ mol } N_2}{}$	$\dfrac{2 \text{ NH}_3}{1 \text{ N}_2}$	$= \mathbf{2 \text{ mol } NH_3}$

Because nitrogen gas (N) produces the smallest amount of ammonia gas, it is the limiting reactant.

30. **A)**

Strontium (Sr) is an alkaline earth metal (group 2) and has two valence electrons. Alkaline earth metals will lose their two valence electrons to form a cation with a 2+ charge.

1. A)

The pharynx is the top area of the throat; food passes through it on its way to the esophagus.

2. B)

Vital capacity is the large amount of air that is moved during deep breathing.

3. B)

The bladder is anterior to the uterus.

4. C)

The incus, stapes, and malleus are bones connected to the skull inside the ear; they have an important role in the sense of hearing.

5. A)

Cytotoxic T-cells are part of the cell-mediated immune response, which does not rely on antibodies to identify pathogens.

6. C)

Skeletal muscles and bones are attached by tendons.

7. A)

The pituitary gland produces growth hormones, so disorders of the pituitary can affect growth and development.

8. C)

Food moves from the pylorus (part of the stomach) to the duodenum (the first part of the small intestine) and into the ileum (the last part of the small intestine).

9. B)

The vertebral cavity protects the spinal cord.

10. C)

The patella, or kneecap, is a sesamoid bone attached to the tendon of the quadriceps.

11. A)

The cilia help move the mucus up to keep the trachea clear.

12. C)

The vas deferens is a tube that transports semen and does not contribute any material to it.

13. B)

The placenta develops from the trophoblast.

14. B)

Urea is the result of protein catabolism.

15. C)

Synovial fluid fills the gap between the bones in a synovial joint, lubricating the joint and allowing for movement.

16. D)

The enteric nervous system plays an important role in the digestive system and the processes involved with it.

17. C)

Muscle fatigue occurs when there is a minimal to no supply of oxygen, glucose, or ATP to the muscle. ADP and lactic acid levels increase.

18. A)

Hemoglobin is rich in iron, which allows it to transport oxygen to cells. Thus, a low iron level will likely correspond to a low hemoglobin level.

19. B)

The cancellous bone that holds the red bone marrow is found at the ends of the long bones.

20. A)

Urine passes through the ureters from the kidneys into the urinary bladder.

21. B)

The epineurium is the outermost layer of connective tissue in the peripheral nervous system; it protects bundles of peripheral nerves.

22. B)

The serous fluid keeps the outside of the stomach wet, preventing friction with the organs close to it.

23. C)

The nerves transport information from sensory organs to the central nervous system and vice versa.

24. A)

The external sphincter closes during sexual activity to keep the urine in the bladder and to prevent semen from entering the bladder.

25. C)

SA and AV nodes are cells that keep the heart's pace and contraction coordinated.

26. C)

The eccrine glands release sweat, which is made up of salt and water, to maintain the body's sodium balance.

27. C)

White matter is composed of myelinated neurons that carry information between regions of the brain.

28. C)

Pancreatic lipase is responsible for breaking down fat molecules into monoglycerides and fatty acids.

29. C)

Testosterone is responsible for secondary sex characteristics in men, such as hair on the chest and a deep voice.

30. B)

There is no lateral lobe of the cerebrum; its four lobes are the frontal, parietal, occipital, and temporal.

1.   A)

Plug the variables into the appropriate formula and solve.

$$v_f^2 = v_i^2 + 2ad$$

$$d = v_f^2 - \frac{v_i^2}{2a}$$

$$d = \frac{0^2 - 12^2}{2(-9.8)} = \textbf{7.35 m}$$

2.   A)

Plug the variables into the appropriate formula and solve.

$$KE = \frac{1}{2}mv^2$$

$$KE = \frac{1}{2}(0.003 \text{ kg})(300 \text{ m/s})^2 = \textbf{135 J}$$

3.   D)

A shaken rope is in the form of a transverse wave.

4.   C)

Plug the variables into the appropriate formula and solve.

$$m = \frac{p}{v}$$

$$m = \frac{12,000 \text{ (kg·m)/s}}{2 \text{ m/s}} = \textbf{6000 kg}$$

5.   B)

Sound waves are due to the compression of air molecules and propagate as longitudinal waves.

6.   D)

Magnetic fields only exert forces on charged particles.

7.   A)

Plug the variables into the appropriate formula and solve.

$$F_f = \mu_k N$$

$$\mu_k = \frac{F_f}{mg}$$

$$\mu_k = \frac{2000 \text{ N}}{800 \text{ kg}(9.8 \text{ m/s}^2)} = \textbf{0.26}$$

8.   A)

Plug the variables into the appropriate formula and solve.

$$P = \frac{W}{t}$$

$$P = \frac{Fd}{t}$$

$$P = \frac{(45 \text{ N})(400 \text{ m})}{3600 \text{ s}} = \textbf{5 W}$$

9.   B)

Plug the variables into the appropriate formula and solve.

$$\frac{1}{R_t} = \frac{1}{R_1} + \frac{1}{R_2}$$

$$\frac{1}{R_t} = \frac{1}{2000} + \frac{1}{3000} = \frac{5}{6000}$$

$$R_t = \frac{6000}{5} = \textbf{1200 } \mathbf{\Omega}$$

10.   C)

Plug the variables into the appropriate formula and solve.

$$F_g = mg$$

$$g = \frac{F_g}{m}$$

$$g = \frac{370 \text{ N}}{60 \text{ kg}} = \textbf{6.2 m/s}^2$$

11.   C)

Plug the variables into the appropriate formula and solve.

$$Q_{TOT} = Nq$$

$$N = \frac{Q_{TOT}}{q}$$

$$N = \frac{1 \text{ C}}{1.602 \times 10^{-19} \text{ C}} = \textbf{6.24} \times \textbf{10}^{18} \textbf{ electrons}$$

12.   D)

Plug the variables into the appropriate formula and solve.

$$v = \lambda f$$

$$c = \lambda f$$

$$f = \frac{c}{\lambda} = \frac{3 \times 10^8 \text{ m/s}}{1 \text{ m}} = \textbf{3} \times \textbf{10}^8 \textbf{ Hz}$$

13. B)

The resistors must be connected in series for the resistance to increase.

$R_t = R_1 + R_2 + ...$

$R_t = 1800\ \Omega + 1800\ \Omega = 3600\ \Omega$

Two resistors are needed to reach **3600 Ω**.

14. A)

The period is reduced by a factor of four (shorter period).

15. B)

Plug the variables into the appropriate formula and solve.

$V = IR$

$R = \dfrac{120\ V}{20\ A} = \mathbf{6\ \Omega}$

16. C)

Plug the variables into the appropriate formula and solve.

$F_c = ma_{rad}$

$F_c = 80\ kg(3 \times 9.8\ m/s^2) = \mathbf{2352\ N}$

17. C)

Plug the variables into the appropriate formula and solve.

$n = \dfrac{c}{v_s}$

$n = \dfrac{3 \times 10^8\ m/s}{2.11 \times 10^8\ m/s} = \mathbf{1.42}$

18. A)

Plug the variables into the appropriate formula and solve.

$m_1 v_{1i} + m_2 v_{2i} = (m_1 + m_2)v_{2f}$

$v_{2f} = \dfrac{m_1 v_{1i} + m_2 v_{2i}}{m_1 + m_2}$

$= \dfrac{2\ kg(4\ m/s) + 5\ kg(-1\ m/s)}{2\ kg + 5\ kg}$

$= \dfrac{3\ kg\ m/s}{7\ kg} = \mathbf{0.43\ m/s\ to\ the\ left}$

19. C)

Plug the variables into the appropriate formula and solve.

$\Delta V = Ed$

$E = \dfrac{\Delta V}{d}$

$E = \dfrac{12\ V}{0.20\ m} = \mathbf{60\ N/C}$

20. C)

Plug the variables into the appropriate formula and solve.

$KE = \dfrac{1}{2}mv^2$

$KE = \dfrac{1}{2}(1.67 \times 10^{-27}\ kg)[0.90(3 \times 10^8\ m/s)]^2$

$= \mathbf{6.1 \times 10^{-11}\ J}$

21. C)

Plug the variables into the appropriate formula and solve.

$m_1 v_{1i} + m_2 v_{2i} = (m_1 + m_2)v_{2f}$

$mv_{1i} + 0 = 2mv_{2f}$

$v_{2f} = \left(\dfrac{m}{2\ m}\right)(v_{1i}) = \dfrac{1}{2}(2\ m/s) = \mathbf{1\ m/s}$

22. D)

For light rays, the angles of incidence and reflection are the same. The sum of the reflection angle and the angle with the normal is 90°.

$90° - 31° = \mathbf{59°}$

23. C)

Plug the variables into the appropriate formula and solve.

$\theta = \dfrac{1}{2}at^2 + \omega_i t$

$\theta = \dfrac{1}{2}(1.5\ rad/s^2)(5s)^2 + 0 = \mathbf{18.75\ rad}$

24. D)

Plug the variables into the appropriate formula and solve.

$F_g = mg$ and $F_g = \dfrac{GmM_{Earth}}{R_{Earth}^2}$

$mg = \dfrac{GmM_{Earth}}{R_{Earth}^2}$

$M_{Earth} = \dfrac{gR_{Earth}^2}{G} = \dfrac{(9.8\ m/s^2)(6.4 \times 10^6\ m)^2}{6.67 \times 10^{11}}$

$= \mathbf{6 \times 10^{24}\ kg}$

25. C)

Plug the variables into the appropriate formula and solve.

$\tau = rF\sin\theta$

$F = mg$

$\tau = rmg\sin\theta$

$\tau = (0.25 \text{ m})(12 \text{ kg})(9.8 \text{ m/s}^2)\sin 90°$

$= \mathbf{29.4 \text{ N m}}$

26. C)

Plug the variables into the appropriate formula and solve.

$PE_g = mgh$

$PE_{Earth} = mg_E h$

$= (1 \text{ kg})(9.8 \text{ m/s}^2)(1000 \text{ m}) = 9800 \text{ J}$

$PE_{Mars} = mg_M h$

$= (1 \text{ kg})(3.8 \text{ m/s}^2)(1000 \text{ m}) = 3800 \text{ J}$

$\Delta PE = PE_E - PE_M = 9800 \text{ J} - 3800 \text{ J} = \mathbf{6000 \text{ J}}$

27. D)

Plug the variables into the appropriate formula and solve.

$n = \frac{c}{v_s}$

$n = \frac{3 \times 10^8 \text{ m/s}}{340 \text{ m/s}} = \mathbf{8.8 \times 10^5}$

28. B)

Plug the variables into the appropriate formula and solve.

$N = \frac{Q_{TOT}}{q}$

$F = k\frac{q_1 q_2}{(2r)^2}$

$F = 1/4\left(k\frac{q_1 q_2}{r^2}\right)$

29. A)

The ball had 100 joules of potential energy before it started to fall. Plug the variables into the appropriate formula and solve.

$PE_g = mgh$

$h = \frac{100 \text{ J}}{(5 \text{ kg})(9.8 \text{ m/s}^2)} = \mathbf{2.04 \text{ m}}$

30. D)

Plug the variables into the appropriate formula and solve.

$\frac{1}{R_t} = \frac{1}{R} + \frac{1}{R}$

$\frac{1}{R_t} = \frac{1}{2R} + \frac{1}{2R} = \frac{2}{2R} = \frac{1}{R}$

$V = IR_t$

$V = IR$

The current does not change.

CPSIA information can be obtained
at www.ICGtesting.com
Printed in the USA
BVHW010745101121
621203BV00016B/311

CONTENTS